Relational Coaching

Relational Coaching

Journeys Towards Mastering One-To-One Learning

Erik de Haan
Translation by Sue Stewart

John Wiley & Sons, Ltd

Other Wiley Editorial Offices
John Wiley & Sons Inc., 111 River Street, Hoboken, NJ 07030, USA
Jossey-Bass, 989 Market Street, San Francisco, CA 94103-1741, USA
Wiley-VCH Verlag GmbH, Boschstr. 12, D-69469 Weinheim, Germany
John Wiley & Sons Australia Ltd, 42 McDougall Street, Milton, Queensland 4064, Australia
John Wiley & Sons (Asia) Pte Ltd, 2 Clementi Loop #02-01, Jin Xing Distripark, Singapore
129809
John Wiley & Sons Canada Ltd, 6045 Freemont Blvd, Mississauga, ONT, L5R 4J3, Canada
Wiley also publishes its books in a variety of electronic formats. Some content that appears
in print may not be available in electronic books.

Library of Congress Cataloging-in-Publication Data
To follow

British Library Cataloguing in Publication Data
A catalogue record for this book is available from the British Library

ISBN 978-0-470-72428-6 (HB)

Typeset in by SNP Best-set Typesetter Ltd., Hong Kong

Through the *Thou* a person becomes *I*. *Thou* comes and disappears, relational events condense, then are scattered, and it is during this change that understanding of the unchanging partner, of the *I*, grows clear, and each time stronger.

(Martin Buber, *I and Thou*, 1923)

We tend to think of any one individual in isolation; it is a convenient fiction. We may isolate him physically, as in the analytic room; in two minutes we find he has brought his world in with him, and that, even before he set eyes on the analyst, he had developed inside himself an elaborate relation with him. There is no such thing as a single human being, pure and simple, unmixed with other human beings.

(Joan Riviere, *The unconscious fantasy of an inner world*, 1952)

Preface

Helping conversations are, happily, still an everyday occurrence, taking place around the kitchen table, in the workplace or on the train. If you look at conversations closely, many turn out to be helping conversations, if only because 'learning' is a recurring objective when people enter into conversations. Interlocutors exchange information, try to steer each other towards different ideas, or attempt to help each other deal with decisions or tasks that are facing them. These are activities that they learn from in one way or another, and they help each other in the process.

But in the complex world of today, conversations, and helping conversations in particular, have also become an area for study and specialisation. Consider the specialist fields of psychotherapy, social work and counselling – including their associated research tradition. Researchers attempt to identify the active or effective ingredients of helping conversations and ask themselves how to enhance the learning side of conversations. However, the 'professionalisation' and study of this area do not alter the everyday nature and importance of helping conversations.

Is it perhaps a sign of impoverishment that the art of conducting helping conversations has grown into a profession and a field of research? Is it perhaps an indication of how difficult it is nowadays to conduct a conversation imbued with trust in the workplace, an indication of greater distance and coolness in interpersonal relationships?

We now have over a hundred years of intensive research into the helping nature of conversations behind us, research that has been anecdotal and qualitative but also rigorous and quantitative. The conclusion from all of these studies must be, as I hope to demonstrate in the following chapters, that we are back to square one, back to the most obvious, naive intuitions that laymen have about helping conversations. At the same time, these are intuitions that have certainly not always played a leading role in the many traditions of conducting helping conversations. In other words, professionally there is a lot to learn from this research. It brings us back to the simple observation that the most important effective ingredients are the capacity for learning of the persons conducting the conversation and the quality of the relationship between the interlocutors. This is why I have called this book *Relational Coaching*. The most important question addressed in this book is: how can we as coaches make the best possible use of the only genuinely effective ingredient that we are able to influence, the *coaching relationship*?

Relational coaching is not just one more in a long line of approaches to coaching, yet another technique or collection of interventions. It is, rather, a radically different way of looking at coaching. Relational coaching means turning one's gaze away from the coach and towards the coachee. Directive coaching, analytical coaching, solution-focused coaching, provocative coaching, even person-centred counselling, and many other approaches, are, in a way, recommendations or ideas for the coach. Those approaches are full of ways to 'handle' the client, and offer often explicit preferences for specific interventions or procedures. Relational coaching says that none of that matters very much. To put it bluntly, research has shown conclusively that the specific things that the coach does or doesn't do, and the specific approaches that the coach believes in most, make little or no difference to the coachee.

What relational coaching is all about is the *relationship from the perspective of the coachee*. As will be shown in Chapter 3, this has been demonstrated to be the most important predictor of the outcome of coaching, and is where coaches should focus their attention. The development of a relationship does not depend so much on the specific things done or said – a relationship is defined by greater things, such as a certain 'chemistry' between personalities, and whether or not it engenders feelings of well-being, recognition or solidarity between equal partners. Specific behaviours can certainly help in this respect, and perhaps any manner of 'chemistry' can ultimately be dissected into behaviours as 'elements' in some 'periodic table'. However, just as in chemistry, the interaction between the various elements gives rise to completely new properties and behaviours. The whole is much greater than the sum of its constituent parts. In other words, relational coaching, the practice in which we focus our gaze on the coachee's appreciation of the relationship, contains all of those specific approaches and interventions, and at the same time none of them. The relational approach is not eclecticism or relativism, but means having the courage to put the coachee truly at the centre of the coaching, rising above all of those models and philosophies *for the coach*.

This book is structured as follows. In part one, after a brief introduction to coaching (Chapter 1) and an explanation of why it is such a popular and expanding profession (Chapter 2), I outline the main effective ingredients of coaching according to the latest research, and how coaches can make the best possible use of those things that have been shown to work. This part describes what relational coaching is, and outlines the tradition from which it stems.

In part two I set off on an exploration within the coaching profession and ask myself again what exactly it is that determines the effectiveness of coaching? How does coaching encourage change, from moment to moment, and what factors can the coach influence in order to contribute towards effective change? This part contains four different exploratory chapters. Chapter 5 is quantitative in nature and explores coachees' comments on what they find helpful in coaching. Chapters 6 and 7 are qualitative and explore the *critical moments* experienced by new and established coaches respectively in their own practice. Finally, Chapter 8 draws on in-depth interviews to investigate how coaches react to their own critical moments and how they attempt to use them or learn from them for the future.

Part three contains a critical overview of the broad arsenal of aids and activities available to modern coaches in order to learn and increase our professionalism. I volunteer my own choices and preferences in terms of the design of coaching education, accreditation and supervision. I also give a list of aspects that I consider relevant in terms of coaches' skills and their continuing professional development. Chapter 9 is devoted to coaches' areas of competence and how their training and accreditation can be tailored to those areas. Chapter 10 describes different forms of continuing professional development for coaches. Chapter 11 discusses a number of other books that coaches can use as source material in their professional development. Finally, Chapter 12 explores how this fascinating profession might develop in future and a number of what I consider to be important research questions with genuine relevance for coaches and their clients.

I open each part of the book with an introduction highlighting some of my own personal ways to 'coaching', 'research' and 'excellence', along a variety of beaten and unbeaten paths.

In four of the appendices to this book (Appendices A to D) the reader will find a variety of *case material* from genuine coaching conversations. I am well aware of the ethical implications of publishing such material (see also Appendix II in Casement, *On learning from the patient*, 1985). Coachees expect complete confidentiality when entering into a coaching relationship, and should be able to count on it. On the other hand, it is virtually impossible to continue to learn as a coach if you can't do so on the basis of case material from genuine coaching conversations, as well as reading through and discussing your own notes during supervision.

In my view, a coach ultimately learns the most from his own coachees, as Casement's (1985) title so aptly reflects, or by stepping into the coachee's shoes and being coached himself.

Learning on the basis of case material puts us on the horns of a real dilemma. On the one hand, there is something to be said for not publishing case histories because it irrevocably breaches the confidentiality of coaching conversations. On the other hand, seeking the coachee's consent to share or publish material is often a violation of the relationship with the coachee and, as a result, must have consequences in terms of the effectiveness of the coaching itself.

My own view is that the importance of continuing to learn from current or future coachees and from real conversations must be the deciding factor[1]. This is why I have taken this decision to publish confidential material. For the longer case studies, in Appendices C and D, I sought

---

[1] This also follows from what my code of conduct in Appendix E says about respecting and at the same time imposing limits on complete confidentiality for coachees.

the permission of the two coachees concerned. Fortunately, they responded positively and indeed were kind enough to help me carry out a number of adjustments to make the case studies more anonymous. They also contributed a few sentences with their reaction on reading the material, and which have been added at the end of the relevant appendix. Those sentences, and the coachees' reactions, do indeed show that the impact on the coachee of reading case material from their own coaching experience is far from minimal. In the case of the shorter case material in Appendices C and D (a total of 158 'critical moments' from real-life coaching conversations) I left the anonymisation and treatment of confidentiality to the 119 coaches concerned. I changed one specific reference to a recognisable organisation and submitted all of the moments – and my interpretations – to all of the coaches before proceeding with publication. I would like to thank all of those coachees and coaches for their willingness and assistance in making these case histories suitable for publication and accessible for other coaches. It sometimes takes courage to give the necessary consent. Although I can't name names here for obvious reasons, I would like to express my appreciation for that willingness and courage.

It will all have been worthwhile if the brief descriptions in Appendices A and B, and the longer studies in Appendices C and D, help the reader to develop further as a coach. The case histories certainly held quite a few lessons for me, as I hope to show in the relevant places and in Chapters 6 to 8 in particular.

The cover illustration depicts a scene of relational coaching in mythical times (it is one of the twelve famous metopes from Olympia's Temple of Zeus dating back to 456 BC). Athena was Hercules' guide. As he lay exhausted by his famous Labours, calling Zeus' name in vain, Athena came down to earth to comfort him. In the illustration, Athena is shown aiding Hercules in his attempt to persuade Atlas. Hercules is to bring the golden apples of the Hesperides, Atlas' daughters, to his client, but has heard that it would be too dangerous for him to pick them himself. Athena suggests that he offer to carry the world for Atlas for a while. Atlas will be so relieved that he will gladly fetch the apples for him. The plan works and Atlas is so enthusiastic that he offers to take the apples to Hercules' client, something Hercules doesn't permit for fear that Atlas will not return. This splendid relief shows how Athena the coach is herself prepared to assume some of Hercules' burden for him, and how Hercules in turn, with her help, is able to focus fully on his opponent Atlas. The artist depicts each relationship beautifully, and the relationship between Hercules and Athena, coachee and coach, is clearly one of enormous trust and support.

More generally, Athena in Greek mythology became an emblematic guide and protectress of heroes and demigods, who literally flourished under Athena's aegis. She helped Perseus and Hercules in their heroic quests on several occasions, and coached Odysseus and his son in her guise as Mentor (more on the latter example in Chapter 11, section 11.2.1 of this book). It comes as no surprise to me that Freud's favourite statuette in his large collection was one of Minerva, Athena's Roman equivalent. Freud's own Minerva is depicted on the back flap of this book. This small bronze cast of Athena was so dear to Freud that it usually took pride of place in the centre of his desk. Marie Bonaparte personally smuggled it out of Vienna at Freud's request, such was the figurine's importance to him. When he collected it in Paris he wrote that the family was continuing its flight to England 'proud and rich under the protection of Athena'. It depicts the goddess of protection and wisdom with her usual attributes: left hand raised to hold a spear (now long gone), right hand holding a decorated libation bowl, and on her breast the aegis with the head of Medusa. The sculpture is Roman but is probably a copy of an earlier, and greater, Greek original.

This book both attempts to offer an overview of the latest research with a bearing on coaching, and to continue in the age-old tradition of helping conversations, which has its roots in ancient Greek mythology. Several chapters of the book have been published previously, in the form of articles or columns in various journals:

- Chapter 1 as 'A new vintage – old wine maturing in new bottles' in *The Training Journal*, November 2005, pp. 20–24. Chapter 1 is also an abridged summary of our earlier book on coaching, *Coaching with colleagues* (De Haan & Burger, 2005).
- The final part of Chapter 4 was published in an extended version as 'Becoming simultaneously thicker and thinner skinned: the inherent conflicts arising in the professional development of coaches' in *Personnel Review*, 2007.
- An extended version of Chapter 5 appears as 'Executive coaching in practice: what determines helpfulness for coachees?' (E. de Haan,

V. Culpin & J. Curd) in *Consulting Psychology Journal: Practice and Research*, 2008.
- An earlier version of Chapter 6 is '"I doubt therefore I coach" – critical moments from coaching practice', in *Consulting Psychology Journal: Practice and Research*, 2008.
- Chapter 7 is a reworking of '"I struggle and emerge" – critical moments of experienced coaches', in *Consulting Psychology Journal: Practice and Research*, 2008.
- An extended version of Chapter 8: *Critical Moments in the Coaching Relationship: Does Supervision Help?* (A. Day, E. de Haan, E. Blass, C. Sills & C. Bertie) has been submitted to *Human Relations*.
- Chapter 11 was previously published as a monthly column in the periodical *The Training Journal*, under the title 'Coaching on the Couch' (January–December 2006).

With Athena as our guide we can assume that the female form is the more suitable for coaches. Still, I decided in this book to use male and female forms indiscriminately for coaches, coachees and supervisors, in order to reflect the diversity of the splendid practitioners that I see around me.

I would like to thank the following people who have made crucial contributions to the gestation of this book.

My fellow researchers at the Ashridge Centre for Coaching, especially the co-authors of Chapter 8, Colin Bertie, Eddie Blass, Andrew Day and Charlotte Sills; and Judy Curd, who made many contributions to Chapter 5.

The staff and participants of our programmes *Coaching for Organisation Consultants* and the Ashridge MSc in *Executive Coaching* including, once again, Andrew Day and Charlotte Sills; and also David Birch, Bill Critchley, Lindsey Masson, Michaela Rebbeck and Ina Smith.

My colleague Yvonne Burger and the participants of the Coaching module of Sioo business school in Utrecht.

James Tattle and Lorraine Oliver of the Ashridge Learning Resource Centre for tracking down and obtaining some quite obscure of articles and books.

Juliet Warkentin of Emap Communications for editing the book reviews in Chapter 11, and my Dutch-Canadian colleague Nico Swaan for reviewing the English translation.

Gerard Wijers of the Instituut voor Beroepskeuze en Loopbaanpsychologie for reading through the manuscript and acting as midwife to a breakthrough in my thinking about the place of coaching in our society (see Chapters 2 and 12).

London, 1 May 2007
Erik de Haan
erik.dehaan@ashridge.org.uk
www.ashridge.com/erikdehaan

Contents

Part I
The Ways of Coaching

Introduction: the paths towards coaching

At the age of 18 I took a gap year and travelled solo round Germany and France, working and living in Berlin, the Pyrenees and Paris. My aims were to improve the language skills I hadn't properly mastered at school, and to lead a 'working' life before spending the next few years in academia. I also wanted to pin down exactly what it was I was going to specialise in. My first two aims were more or less achieved, but I didn't actually devote much thought to the third, and at the end of the year signed up for physics, the same subject that had attracted my lukewarm interest a year before.

Most of my year out went well and in fact flew by, but there was one moment when I really did lose my way, a moment which in retrospect is indicative of how I often feel as a coach. I was heading from the Pyrenees to Paris and decided to walk to Carcassonne for the first few days, then hitch-hike from there. All I had with me on this hike was a road map of the whole country, on a scale of one to a million. But I wasn't worried because I intended to keep to roads and beaten tracks. One day, however, while hiking through the foothills of the mountains, I must have had a bout of over-confidence, when I decided to leave the road I was on and head straight north in a short-cut towards another local road. I ended up in a wooded area with a maze of tiny paths and denser and denser undergrowth. This was the infamous French *maquis*, which sheltered many a resistance fighter during the Occupation, so becoming a byword for the Resistance.

As the scrub got thicker it became harder to follow some of the paths, and the ones I was on seemed to have been made by creatures smaller than a human being, so frequently did they disappear beneath low bushes. Because I couldn't see any way through it, I decided just to walk up towards the highest point, where I would undoubtedly get a better overall picture. This strategy seemed to work well at first, because there came a point when the scrub died out. I found myself just below the summit of an elongated hill that I could easily climb. Everything seemed to be becoming clear, but the opposite was in fact the case. The hill, covered with grass and low bushes, turned out to be around a kilometre long, perhaps a hundred metres wide, and surrounded on all sides by dense vegetation. I *could* see a long way from the top, as I'd hoped, but what I saw caused me to break out in a cold sweat. An endless succession of similar hills and valleys stretched out before me, all arranged more or less in parallel and with no sign of buildings or roads, let alone wind direction. At least, not to an inexperienced hiker such as myself. Closer by, there was only a jumble of crisscrossing paths, used for horse-riding judging by the hoofprints and other evidence. It was late in the afternoon, I had no idea where to head next and was quickly losing sight of where I'd come from. I was able to walk to and fro over the bare back of the hill, but that made absolutely no difference to my current predicament. My throat closed up, I felt feverish, my breathing quickened and I felt almost compelled to cry out. Because no one would hear me, I didn't, as far as I recall. In the end I did the only thing I could think of: dive into the undergrowth somewhere at random and walk down in what felt like a straight line, for better or worse, looking for some form of habitation.

In the end I did make my way out and found roads and signposts again, but the existential angst I felt at the top of that hill has stayed with me ever since. It reminds me of a feeling I get during most coaching conversations. Fortunately, the angst experienced during coaching is accompanied by less panic, because it has now happened many times and I know I will always return to an 'inhabited world', but it is exactly the same feeling nonetheless.

I believe it is worthwhile to describe that 'angst' or anxiety in more detail. I know it isn't 'stage fright' or 'performance anxiety' because I know what those feel like. I get them regularly when I have to stand up before a large group of people. Stage fright is accompanied by a surge of adrenalin, butterflies in the stomach, disturbed sleep beforehand and a state of hyper-alertness. And it disappears the moment I get to know the group and the podium and when I start to feel that things are going well. It often leaves me with a sort of 'hangover' of irritability and tiredness.

'Coaching anxiety' is quite different because it brings none of those symptoms, not even any particular tension before the coachee's arrival. On the other hand, this anxiety doesn't decline when I feel that things are going well. It is the pure fear of the unknown, the fear of not knowing what will happen next whilst realising that knowing is impossible.

To continue the parallel drawn above, the ways of coaching can probably best be compared to the jumble of crisscrossing paths in the *maquis*, or the absence of paths beaten by human beings. We need to find our own way, without a map or outside assistance.

It is this exploration off the beaten track that makes coaching such an unpredictably rich profession, constantly full of surprises. It also explains, for me, why there are so many different ways of coaching, probably as many as there are coaches. Or perhaps even more than the number of practitioners, because each retelling spawns new and different approaches: each time we recount our coaching experiences we cannot help adding new interpretations and ideas, and leaving others out.

In the first part of this book I hope to give an overview of the state of the art of the profession, paying special attention to its fundamentally 'unexplored' nature and the various paths and roads proposed by professionals. In Chapter 3 I examine what *is* known about helping conversations. Precisely because so much is unknown about each coaching conversation, it is good to know that some important results have been achieved in determining the most effective factors in one-to-one conversations. This chapter contains a summary of the findings from decades of quantitative research into effectiveness. Not that such facts, based on the retrospective analysis of thousands of therapeutic relationships, can help with the existential angst itself, because that is different every time and has to do with *this* relationship and *this* conversation. But the results of research can certainly give the coach confidence and point him, or her, towards the attitude towards coaching that is most effective. To illustrate this, Chapter 4 lists 'ten commandments' for the executive coach based on empirical research in the field of psychotherapy.

In a nutshell, Chapter 1 contains an overview of the entire specialist area of the executive coach. Chapter 2 deals with the history and development of the profession and the current surge of interest in executive coaching. Chapter 3 summarises the meta-analytical studies in psychotherapy which hold lessons for coaches. Finally, Chapter 4 outlines my perspective on the most effective form of coaching, *relational coaching*.

Chapter 1
From Intake to Intervention: the Outlines of a Profession

The discipline of coaching is currently enjoying a resurgence of interest in the form of new and diverse initiatives on the part of government, industry and consultancies. A potential risk, however, is that the label of 'coach', which already has precious little statutory or professional protection, will be further eroded. What exactly does the word 'coaching' stand for in the twenty-first century; and what is needed to give coaching the support that its intensive and widespread practice demands, and that can make the discipline an independent and clearly delimited profession?

1.1 Coaching: a new trend?

The term *coaching* may appear fashionable but it has a long history behind it. In Chapter 2 I will look at the history of the word coaching. It is important to realise here that inspiring coaching conversations have been passed down from classical times[1], in the dialogues of Plato, Cicero's conversations in Tusculum, and Seneca's letters to Lucilius for example. The first coach appears in Homer's *Odyssey*, where the goddess Pallas Athena assumes the form of Mentor in order to assist adventurous mortals. There is currently a growing interest in this age-old tradition of work-related learning that relies primarily on one-to-one conversations. In those conversations, the coach is focused on facilitating the coachees' learning and development and tries to take care that the coachees take care of themselves. The aim of coaching is to improve the coachees' performance by discussing their relationship to certain experiences and issues.

---

[1] See Chapter 11 section 11.2.1 for a reading of the *Odyssey* with special attention to the mentoring in that work, and Chapter 11, section 11.2.2 for a discussion of Plato's *Meno*.

The coach's intention is to encourage reflection by the coachee, to release hidden strengths and to overcome or eliminate obstacles to further development. The focus is on such topics as:

- how the coachee works with others and makes sense of organisational life;
- how the coachee acts in specific situations, such as those involving managing, negotiating, giving advice or exerting influence;
- how the coachee handles difficult situations, such as with colleagues and clients;
- how the coachee forms judgments and makes decisions.

These topics are linked not only to the coachee's professional role and the content of the specialist area but also to the person of the coachee and the knowledge and skills at their disposal, the way in which they think and act. Because there is a personal component, it is important for coachees to become aware of their own actions and to consider alternatives. The coach helps in this respect, in the first instance mainly by clarifying the problem. There is often a link between the person who has an issue and the nature of that issue. For example, a given question can be very difficult for one individual to address, while someone else barely registers it or is able to resolve it without difficulty. The degree to which a problem affects us, makes us insecure, causes sleepless nights or intrigues us, says something about the problem, of course, but also something about the person who perceives and 'owns' the problem. I distinguish the following possible relationships between 'problem owner' and 'problem':

1   Some problems are 'objective' or technical in nature. For example, if someone is having trouble with certain software packages, this might relate to resistance to information technology, but usually has more to do with a lack of knowledge or skill. Sometimes, therefore, there is simply a need to acquire knowledge or learn a particular skill. *Expert advice* can provide a solution here.

2   Sometimes, however, acquiring knowledge or learning new behaviour is not enough. There are underlying patterns which suggest that, though this specific problem may be solved, the same problem (possibly in a different form) will reappear the next day. Here it is important to consider not the incident, but the work context and the patterns that led to the incident. This is not always easy, because a feature of such patterns is that they often go unrecognised by the person concerned. Many people have a tendency to define

problems as separate from themselves: 'It's not my fault; it's the work environment; it's my colleagues'. *Coaching* can provide a solution here.

3 Sometimes issues and problems are so personal that a thorough exploration within the context of work and professional experience is insufficient. An individual's abilities and limitations underlie the problems at hand. A characteristic aspect of such problems is that they are experienced as much privately as they are at work. *Therapy* can provide a solution here.

A *coaching conversation* therefore centres partly on personal performance, but always in the context of practice. In my experience, the scope of coaching issues is more or less as follows:

1 Issues where content is at the centre will often relate to unexpected experiences, for example in drafting proposals and giving advice. These are often put forward in terms of 'what' questions: 'What kind of system should I use here?'.

2 Issues where the actions of the issue holder and the way in which he or she handles a problem are central, are often put forward in terms of 'how' questions: 'Will you, as my coach, help me to decide how to do this, or how to tackle this issue?'.

3 Issues where the very person raising the issue is at the centre are often put forward in terms of 'what' questions too: 'What kind of assignments suit me?' or 'What is it about me that makes me

1. Issues where content and specialist knowledge are at the centre, where the focus is on applying them in specific, difficult situations.	2. Issues with a content element, but where the actions of the coachee and the way in which she handles the content are central.	3. Issues where the personal characteristics of the coachee are central.
'What' questions	**'How' questions**	**'Who' questions**

⟵ **Range of coaching issues** ⟶

Figure 1.1

come up against this time and again?'. As these are more personal 'what' issues, they can also be put forward as 'who' questions, along the lines of 'Who am I, and what type of work is suitable for me?'.

In coaching, a number of different levels are present simultaneously. The focus is often not only on the technical or organisational issue raised, and on ways of dealing with it, but also on the personal dynamic and emotional undercurrents at the root of such issues. The coach is constantly having to choose which of these levels to pursue, or at which level to make a contribution. In making that choice, the coach determines to a large extent how the conversation will continue. The importance of choosing the 'right' level of intervention therefore often becomes clear only in retrospect.

Various traditional forms of coaching, such as mentoring, individual consultation and counselling, are often differentiated by the level at which they tend to intervene, as is also demonstrated by the overview of the scope of coaching conversations given in Figure 1.2.

The role of coach was previously assumed largely by managers and external coaches, and we are now seeing an increase in the training and use of *internal coaches*. Coaching has become an instrument for enabling organisational renewal from within.

1.2 Developing a coaching relationship

The *first impressions* that people gain of each other have a significant impact on the course of the subsequent coaching. First impressions can, after all, be strong and persistent. They can tell you a lot about the underlying themes, but can also be deceptive. A particularly positive or negative first impression often indicates that something is going on that might obstruct an open, exploratory approach. It is worthwhile registering a number of things consciously right at the outset, such as:
- Are both parties on time, or does one arrive early or late?
- Do they shake hands? What does the handshake feel like? Do they look at each other?
- What associations does this person have for you? Who do they remind you of?

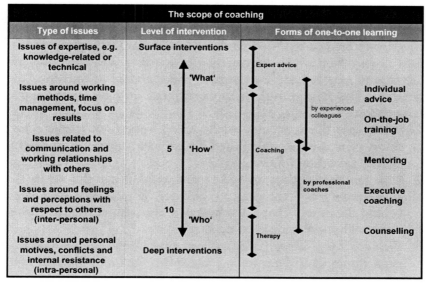

Figure 1.2 *The scope of coaching.*

- How do the two parties get on? What body language do you notice?
- Do you use first names? Do you break the ice, or give a formal introduction?

There is no single correct answer to these questions, but it seems important to consider them as experience shows that 'minor' impressions at the start can have major consequences later on. The start of a coaching relationship is often dominated by the *needs* of both coachee and coach, and by their degree of openness about those needs. The coachee often needs help, and is quite possibly hoping for a specific *type* of help and a specific approach from the coach. In a sense, such a coachee supplies the problem and the solution right at the outset!

The coach clearly needs a coachee in order to be a coach. In a wider sense, a coach often has a need to be helpful to someone and to consolidate that helpfulness. It helps to be aware of the existence of such needs, their translation into specific wishes or their concealment using diversionary tactics, right from the start. Managing them explicitly and in a productive way can then commence, if necessary, right at the start of the coaching relationship.

It is advisable for you, as the coach, to enter into and build up the relationship as *consciously* as possible. To that end, it may be useful to investigate for yourself – patiently and almost a little suspiciously – how the coachee arrived at the issue in question, and what role you are seen to play in handling the issue and therefore in the life of the coachee. The following thought experiment may be useful in this connection[2]:

1 What does this coachee actually want? To get away from something, or to achieve something? To explore something, or to arm against something?

2 How has the coachee arrived at this wish? What else might the issue relate to? What does it point to? What might be hidden behind the issue? What is the history of the wish or issue and what attempts have already been made to address it?

3 Why coaching? What has led to this request? What does the coachee expect from it? What recommendations is she following, and from whom?

4 And why me? What expectations does this coachee have of me – what prejudices, perhaps – what assumptions about my method? What is the coachee hoping for?

5 What feelings does this coachee prompt in me? Do I think we get on? What do I think of the quality of our contact? What is the coachee appealing to in me? Can I and do I want to offer that? What is my own interest? And what am I hoping for myself?

6 What approach is the coachee requesting? What approach do I think myself is best? Does the coachee have sufficient strength to handle my preferred approach?

7 What does this mean for our relationship? How is it going to develop? How am I to enter into that relationship? How can I show in my behaviour what kind of relationship I envisage? How can I adopt my own choice of coaching approach from our very first meeting?

Once the coaching has started, many types of coach/coachee relationship can develop, often geared very specifically to the interaction between this particular coach and this particular coachee. All of these

---

[2] Appendix F contains an intake checklist for the coach, based on this thought-experiment.

productive coaching relationships are examples of *working alliances*[3], and they probably replicate previous helpful relationships in the life of coach and coachee. By quickly creating a strong working alliance, the coach attempts from the outset to make use of the coachee's previous experience of helping conversations. The following typical forms of working alliance can be differentiated:

1 The *guild master/freeman* relationship, in which the coachee presents practical issues, and the coach becomes deeply involved in those issues and says something meaningful about them. This relationship is often seen between mentor and mentee, or in supervision.

2 The *doctor/patient* relationship, in which the coachee discloses all, revealing uncertainties and emotions as completely as possible; the coach interprets the problems and outlines possible solutions. This relationship often arises with more emotional themes and issues.

3 The *midwife/mother* relationship, in which the coach anticipates the coachee's problems and seeks to provide strength to tackle them. This relationship is characteristic of a concerned and caring coach.

4 The *peer review* relationship, in which coach and coachee look together at the coachee's day-to-day practice and subject it to as independent an examination as possible. They 'dot the i's' together and take a critical look at the coachee's approaches and plans. This relationship often arises in a coaching assignment geared towards finding out something new.

5 The *old boys* relationship, in which the coachee seeks out the coach as a *sparring partner* in order to exchange experiences and try out ideas. The coachee often rehearses certain approaches and conversations with the coach. This relationship often arises in the coaching of senior managers.

In my day-to-day practice I see various mixtures of these typical relationships. A strong coaching relationship may evolve from one to another, depending on changes in the nature of the themes.

---

[3] Freud (1913) distinguished between positive and friendly aspects of the helping relationship and neurotic aspects of the same relationship, whereby the former work together with the therapist to do something about the latter. The term 'working alliance' comes from Greenson (1965).

Take care that coaching relationships do not deteriorate unnoticed into 'ordinary' significant relationships, like that of a courting couple, rival scientists, a rich uncle and favourite nephew, or a parent and dependent child. The coaching relationship comes into everyone's life after many other important relationships have already been entered into. Almost inevitably, the coaching relationship comes to resemble one or more of its predecessors. This is not a problem in itself, as long as it does not happen completely unnoticed, and it does not undermine the essence of the coaching relationship (as bounded and for the benefit of the coachee).

As long as the coach continues to reflect – patiently and almost suspiciously! – on the nature of the relationship and is not led astray into non-coaching interventions, any resemblance to other, earlier relationships can only be enriching and instructive. Forces that exert an influence in all other relationships, such as the quest for inclusion, control, or affection (see Schutz, 1958), will unavoidably also come into play in this coaching relationship – and there is an increased opportunity to learn about them here.

1.3 The organisation coach

Coaching of individuals is also coaching of an organisation, because the coachee's organisation is present in and through every coachee. This is the main difference between coaching and psychotherapy: coaching is work- and organisation-oriented, while therapy is more remote from the working organisation – the organisation being only one dominant system of which the client forms part.

The coachee is the person who translates and applies the outcome of coaching conversations in their own practice. With the aid of coaching renewed sense is made of the situation, and the coachee prepares to adapt accordingly, becoming the link between the coaching relationship and organisational practice. In fact, for the coachee, entering into a relationship with a coach means an additional adjustment and finding a new role, namely that of coachee of this coach. Because it is a role that is situated partly outside of the coachee's ordinary working practice, it offers opportunities for gaining insight and for experimenting. It is often useful to look at your coachee as a translator or messenger between coach and organisation. This is particularly helpful if it emerges that certain actions planned during the coaching conversation are not carried out in the coachee's refractory day-to-day practice – in other words, when the coachee experiences (in the view of the coach) a 'relapse'.

The coachee attempts to develop within a role provided by the organisation, and develops as an individual and in personal roles at the same time. On the basis of life experience, the coachee brings along all sorts of (behavioural) patterns, which are visible in role-behaviour. After some time in the role, moreover, the coachee carries the organisation internally, as in a hologram or a fractal, each fragment of which still contains the entire original image (see Armstrong, 2004). In other words, the coachee reflects elements of their entire emotional experience in an organisation in every fragment of conversation. Like a fragment of the hologram, the coachee presents a complete and personal image of the organisation. Making use of this, the coach can often relate the coachee's problems and emotions to the problems and emotions prevailing within the coachee's organisation. The coach should ask him or herself regularly during coaching conversations: what sort of function do I fulfil as a coach in the coachee's organisation? This question can also be put to the coachee: what is the emotional 'value' of your role for yourself and for your organisation?

An example is the coachee who describes the way in which he was recently treated by his own organisation as 'an itch that I cannot scratch' and who, later in the coaching conversation, describes his own behaviour within the same organisation as 'disruptive but not destructive'. Here, the informal role of the organisation for this person appears to be virtually identical to the informal role of the person for the organisation, namely an itch you can't scratch, an irritation that just won't go away. Later in the conversation it emerges that the coach is increasingly tempted to start being irritating himself, thereby acting as an 'itch' for his coachee to (not be able to) scratch.

1.4 The coach's playing field

In my view, there are two main choices that a coach can make at any time in the conversation. The first is the *direction* of their contribution: exploring or guiding? The coach can choose at each moment to follow and open up the coachee's thoughts and contributions, or to comment upon them and introduce their own thoughts and contributions. This enables the coach to influence the direction of the conversation, by deciding whether to 'lead' or to 'follow' the coachee. In the first instance the coach will *suggest* or propose something; in the second the coach will be at the service of a joint *exploration* or discovery process.

The second is the *nature* of the contribution: supporting or confronting? The coach can decide at each moment to build on and reinforce the coachee's (perceived) strengths, or else to bring up and help to overcome the coachee's (perceived) weaknesses. This enables the coach to influence the *construction* or *deconstruction* of the conversation, by deciding to *support* or *challenge* the coachee more.

Combining each of these two choices gives a basic playing field for the coach, encompassing four options. Each of these four orientations leads to a different focus on the part of the coach. In addition, each orientation has given rise to specific approaches and 'schools' of coaching, as follows (see Figure 1.3):

1 *Person-focused coaching* (see for example Kline, 1999). Exploring and supporting, or facilitating the coachee with encouragement and understanding. The coach attempts to explore the issue together with the coachee and contributes warmth and understanding to the conversation.

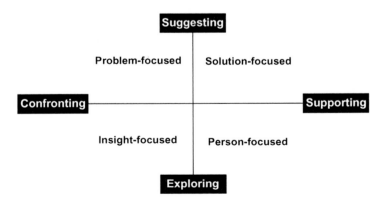

Figure 1.3 *The window onto the coach: different contributions from the coach*

2 *Insight-focused coaching* (see for example Brunning, 2006). Exploring and confronting, or facilitating the coachee at a greater distance. The coach attempts to look at what the coachee is leaving out and is not aware of, thus contributing understanding and objectivity to the conversation.

3 *Problem-focused coaching* (see for example Whitmore, 1992, or Skiffington & Zeus, 2003). Suggesting and confronting, or helping the coachee with suggestions and instructions. The coach attempts to offer the coachee a new framework or approach to the problems being considered, and contributes ideas and guidance to the conversation.

4 *Solution-focused coaching* (see for example Greene & Grant, 2003, or Pemberton, 2006). Suggesting and supporting, or helping the coachee with options and positive feedback. The coach attempts to send the coachee off on a more positive, constructive train of thought and to help with suggestions for the future.

The main coaching methodologies have a place within this playing field (for more information on these specific methodologies, see De Haan & Burger, 2005):

1 *Person-focused coaching* is based on the *counselling methods* as developed by Carl Rogers in particular (1961). In this approach the coach attempts to shift the coachee's attention inwards and is available primarily as an accepting and attentive listener.

2 *Insight-focused coaching* is based on the long tradition of psychodynamic coaching. The coach attempts, with the coachee, to understand the issue from the inside. A number of more specific insight-focused methods are:

a) the *analytic method* – in which the coach concentrates on the signals he is picking up, what is not being said, the conflict or ambivalence that is central to the issue, and what the coachee does with the coach.

b) the *organisation coach method* – in which the coach continues to concentrate on signals, omissions, conflicts, ambivalence and transference, but pays special attention to transference from the coachee's organisation.

c) the *ladder method* – in which the coach and coachee explore the assumptions behind the latter's issue, the reasons for those assumptions, and the underlying conflicts and emotions that led to those assumptions, and then go on to ask whether alternative assumptions are also possible.

3 *Problem-focused coaching* is primarily directive in nature. The coach attempts to improve the situation from the outside. Coaching approaches include:
   a) The *GROW method* – in which the coach asks in turn about the coachee's Goal or objective, the Reality relating to the issue, potential Options and the coachee's Will or determination, spelling out the word GROW (see Whitmore, 1992).
   b) The *ironic method* – in which the coach parries ambivalence and defences with irony, reflecting the irony in the issue back towards the coachee.
   c) The *paradoxical method* – in which the coach parries ambivalence and defences with a paradoxical instruction, an assignment for the coachee that contains an unsolvable dilemma.
   d) The *provocative method* – in which the coach consciously provokes resistance and intentionally frustrates the coachee's thought processes (see Farrelly & Brandsma, 1974).
4 *Solution-focused coaching* is a particular form of directive coaching, in which coach and coachee look predominantly to the future and consider times when the problem does *not* arise. The coach attempts to convert problems into positive plans and challenges.

1.5 A coach from inside or outside the organisation?

For the coaching intervention to succeed, the coach must not only consider the most suitable approach together with the coachee, but also the question of whether the coach should come from inside or outside the coachee's work or other organisation. There are two striking differences between internal coaches and coaches from outside the organisation:
1 First, the internal coach is *not truly independent* with respect to the organisation. The coach has a personal role to play in it, and also has their own (emotional) experience of and connection with the organisation. This sometimes makes it difficult for the coach to 'empty the mind' and listen with complete objectivity to what the coachee is saying. And it also makes it more difficult for the coachee to be sure of complete confidentiality.
2 On the other hand, the internal coach has *more knowledge* of the organisation and therefore a clear idea of the context within which

the coachee is operating. Not every external coach is able to assess that context properly. However, knowledge of the organisation can sometimes also impede a fresh and independent assessment of the organisational context and the coachee's issues.

Besides these differences, there are other reasons why organisations choose to work with internal coaches. For example, the organisation sees coaching as an effective form of learning and wants to build up that knowledge and experience within the organisation, to enable the organisation to gain maximum benefit. In addition, organisations choose an internal coach as part of the continuing personal supervision of staff, so as to increase the effectiveness of the organisation. These are considerations of a purely practical nature. The organisation wants to have constant access to coaching expertise and not to be dependent on outsiders. Often, the organisation also wants to keep the costs of coaching under control, especially if it plans to offer coaching to wider target groups.

1.6 What works for whom?

Different coachees, issues and objectives require different approaches (see Wasylyshyn, 2003, or Roth & Fonagy, 1996). My own hunches relating to applicability, which are merely initial assumptions for a correct application of the different coaching methods, are given in the following table (Figure 1.4).

I return to applicability in Chapter 3, where I summarise what is known about the effectiveness of (different approaches in) psycho-therapy. The question of when to apply which approach is very complex and depends on a range of factors (such as the person of the coach, the person of the coachee, the aim of the coaching, the nature of the coaching relationship, and the wider work context). It is doubtful that we can ever have a much better guideline than the hunches in Figure 1.4, and it is also doubtful whether we should be asking ourselves the question in this way: modern research shows that all known professional methods in psychotherapy are equally effective and that what matters more are other factors such as the personalities of coach and coachee. This topic too is revisited in Chapter 3.

Method	When can it be used?	Recommended where there is/are	Not recommended where there is/are
GROW method	broadly applicable, even to short, specific issues	high motivation, but little idea of possible ways to move forward	emotional issues, non-specific issues, double meanings
Ironic method	broadly applicable	those that ask for advice; those that do not take responsibility	low self-confidence, lack of confidence in coaching
Paradoxical method	in the case of ambiguous, internally contradictory questions to the coach	strongly ambiguous messages and unclear motivation for coaching	no strong and absolutely necessary reasons for using it
Solution-focused method	broadly applicable, especially to practical issues	discouragement, anxiety about the future	'visitors' and 'complainers', i.e. coachees not prepared to consider their own share in the problem
Counselling method	broadly applicable, especially in a longer-term coaching relationship	lack of self-confidence or self-motivation	need for a critical sparring partner
Analytic method	broadly applicable, especially to multi-layered and emotional problems	'visitors' and 'complainers'	need to achieve quick results and find solutions, low self-confidence
Ladder method	multi-layered problems, including short, specific issues	willingness and ability to consider their own assumptions	non-specific issues, highly emotional issues

Figure 1.4 *Application of different coaching approaches.*

Summary: from intake to intervention

Coaching is a method of work-related learning that relies primarily on one-to-one conversations.

The **aim** of coaching is to increase the coachee's performance by discussing their relationship to the experiences and problems raised.

Coaching is situated somewhere between **expert advice** and **therapy**. The **scope** or **intervention level** of coaching embraces the following issues:

1 expert advice: issues of expertise, e.g. knowledge-related or technical;
2 handling of knowledge-related and technical issues;
3 issues around working methods, time management, focus on results;
4 issues related to communication and working relationships with others;
5 issues around feelings and perceptions with respect to others (interpersonal);
6 issues around personal motives, conflicts and internal resistance (intrapersonal);
7 therapy: purely personal issues.

A short **intake checklist** is as follows:

1 What does the coachee want?
2 Where does this wish or question come from?
3 Where does the idea of coaching come from?
4 Where does the idea of me as coach come from?
5 What is my response to this question?
6 How can I help? What do I need in order to help?
7 How can the coachee help himself or herself?
8 How are we going to work with each other?
9 How are we working with each other now?

In relation to the last two questions, there are five known **coach/coachee relationship patterns**:

1 a **guild master/freeman** relationship;
2 a **doctor/patient** relationship;
3 a **midwife/mother** relationship;
4 a **peer review** relationship;
5 an 'old boys' relationship.

The coach's possible contributions can be presented clearly using the **window onto the coach**:

1 **Person-focused coaching**: observing and supporting the coachee from the coachee's perspective.
2 **Insight-focused coaching**: considering the coachee from an independent perspective and trying to understand the problem.
3 **Problem-focused coaching**: helping the coachee with an approach to the problem.
4 **Solution-focused coaching**: supporting the coachee in their search for solutions.

Chapter 2
From Stigma to Status: the Growth of a Profession

2.1 The exponential growth in coaching practice

In Chapter 1 I attempted to define the field of activity of professional coaches and to give an overview of the approaches that coaches choose. Defining the entire field of coaching has become more difficult over the years because the profession has grown so much and has only become broader and more varied in the process. There are now many hundreds of books about coaching, mentoring and counselling, and still more numerous development programmes in this area. Popular modern buzzwords are 'team coaching' and 'organisation coaching' and coaches are therefore gaining ground that was previously the domain of facilitators and consultants. Increasingly, I find I am being asked for assignments about 'creating a coaching culture', where executives would like to be using more 'coaching' techniques in their management style, or to work together more closely with their staff around personal development.

Due to the huge success of coaching and the increasing attention paid to it by professionals and authors from other fields, it seems as if the word 'coaching' is now being tacked on to a range of traditional development activities as a marketing prop to increase their chances of success.

If one considers publications with coaching in their title or subtitle, one can observe an exponential growth over the last 50 years (Grant, 2006): 2 articles in the years from 1955–1965, 9 from 1965–1975, 25 from 1975–1985, 39 from 1985–1995, rising to 318 in the years from 1995–2005.

We have already seen in Chapter 1 that coaching can be anchored within the discipline of psychotherapy. This should make this 'new entrant' to the management consultancy world at once the best-investigated and best-understood form of management consultancy, as demonstrated by the lessons learnt in the next chapter from thousands of quantitative research articles in the psychotherapy literature. Is it in fact correct to base the discipline of coaching on that of psychotherapy? A look at the etymology of the word 'coaching' reveals that other foundations are also possible.

'Coach' is defined in the dictionary as 'a carriage which conveys individuals from where they were to where they want to be'. The coach is therefore a vehicle, a way of getting from A to B, and not a person who contributes knowledge or experience and gives instructions. In my view, this is the main difference between a mentor and a coach: one is a more experienced professional who contributes his own expertise; the other is an instrument in the coachee's learning, who is not necessarily familiar with or experienced in the coachee's field of work. It is interesting to note that the word 'coach' comes from the name of the Hungarian village Kocs, where a particularly popular type of wooden carriage was produced in the fifteenth century. In the mid-nineteenth century the word is used for the first time to describe a type of educator (in 1850 at Oxford University), and the term 'sports coach' also dates back to that time (1867, first used in connection with rowing; see Garvey, 2006). For me the word 'coach' therefore symbolises the gradual change in our society from craftsmanship ('Kocs carriage') to industrial ('railway coach') to knowledge-intensive ('educator-coach') to emotionally intelligent ('executive coach') production methods. From this etymology it seems possible to identify at least four – overlapping – bases for coaching activities.

1 A *transport expert* or change expert: how do you get someone from A to B? The old meaning of 'coach' that still perhaps best sums up the essence of coaching.
2 An *educator* (including the sports context): how do you improve someone's performance?
3 A *therapist*, sometimes reinforced in the term 'remedial coaching': how do you help someone to overcome obstacles and make them stronger and more effective?
4 An *organisation developer* (particularly in the term 'executive coaching'): how do you develop an organisation by supporting individual professionals within that organisation?

None of these influences has a privileged position. A study of 71
coachees, reported in Chapter 5, found that coachees recognise
each of these aspects and look for combinations of them (almost all of
those interviewed ticked more than one of the five options given
below):

- (in the transport expert tradition:) 56% of the interviewees (the
  largest group) indicate that one of their aims is to change their
  behaviour or approach;
- (in the educator tradition:) 30% of the interviewees indicate that
  one of their aims is to learn something new;
- (in the therapist tradition:) 41% of the interviewees indicate that
  one of their aims is to become stronger, and 15% that they want
  to stop doing something;
- (in the organisation developer tradition:) 52% of the interviewees indicate that one of their aims is to reflect on their own
  practice.

These figures add up to much more than 100% because the interviewees were able to tick either one or two options.

The discipline of executive coaching has experienced a huge expansion in recent years. On the part of the coach there has been increasing
professionalism and quality assurance in the form of codes of conduct,
supervision and personal accreditation. There has also been wider self-
certification of coach development programmes by international associations of coaches such as the European Mentoring & Coaching
Council (EMCC), the Worldwide Association of Business Coaches
(WABC) and the International Coach Federation (ICF).

On the part of the coachees I am witnessing increasingly meticulous
assessment and evaluation of coaches and greater explicitness about
the expected contributions and results of coaching. On the part of
many organisations there has been increasing attention to selecting
and benchmarking external coaches and to the professional design of
in-house coaching and mentoring systems. This self-certification and
benchmarking may help to ensure a more careful choice of interventions and to reduce the small number of cases of abuse, lack of proper
conduct and supervision, and undue flattery of vulnerable clients that
do still occur (Berglas, 2002).

2.2 Underlying social trends

We live in unusual times, where we are perhaps both the most actively learning generation and the one most resistant to learning. The following longer-term trends relevant to coaching will be recognisable to most readers.

1 We live in a time of ever-increasing *connectedness*: modern telecommunications technology has enabled 'world citizens' to be privately and economically connected worldwide, to have numerous products and ideas in common, and to communicate with each other despite cultural and social differences. This trend is often called globalisation.

2 (following on from the previous trend:) We are exposed to an overwhelming number of influences, changes and responsibilities. Never before has the number of different influences on a human life been so great as it is for the twenty-first century inhabitant of the West. Thanks to the internet, telephony and television, we have more information 'at our fingertips' than evolution has equipped us to process.

3 (following on from the previous trend:) We are under increasing pressure to form opinions and make decisions on ever more existential questions, such as our political economy, our capacity to kill on a large scale, and our 'footprint' on the planet. Choices made by individuals now have far-reaching consequences.

4 (following on from the previous trend:) Traditional 'spiritual care' has come under pressure due to the development of modern alternatives such as therapy, counselling and coaching, but also because clients themselves are choosing between all of these options. The consumer of such care is becoming increasingly central to the delivery.

5 (still following on from the trend before last:) The traditional work context has also come under pressure. Our relationship to work is undergoing a radical change in the Western world: the nature of the work that people do is increasingly a result of free personal choices and the boundaries of work are becoming less sharply defined, such that work and private interests and activities are increasingly overlapping.

All of these long-term trends are having significant consequences for personal learning. Modern managers and professionals are inevitably having to devote increasing time to learning activities:

- to prepare themselves for and mount a response to the rising surge of impressions and changes;
- to form a basis for increasingly far-reaching choices and decisions;
- to accommodate themselves within a constantly changing work context; and
- to find personal satisfaction in their work and in their private lives.

Learning has therefore become an activity that more and more professionals are explicitly getting to grips with, and an activity that is considered important in an increasing number of fields of work. This is remarkable because learning is in the first instance a painful and risky activity. Painful because you often have to give something up for it, and risky because it is an excursion into the unknown and you don't know in advance what the situation will be like once you have completed the activity.

Edgar Schein (e.g. in Schein, Schneier & Barker, 1961) described learning as a compromise between two anxieties:

1 anxiety about staying the same (dissatisfaction with one's symptoms, fear of progress or even of making the existing situation worse); and
2 anxiety about change (fear of the new and reluctance to change).

The extent to which we can expose ourselves to the first fear is a measure of how much discontentment or dissatisfaction we are able to bear. The extent to which we can expose ourselves to the second fear is, as Nietzsche put it (in *Ecce Homo*, 1888), a measure of how much 'truth' we are able to bear about ourselves. We need a degree of certainty in order to bear the 'learning anxiety', and we need a degree of change to bear the 'survival anxiety'[1]. Another way to express this comes from Harrison (1963): in order to learn, we need a 'castle' and a 'battleground':

---

[1] Personality traits also play a role: disposition to handle survival anxiety is a measure of 'emotional stability', disposition to handle learning anxiety is a measure of 'readiness to change' (compare with factors C and Q1 of the well-known 16PF personality description – Cattell, 1989).

- A castle as a safe fortress to which we can retreat, a base from which we can tolerate uncertainties.
- A battlefield as a place where we can come to the painful realisation that we still have something to learn and that it will not be easy.

In my view, the five social trends outlined above conspire to feed those two anxieties, the 'survival anxiety' and the 'learning anxiety'. Survival anxiety increases because there is more change, and the inability to continue as before becomes a virtual certainty. Learning anxiety increases because those changes call for greater autonomy and we have to be increasingly self-reliant. As a result, many professionals become weighed down in an existential manner under one or both anxieties, so that the possibility of learning for them becomes not easier but nevertheless more regular and more necessary.

One might argue that what is learned subsequently is more of the same, because more and more people are having to find answers, individually and for themselves, to the great existential questions such as 'How do I live my life?', 'How much pollution do I want to be responsible for?', 'Where do my political affiliations lie?', 'Where do I work?', 'What sort of role can I play?'. This wheel, the wheel of personal development, is therefore reinvented over and over again, but that does not make us less engaged in learning activities.

It is no surprise that there is increasing reliance on professional facilitation of personal learning, coming from domains such as organisation development, peer consultation and individual coaching. I believe that the increase in both survival anxiety and learning anxiety explains, at least in part, why coaching has taken off so much over the last decade. The most personal and individual of the various learning initiatives is coaching, which is why, in my view, it is the fastest-growing of all forms of organisation development.

We can also highlight three further long-term trends that are having an influence within the field of coaching but whose scope extends much wider than simply learning and personal or organisation development.
1   From *remedial* to *developmental*. The negative status and stigma that attached to managers who needed a coach for their professional development appear to have been replaced by a positive status,

arising from the fact that the manager is evidently important enough to the organisation to merit the investment in coaching (Frisch, 2001). It is also noticeable that, given the importance of personal learning on the shop floor, managers are generally more willing to reveal their vulnerabilities than they were a decade ago, and that too is having an effect on the quality of executive coaching.

2   From *sectarian* to *integrative*. Most development programmes for coaches, but also handbooks and scholarly articles, were traditionally developed on the basis of a single guiding approach. As a result, many schools invest a great deal of energy in differentiating and criticising fellow institutes which tackle things differently. After the general integration within psychotherapy in the past decades (*cognitive-behavioural, integrative*; see Norcross & Goldfried, 1992, or Lapworth, Sills & Fish, 2001) it now seems the time has come to practise the discipline of coaching from an integrative perspective. Books such as Peltier, 2001, and De Haan & Burger, 2005, already advocate this approach. Chapter I also outlines the discipline of coaching in an integrative manner. More and more often, different approaches are being given a place in an all-encompassing description of the profession.

3   From *hobbyism* to *expertise*. This is perhaps the slowest-developing of the three, because it is being held back by the growing popularity of coaching and the rapid expansion in the numbers of coaches. From way back, a wide range of professionals have entered the discipline of coaching, often without acquiring specific preliminary accreditation, certification, or a code of conduct. These prerequisites are, however, increasingly being stipulated by clients as a condition, and the efforts towards better qualification of coaches are being accompanied by further-reaching professionalisation of this specialist field, in terms of both preliminary training and continuing professional development. The third part of this book is a reflection of the range of activities that have been developed in recent years with a view to further professionalising and regulating the development of coaches.

It would not surprise me if the process of professionalisation that is currently taking place in the discipline of coaching, of which this book is both an illustration and an account, were to extend further to adjoining fields within management consultancy such as expert advice, group facilitation and the facilitation of change. I am already looking forward to that development.

2.3 What can we learn from these trends?

If we extrapolate the trends above into the future, a number of things are striking. In the first place, it appears reasonable to expect that coaching will continue to grow and become consolidated as an independent profession within the wider specialist field of management consultancy. There are simply too many long-term trends pointing in the direction of coaching as a relevant intervention.

Second, I expect to see increasing friction between the continuing regulation and standardisation of executive coaching, and the *uniqueness* of every new coaching assignment and indeed every new 'moment' in coaching. The same thing happened in psychotherapy in the second half of the twentieth century: increasing *regulation* of therapeutic conversations, in terms of the steps to be taken within certain approaches, prescriptions of specific interventions and actions in the form of 'if such and such, then such and such . . . , culminating in the adoption of strict protocols and manuals. Psychotherapy professionals are in the process of renouncing that trend because they can now demonstrate that rules and regulations have no effect or even, in some cases, a harmful effect, on the outcome of therapy (Wampold, 2001). With the increasing certification and accreditation of executive coaches, we are seeing the first signs that many coaches are starting out on the same path, and my prediction is that they may backtrack from manuals and protocols in the future just as the psychotherapists did.

I would like to illustrate the 'uniqueness' of coaching, the fact that every step must be discovered and trodden by client and coach together, with a pair of recent examples from my own practice. With one coachee I drew up a plan for ten conversations with clearly defined results. At the end of the first session, in which he had given himself time to consider his busy job, his responsibilities and his position within the organisation, he decided to look for alternatives. A few weeks later I received the news that he was going to work for a completely different organisation. Our conversation had helped him to consider alternatives. I look back on this coaching relationship with satisfaction, even though we did not achieve any of the results in our contract and stopped after only one session. Another example is the coachee who also appears in Appendix D of this book. In our first session I was under the impression the impression that he didn't really need coaching, but in the end the contract was extended from five to more than twenty sessions.

Nor are these examples unusual; time after time, it proves impossible to plan coaching in advance. Sometimes it takes a number of sessions before a coachee gathers sufficient confidence and trust to say what is really the problem. This doesn't mean it is a bad idea to draw up an explicit coaching contract or even to plan coaching meetings, but it does appear at the same time to be essential to keep refining or adjusting that contractual relationship on an ongoing basis. Unlike in other forms of consultancy, it is my experience in executive coaching that advance planning creates unnecessary restrictions for the client (and sometimes for the coach as well). If it is not possible to plan in advance, both parties, coachee and coach, are much more at the mercy of the conversation itself as it unfolds. This may make them feel anxious and vulnerable, but it can also engender an enormously valuable learning experience.

Finally, one further expectation I have for the coming years is that, in addition to the vulnerability of clients, the vulnerability of coaching itself will become more and more evident. What I mean by this is that coaches and coachees will be more aware of what it means to sit together in a room with no idea of what will happen next. This may help them to drop their guard sooner and to focus more actively on the relationship developing between them and on ethical aspects of that relationship. What does it mean, for example, to undergo a personal learning process with another professional? What risks, what hopes and expectations does that entail? In connection with this vulnerability, it is to be hoped that we will see more integration in future between the various associations attempting to regulate the profession, and a move away from self-regulation towards more independent regulation of the practice of coaching.

Despite the relative youth of the coaching profession, other forms of consultancy can already learn a great deal from developments within this field, as I hope to show later on in this book. Because coaching is relatively limited and straightforward in terms of the scale of the intervention, coaching as an activity is easier to study, can be defined more precisely in a professional code and can be mapped more clearly. In addition, other similar forms of one-on-one helping conversations, such as those that take place within counselling and psychotherapy, already have a long tradition of research and modelling behind them.

Summary: from stigma to status

On the basis of mentions in the specialist literature, the discipline of coaching has experienced exponential growth over the last fifty years. Based on the history of the word itself, four **historical roots** can be distinguished.

1 A **transport expert** or change expert: how do you get someone from A to B?
2 An **educator** or sports instructor: how do you improve someone's performance?
3 A **therapist**: how do you help someone to overcome obstacles and to become stronger?
4 An **organisation developer**: how do you develop an organisation by supervising its professionals individually?

Social developments fostering an increasing demand for coaching:
• growing ICT connections between more and more people;
• an increasing flow of information, leading to more change and more responsibility;
• increasing pressures on opinion-forming and decision-making;
• a more central position for the customer in the various forms of care and advice; and
• changing attitudes to work.

There are also three trends within the field of coaching itself.
1 From remedial to developmental.
2 From sectarian to integrative.
3 From hobbyism to expertise.

On the basis of these trends, I expect to see the following in future.
• Continuing growth and consolidation of the executive coaching profession.
• Increasing awareness of the friction between general knowledge about coaching and the uniqueness of a coaching relationship.
• A more external and independent form of regulation than self-regulation.
• Increasing awareness of the 'vulnerability' of coaching.

Chapter 3
From Prize-fighting to Prizes for All: the Active Ingredients

The questions that most preoccupy professional coaches are these.
- 'What works best for this coachee with this issue?'
- 'Which method, which approach, which interventions can I use in order to help this client?'
- 'What will help us in this session, at this moment?'

The main question for coaches is therefore: 'Which, of the whole range of things I can do now, is best for my coachee?' What wouldn't coaches give if they could just lift a tiny corner of the veil, if they could give a definite (even if partial) answer to this question, or at least obtain sound and uncontested research results relating to it.

Unfortunately, no-one has yet been able to supply an answer to the above question which most concerns us as coaches. In fact, very little proper research has been carried out into coaching as yet: there are many times more descriptive articles in this area than research articles. See Chapter 5 for a summary of all of the quantitative research articles on coaching that I have managed to find.

There is, though, a long tradition of research in psychotherapy, and an equally long debate about the effectiveness of different forms of psychotherapy. In the last thirty years clear breakthroughs have been achieved in that debate, such that certain questions have now been broadly answered after years of conflict. In his reliable and comprehensive review entitled *The great psychotherapy debate* (2001), Bruce Wampold summarises most of the answers and puts forward the powerful arguments that have convinced more and more psychotherapists.

It is important that professional coaches take note of these conclusions from decades of research, if this young profession is to avoid repeating needless tribal warfare and wrestling with research questions that have already been answered. Thanks to the broad consensus in psychotherapy, the discipline of coaching too is now able to reach a consensus, ask new questions and embark upon a new type of research – into demonstrably relevant aspects of coaching. This is why I intend to give a rather detailed summary of *The great psychotherapy debate* (2001) in this book, and to set out the main achievements of the existing research into the effectiveness of psychotherapy.

The reason why more 'hard' information is finally becoming available about the effectiveness of psychotherapy is not that more or better research into effectiveness is being done. There have always been intensive efforts to measure effectiveness, efforts driven in part by professional curiosity and in part by pressure from clients and sponsors: in the same way as doctors, psychotherapists often have to answer to large and monolithic insurance companies. The reason why all of these efforts have finally produced clear answers is that we now have a powerful statistical instrument available to us which can collate the various research findings, in the form of meta-analysis.

For a long time, psychotherapists couldn't even agree among themselves on whether psychotherapy had any useful effect. There were influential advocates of the view that psychotherapy has *no* effect compared with 'doing nothing', or even a harmful effect. Hans Eysenck (1952) was perhaps the most influential of these voices, and his articles about the non-effectiveness of psychotherapy were cited with approval until as recently as the 1990s.

It was only by carrying out *meta-analysis*, the analysis of large volumes of quantitative research, that the general question about the effectiveness of psychotherapy could finally be resolved in its favour (see Mann, 1994). Meta-analysis is a refined method in which the size of the effect (i.e. the difference between the average of two distributions, such as outcome with and without psychotherapy, or the outcome for the client group and for the control group) is estimated under the assumption that different studies measure the same effect, i.e. that they understand the same by 'psychotherapy', and have measured essentially the same population.

That is a huge assumption of course, because different groups of therapists, with different procedures and backgrounds, working in different countries or with different target groups, are all lumped together in meta-analysis. But the beauty of meta-analysis is that the original assumption (that different studies measure the same effect) can later be verified. It often emerges then, for example, that you *cannot* put together the different countries where therapists work or the degree to which they are persuaded by certain approaches (such as advocates of certain techniques, and their opponents), and that the studies are *not* measuring the same effect. The nice thing about a well-conducted meta-analysis, therefore, is that this procedure justifies and, where necessary, corrects itself.

Meta-analyses can also help to 'categorise' populations, i.e. to find homogeneous populations among the different studies investigated. For example, the attachment of therapists to certain approaches turns out to make a considerable difference in their effectiveness (we return to this later, in section 3.4 below). Confirmation that meta-analyses are a reliable instrument is found in the fact that we encounter no difference in statements when comparing properly conducted meta-analyses, whereas major differences do occur with properly conducted effectiveness studies (differences which often result from hidden or unmeasured variables). With meta-analyses we find differences, at most, in the precise size of effects, as we will see below. Meta-analyses therefore appear to be just as robust as they claim to be.

It is important to specify in advance what we mean by *outcome* of the therapy. This can of course be the client's degree of satisfaction with the psychotherapy undertaken, but most studies use more objective measures than that. Instead of measuring satisfaction with the therapy, they opt to measure directly the degree of occurrence of the original problem, for example by using the generally recognised *depression scale* for depressive patients, and other relevant scales for other patient groups.

In the social sciences there is some agreement on what we consider a small effect, a medium effect and a large effect (see for example Cohen, 1988). Effect size[1] is always indicated in standard units, i.e. scaled with

---

[1] Specifically, meta-analysis, like more primary research into effectiveness, always gives a *reliability* interval in addition to an estimated *effect size*, i.e. it gives a judgment on how reliable the estimated effect size is. If the reliability interval at a certain reliability level (such as *: $p < 0.05$; **: $p < 0.01$; ***: $p < 0.001$) overlaps with 0, we report 'no difference' or 'no effect', and otherwise we can say with 95 % ($p < 0.05$), 99 % ($p < 0.01$) or even 99.9 % ($p < 0.001$) certainty that we have demonstrated an effect.

the standard deviation. Upwards of an effect size of $d = 0.80$ is termed a large effect, between $d = 0.50$ and $d = 0.80$ a medium effect, and below $d = 0.20$ a small effect. In order to interpret these figures, it helps to look up in a table that:

- $d = 0.20$ means that the average person 'undergoing' the treatment does better than 58% – i.e. clearly more than average – of the control group;
- $d = 0.50$ means that the average person 'undergoing' the treatment does better than 69% of the control group;
- $d = 0.80$ means that the average person 'undergoing' the treatment does better than 79% of the control group; and
- $d = 1.0$ means that the average person 'undergoing' the treatment does better than 84% of the control group.

Armed with this statistical vocabulary, we can take on board the results of meta-analyses of large numbers of effectiveness studies involving enormous numbers of therapists and patients – see the paragraphs below.

3.1 Ample evidence of great effectiveness

The first important result is that it can be demonstrated that psychotherapy does indeed have an effect, and in fact a *large effect* on the various outcome scales. This conclusion was drawn by Smith & Glass (1977; 1980). They found an effect size of $d = 0.85$ by meta-analysis of all of the effectiveness studies with control groups up to 1977 that they could find, published or unpublished (a total of 475 effectiveness studies). That value would mean that the average psychotherapy client is better off than 80% of the people in the control group.

Similar effect sizes have also been found in more recent studies: 0.82 (Lambert & Bergin, 1994) and 0.81 (Lipsey & Wilson, 1993). Psychotherapy appears to be remarkably effective!

3.2 No difference in effectiveness between approaches

With a large demonstrated effect it often becomes possible to ask subsidiary questions, such as the one that has had generations of psychotherapists at each others' throats: which psychotherapeutic approach or method is the most effective? This is a question which, with the vast amount of experimental data now at our disposal, can be answered beyond doubt. The answer comes as a shock to all of those who devoted themselves heart and soul to one specific approach in psychotherapy because they believed it would be more effective: there is no difference![2]

The best way to carry out a meta-analysis into differences in effectiveness between approaches is to gather together studies looking for such differences. It is also possible, of course, to investigate whether some approaches are able to produce a larger effect size when they are compared with a control group, but in the latter case there is a much greater risk of confusing variables. Wampold (2001) gives results for both methods of investigation, but I will confine myself here to meta-analyses of direct comparisons between different forms of therapy. That form of meta-analysis also holds a risk of hidden variables, especially the competences and beliefs of the therapists.

The fact that researchers from each main 'denomination' of psychotherapy have carried out effectiveness studies which incontrovertibly demonstrate the effectiveness of 'their' form of therapy should already raise some suspicion: there is evidence of effectiveness, not just for psychotherapy as an intervention, but also for each known professional form of psychotherapy separately. That information should scale down our expectations of finding *relative* effectiveness, i.e. evidence that certain forms of therapy that work *even better* than others.

Meta-analysis shows that relative effectiveness cannot be demonstrated, so there is no single form of therapy that works consistently better than others, not even for specific groups of clients (such as phobic clients, or depressive clients), as was previously thought. In a meta-analysis of all direct comparative studies from 1975 to 1979 (143 in total), Shapiro & Shapiro (1982) found only one therapy form comparison with a significant difference in outcome[3] (that between cognitive therapy and systematic desensitisation).

---

[2] Note, there is no difference between *professional* practitioners of the different approaches. It *is* possible to find differences between professional and lay therapy (Wampold, 2001).

[3] Berman, Miller & Massman (1985) did demonstrate later, however, that that one difference could be explained by the fact that the therapists in question were keen advocates of the cognitive method over that of systematic desensitisation.

A more comprehensive meta-analysis, by Wampold, Mondin, Moody, Stich, Benson & Ahn (1997), took all of the studies that appeared between 1970 and 1995 in six leading journals, with direct comparisons between forms of therapy – a total of 277 comparisons. Wampold et al. (1997) allocated the effect sizes a random sign, as follows. If therapy form A does better in a given study than therapy form B, they described that form of therapy as having a positive effect and, conversely, if elsewhere A scores less well than B, they referred to a negative effect for the same comparison. The analysis showed that the effect sizes defined in this way are clearly distributed around zero, precisely as you would expect if there were *no* effect in the population. The average absolute effect size was only $d = 0.20$ – a small effect. This is a very generous upper limit for the differences between different forms of therapy, also found by Grissom (1996) who examined six different meta-analyses.

Later, comprehensive meta-analyses were carried out in specific client groups such as depressive or phobic patients, but here too, only negligible effects were found[4]. The conclusion therefore must be: 'Despite volumes devoted to the theoretical differences among different schools of psychotherapy, the results of research demonstrate negligible differences in the effects produced by different therapy types' (Smith & Glass, 1977).

Ahn & Wampold (2001) also carried out a meta-analysis of all of the studies comparing therapies with and without specific ingredients. They looked at one form of therapy and, within it, made a comparison of therapy with and without a relevant component, such as relaxation training, cognitive restructuring or behavioural instructions. Again, meta-analysis revealed no effect: further strong evidence against the existence of specific ingredients of specific approaches that have a decisive effect on the outcome of psychotherapy.

---

[4] And insofar as small effects are found in some meta-analyses (with d around 0.20), it is possible to demonstrate that these effects are associated with differences between individual therapists and not with differences between approaches (Wampold, 2001, Chapter 8).

3.3 The active ingredients are common to all approaches

Interestingly, the suspicion that all forms of therapy, when used competently, are equally successful, was put forward as long ago as 1936 by Rosenzweig. Rosenzweig (1936) refers to Chapter 3 of *Alice in Wonderland*, where the the Dodo organises an absurd race. When the participants challenge him to say which of them has actually won, he replies, '*Everybody* has won, and *all* must have prizes.' Nowadays, now that we know how close Rosenzweig came to hitting the nail on the head, there are increasing references within the profession to the 'Rosenzweig conjecture' – or the 'Dodo conjecture'.

Rosenzweig also goes on to take the next step in his article. If all therapies are equally effective, there is a good chance that the ingredients they have *in common* will determine the effectiveness of therapy – and not the specific interventions of an individual form of therapy. The active ingredients of therapy must therefore be common to all approaches to a large extent.

It is worthwhile investigating what those common constituents might be. Rosenzweig set the standard for the current debate on these common factors. He cites the following common factors that occur in *every* therapeutic situation[5].

- The therapeutic *relationship* and, in particular, all of the non-verbalised aspects of that relationship. The fact that meetings take place, with a certain regularity, devoted to the client's problems or issues, aimed at the possibility of a solution, progress or change.
- The presence of the therapist as a person, with a certain *personality*. Rosenzweig writes that clients are often quick to sense the characteristics of a good therapist.
- The presence of a particular *ideology*, to which the therapist refers and on which he bases his actions. The formal consistency and the bias or partiality of the ideology in particular may be factors which make more of a difference than the precise nature of the ideology.

---

[5] There are of course wide differences within each of these factors, but those are differences that are independent of the differences between therapies, or at least are assumed to be independent by the champions of those therapies.

The ideology provides a systematic basis for *reintegration* for the patient. Rosenzweig also refers in a more general sense to the complexity and over-determined nature of human problems, which results in many different interpretations holding some truth and forming a possible starting point for change or reintegration. The potential (or scientifically demonstrated) adequacy of the ideology is independent of the aspects mentioned above – it is possible that such an adequacy may lead to greater effectiveness, but only on top of the factors already mentioned.

To summarise, therapists who offer a reliable relationship, an effective personality and consistency of adherence to a particular approach may with those characteristics alone account for most of the effectiveness of psychotherapy, according to Rosenzweig – and, as we have seen above, the hunch that he had back in the 1930s was scientifically proven only in the 1980s.

Nowadays we see more detailed lists of common factors in the psychotherapy literature. The following list is inspired by the research and classification of Grencavage & Norcross (1990):
1 Relationship-related factors:
    a) Development of a working alliance or helping relationship
    b) Commitment to the relationship
    c) Transference to the relationship
2 Client-related factors:
    a) Expectations of change ('hope')
    b) Problem pressure
    c) Active contribution expressed, e.g. in the search for help
3 Therapist-related factors:
    a) Personal characteristics
    b) Cultivation of the positive expectations of the client
    c) Warmth, positive outlook, attention, care
4 Change-related factors:
    a) Possibility of expression and change
    b) Acquiring new experiences and new behaviour
    c) Acquiring a 'change rationale' inspired by ideology
5 Structure-related factors:
    a) Use of techniques, rituals and contracts
    b) Focus on internal world and exploration of emotions
    c) Commitment to a theory or ideology

This list can be extended with the many factors that are also common factors but have nothing to do with the therapy itself, the *external factors*:

6 External factors:
   a) Help from family, friends, colleagues and acquaintances
   b) External changes that influence the problem
   c) External changes in other areas of the client's life

All of these factors are present in or around every therapy (and in or around every session of coaching!). There are quite a few of them, so it is perhaps not surprising that they should have a substantial combined effect. Moreover, these factors which are common to many approaches also have much in common and overlap to some extent. As a result, there is a good chance that they reinforce each other: they can build on each other. There is some evidence as to which of these factors is probably the most effective in obtaining the effect of psychotherapy, and this is the subject of the following section.

3.4 Working alliance, therapist and client are the most effective active ingredients

We already seem to have some pretty definite answers on whether or not therapy works, and which aspects of therapy work. However, Wampold (2001) writes about other interesting meta-analyses, including the research carried out into the relative effectiveness of the various common factors, the factors which now appear to be at the centre of psychotherapy effectiveness:

3.4.1 The quality of the relationship
The *working alliance*, in other words the quality of the relationship between psychotherapist and client, appears to be closely related to the success of therapy, especially if you ask the client to evaluate that alliance. The quality of a relationship is admittedly a complex, subtle and personal experience and we cannot do it justice by reducing it to a single number on a Likert scale[6]. Aspects that many therapists count as part of a 'working alliance' include (Wampold, 2001):

---

[6] A Likert scale is the psychometric response scale most widely used in questionnaires, where respondents specify their level of agreement to a statement (traditionally on a 5-point scale from 'least' to 'most').

1 the client's affectionate relationship with the therapist;
2 the client's motivation and ability to accomplish work collabora-
  tively with the therapist;
3 the therapist's empathic responding to and involvement with the
  client; and
4 client and therapist agreement about the goals and tasks of
  therapy.

If you ask the client or an independent observer to score these or
similar aspects, and also independently measure the outcome of therapy
using one of the standard instruments, the correlation found between
those scores is, on average, as much as 0.26[7] (with a negligible chance:
$p < 0.001$ that the two do not correlate). This corresponds, under
certain assumptions, to an effect size of $d = 0.54$ – i.e. a moderate effect
(see Horvath & Symonds, 1991, and Martin, Garske & Davis, 2000).
It was noticed in this respect that the scores awarded by clients and
independent observers correlate strongly and, taken together, are the
best predictors of outcome one can find. Scores for the working alliance
given by the therapists correlate much less well with the outcome
(even if the outcome is scored by the therapist himself or by an independent observer).

Another interesting finding is that it doesn't matter when you score
the working alliance; the initial working alliance is just as good a predictor as the working alliance at the end of the therapy. It is not simply
the case that a better outcome leads to a better (perceived) working
alliance. Rather, the opposite seems to be true: a better (perceived)
working alliance leads to a better subsequent outcome.

3.4.2 The person of the therapist

Of course, the person of the therapist cannot be viewed separately from
the working relationship. If the person changes, the relationship
changes to such an extent that it is better described as the end of one
relationship and the start of a new one, rather than a change in the

---

[7] The correlation coefficient of 0.26 and accompanying effect size of 0.54 was found
in the study by Horvath & Symonds (1991), a meta-analysis of 20 studies with an
average of 49 clients, i.e. around 1000 clients. Later, with a meta-analysis of 79 studies
and a total of around 4700 clients, Martin, Garske & Davis (2000) found a correlation
coefficient of 0.22, i.e. an effect size of 0.45 – still a moderate effect.

relationship. Clearly there is a lot of overlap with the previous 'common factor', and also with other factors such as 'ideological commitment', to which I will return later.

The person of the therapist is at least as complex and subtle a dimension as the working alliance discussed above. The dimension of 'person' can be interpreted very broadly. Wampold (2001) refers to accepted distinctions between personality characteristics and attitudes ('traits' and 'states'), and between objective and subjective characteristics[8], but even that is not nearly enough to categorise such a thing as personality exhaustively. In Chapter 9 I make my own attempt to list various aspects of the coach's personality, using a multi-layered model derived from organisation culture models.

Demonstrating that the person of the therapist is a significant factor is easy, and I will return to this later. What turns out to be extremely difficult, however, is to pin down and identify what exactly are the 'effective parts' of that 'person', i.e. which characteristics of the therapist are most likely to result in greater effectiveness.

Again, what seems to matter most is the client's perspective on the therapist, i.e. the way in which the client *sees* the therapist and not how the therapist *is*. For example, if we ask experienced therapists to rate the quality of a colleague on a set of Likert scales, which should be the most objective *a priori* assessment of the therapist's effectiveness, we obtain a very poor predictor of therapeutic outcome. Thorough research using expert ratings of 302 video-recorded therapy sessions conducted by 8 therapists showed that such expert ratings are statistically irrelevant as a measure of the quality of the therapist (Shaw, Elkin, Yamaguchi, Olmsted, Vallis, Dobson, Lowery, Sotsky, Watkins & Imber, 1999).

The best we can do is to adopt an *a posteriori* criterion, simply using the outcome of therapy as a measure of the quality of the therapist. Using that measure, vast quantities of raw research data have been re-analysed in order to establish how variability due to therapists can be

---

[8]Objective characteristics include age, sex and ethnicity, while values, religion and philosophical orientation are more subjective.

compared with the variability of different approaches. It emerges that therapist-related variability is many times greater than the variability due to different approaches. In fact, therapist variability fully explains the small effect size due to differences between approaches ($d = 0.20$). To put it briefly, this analysis demolishes the last shred of evidence of differences in effectiveness between approaches (Wampold, 2001).

On the basis of the variability between therapists, we can also estimate an effect size associated with the person of the therapist, i.e. how much effect does a good therapist produce on average compared with a less-good therapist? It appears to be between $d = 0.50$ and $d = 0.65$ (6% of the variability in Project MATCH Research Group, 1998, and 9% of the variability in Crits-Christoph & Mintz, 1991), i.e. of the same order of magnitude as the effect resulting from the quality of the relationship between therapist and client. The Project MATCH (1998) conclusions also hint at a distribution of therapists where most are similarly effective whilst some outlying exceptional ones – particularly, exceptionally *bad* ones – account for most of the variability.

There are also a number of personal characteristics of therapists which have been proven by statistical research to make a difference to the outcome of psychotherapy. The following is a short list of variables which appear to have a favourable effect on the results of psychotherapy:
- Empathy, understanding, respect, warmth and authenticity – the criteria already emphasised by Carl Rogers (Rogers, 1957; Lambert & Bergin, 1994).
- Being attractive (!), inspiring confidence and appearing competent, in that order (McNeal, May & Lee, 1987).
- The therapist's own mental health (Beutler, Crago, Arizmendi, 1986).
- The ability to let go of one's own system of values and to communicate within the other person's value system (Norcross, 1993; Beutler, Machado & Allstetter Neufeldt, 1994).

In apparent contrast with the last finding above, one aspect of the person of the therapist which appears to be particularly essential to a good outcome is the degree of 'ideological commitment' or, one might say, 'dogmatism', of the therapist. It seems to be the case that more ideologically committed therapists achieve better results than less dog-matic colleagues, which is a particularly salient finding because in other respects 'dogmatism' is probably not a good quality for a thera-pist. Ideological commitment can be studied by awarding an author a mark for 'dogmatism' on the basis of their previous publications, and correlating that mark with the results of their preferred therapeutic approach. Careful meta-analysis appears to give significant correlations and effect sizes ranging from $d = 0.29$ (Smith *et al.*, 1980) to $d = 0.65$ (Berman, Miller, & Massman, 1985), i.e. moderate to large effects.

Another area studied has been whether commitment to specific inter-ventions, due in particular to the use of strict manuals ensuring that interventions are more specific and more limited, has an influence. Wampold (2001) summarises a number of different studies: some con-clude that there is no effect, some a small positive effect, and others even that there is a small negative effect due to the use of manuals. Commitment to specific interventions therefore appears to have little influence on effectiveness.

The conclusion here should be that 'belief', 'conviction' or 'commit-ment' with respect to a specific approach makes a considerable differ-ence to the outcome of therapy: therapists who are confirmed in their views appear to do better than those who are not. On the other hand, slavish adherence to therapy manuals appears to have little effect, or indeed a negative one. Dedication to the ideology appears to be more important than dedication to the rulebook.

Another way to view these research results is to point out that theo-retical orientation evidently makes little difference, while conviction or commitment to the orientation makes a lot of difference. That in itself is a satisfactory and non-dogmatic conclusion in my view. In addition, it gives every reason to allow professional therapists free rein in choosing their own approach and in the precise translation of that approach to their own therapeutic practice.

3.4.3 The person of the client
I should perhaps have started with this factor, because it is undoubtedly the most important and the most influential. Which is not really sur-prising: therapy is about the client and about changes for the client, i.e. who the client is and what the client does is crucial. What *is* sur-

prising is that this is the least studied common factor, with very few meta-analyses as yet, and Wampold (2001) is able to refer to it only indirectly in his thorough review.

Without doubt, the single most important effective factor in therapy is an *external* factor which, by definition, therapy cannot influence, namely on the one hand the support and assistance and on the other the trials and tribulations experienced by the client *outside* the therapeutic relationship (the *external factors* referred to above). In most cases the time spent outside therapy is more than 99% of the time available, so it is not surprising that much happens there that is of greater importance in terms of change than what takes place in or what is said during the therapy. Estimates of the effect of external factors are as high as 40% of the explained variation (Lambert, 1992), i.e. an effect size of as much as $d = 1.65$. In other words, clients with support outside therapy will do better on average than 95% of the group without such support.

An important indirect indication of the huge influence of factors external to therapy is the observation that *self-help* (i.e. change without therapy) is almost as effective as 'therapy help'[9]: meta-analyses by Scogin, Bynum, Stephens & Calhoun (1990) and by Gould & Clum (1993) have demonstrated this for a wide range of problems.

But even inside psychotherapy the person of the client appears to be crucially important. For example, hope or positive expectations of therapy have a considerable influence on the outcome: Lambert (1992) gives an estimated effect size of $d = 0.85$ for the presence of hope.

Further indirect evidence of the overriding importance of the client and the client's contribution to the therapy can be found in the results achieved by comparing change in the client during the intake and first meetings with change over the entire course of therapy. The majority of change is found to occur as a result of the first session, or (in other

---

[9] Or in fact 'self-help + therapy help' because psychotherapy clients receive both of course. Despite the fact that therapy can make a clear difference, effective self-help in itself proves to be almost equally effective in many cases. It is not yet clear whether there are different groups of clients and/or basic issues for which self-help or 'therapy help' is most effective.

research) in the first three to four weeks of treatment (Snyder, Michael & Cheavens, 1999). Studies have even found clear indications that significant changes occur *before* the first therapy session, merely as a result of being invited to and preparing for that session (see for example Lawson, 1994).

Finally, it was stated above that what matters most in the case of a working alliance is the client's perspective on the alliance, another indication that the client is perhaps the most effective 'common factor' in therapy, and that it is therefore crucially important for therapists to focus on that factor more than previously, i.e. to make the client central in any evaluation of interventions, for example.

> ### Summary: from prize fighting to prizes for all
>
> The key question for coaches is undoubtedly: **'Which, of the whole gamut of things I can do now, is the best for my coachee?'** This question addresses the effectiveness of coaching. This question is asked in a number of ways in practice, for example:
> - What will work best for this coachee at this moment?
> - What will work best for this organisational context and given my own strengths and limitations?
> - Which method/strategy/approach/interventions can I use here?
>
> Similar questions have been asked over a much longer period and more intensely in the field of psychotherapy. **Meta-analytical research** in psychotherapy has shown that:
> 1 Psychotherapy clearly has a large effect on various criteria for success (effect size $d \approx 0.85$ so clients do better on average than 80% of the control group).
> 2 There is a negligible difference in effectiveness between different approaches (effect size $d < 0.20$).
> 3 The active ingredients of therapy are therefore **common** to many approaches:
>   a) Relationship-related factors: working alliance, commitment, transference.
>   b) Client-related factors: hope of change, motivation, problem pressure.
>   c) Therapist-related factors: personality traits, cultivation of positive expectations, warmth, appreciation, attention.
>   d) Change-related factors: opportunity for expression, practice and acquiring a rationale for change.

e) Structure-related factors: use of techniques or rituals, exploration of issues of the coachee and commitment to theory.

f) External factors: outside help, changes occurring independently of the therapy.

The strongest effective factors are as follows:

- The quality of the **relationship** produces an effect size of as much as $d \approx 0.54$.
- The **person** of the therapist produces an effect size of as much as $d = 0.50\text{--}0.65$.
- The **client**: the least-studied but probably most effective factor in therapy. Well-founded estimates of effect size of 'hope' alone are as high as $d \approx 0.85$. Unfortunately, this 'factor' is also the factor which the therapist is least able to influence.
- The support, trials and tribulations experienced by the client **outside the therapy**: an estimated effect size of as much as $d \approx 1.65$.

Chapter 4
From Intervention to Interaction: Relational Coaching

4.1 Ten commandments for the executive coach

The results of the research presented in the previous chapter are significant in relation to the effectiveness of coaching only if it is safe to assume that similar factors are at work in coaching and in psychotherapy, and that has not been demonstrated to my knowledge. There may indeed be many similarities between the disciplines of coaching and psychotherapy, but there are also these differences (Kets de Vries, 2005).

1 Coaching generally takes place with strong and well-functioning individuals – or at least under this assumption, therefore, in the absence of a diagnosis of potential pathology.

2 Coaching is largely work-related, which makes it much more of an 'organisation intervention' than psychotherapy. This means that 'effectiveness' has a different meaning in coaching: it also includes effectiveness for the organisation, i.e. for other people who are not present at the sessions.

3 Coaching is generally more oriented towards concrete results and specific actions than is therapy.

4 Coaches and therapists have different previous training and work experiences, plus there is probably a greater diversity within the discipline of coaching.

5 There are practical differences, such as the location, duration and frequency of sessions, and regarding fee structures.

Although it is easy, therefore, to find Differences between psychotherapy and coaching, these are nevertheless differences in emphasis and not really in the nature of the service provided. My own view is that the differences between psychotherapy and coaching in practice are relatively small: probably smaller than those between different approaches or practitioners in each of the two areas. Coaching is in fact the same service as therapy, with the main difference being, roughly speaking, that coachees do not aim to progress from 'negative' or 'poor' to 'average', but set themselves the goal of progressing from 'average' or 'well-performing' to 'excellent'. The similarities in dominant approaches and ways of working are clear (see also Chapter 1 of this book), such that it appears to make sense to assume at least provisionally that the principal results from the meta-analyses of effectiveness research in psychotherapy can be transposed to coaching.

Unfortunately, the differences between psychotherapy and coaching are so difficult to quantify and so little quantitative research has been done within coaching (see Chapter 5 for an overview) that we have no hard, quantitative data on factors of effectiveness in executive coaching. Moreover, we are certainly unable yet to carry out a significant meta-analysis of effectiveness studies in the realm of coaching. For all these reasons, we lack conclusive arguments at present that would enable us to say where the similarities between coaching and psychotherapy end.

It is my conviction that there are most likely more similarities than differences between the disciplines of psychotherapy and coaching. However, I can't be sure that the translation of the results from the previous chapter to coaching is more than a thought-experiment. Even if it is only a thought-experiment, though, it may prompt coaches actually to think about how they work and what effects they are achieving through their work. Based on the meta-analyses in psychotherapy and other reliable research data, as summarised above, I propose the following *ten commandments for the executive coach*.

1 First, do no harm
This commandment might appear self-evident but, given the reports of abuse in coaching (Berglas, 2002), it is perhaps not entirely superfluous. Moreover, it has been demonstrated that therapeutic approaches do very badly if they are used not therapeutically but, say, as a way of passing the time or in order to create a 'stationary' control group (see Wampold, 2001). The conclusion often drawn in medicine from the rule of *primum non nocere*[1] is *in dubio abstine*, i.e. if in doubt, it is better to do nothing than carry out an intervention that may be harmful.

---

[1] Not found in Hippocrates, but certainly derived from the classical Hippocratic corpus.

2 Have confidence
As long as you follow tried and tested ethical principles (as in Appendix E) and your honest intention is to help the coachee, there is a good chance you *are* actually helping. Coaching interventions are highly effective, by all accounts. You are not necessarily any better at it than other coaches (an illusion that you can easily acquire, however, in the isolation of your coaching sessions!), but you have a good chance of doing it more or less as well as they do.

3 Commit yourself heart and soul to your approach
Although we can't demonstrate that there is one specific approach that works better than others, it *is* possible to show that commitment, faith, attachment or loyalty to an approach – whatever it might be! – does make a positive difference (see the previous chapter). Commitment to a coaching ideology and a coaching approach, to which you gear your interventions, will contribute towards your effectiveness, provided that commitment is genuine and focused on helping the client. In other words, commit yourself heart and soul to your approach but resist the temptation to believe that it is truly superior.

4 Feed the hope of your coachee
Hope is such an important 'common factor' that it would be a sin to do anything to lessen it. As a coach, your coachee frequently confronts you with doubt, in the form of questions such as 'Will this help me?' or 'What will five coaching sessions do for me?' In response to such questions, there is no more ill-advised potential answer than the one that is probably the most correct: 'I don't know yet. I have no idea if this will help you'. With that answer you run the risk, in all honesty and openness, of diminishing that valuable hope. In such a case it is much more advisable to remain hopeful oneself and, equally truthfully, to respond that 'Coaching has helped many other people with similar issues', or 'I personally have very positive expectations about the outcome'.

5 Consider the coaching situation from your coachee's perspective
All the signs are that it is primarily the client's expectation that determines how effective a given coaching relationship will be. What is important, therefore, is how your coachee sees you and how your coachee experiences the working alliance with you, so collect as much 'feedback' and and many 'ratings' from your coachee as you can.

The following three 'commandments' are consequences of this important conclusion from research in psychotherapy.

6 *Work on your coaching relationship*
It is not just about the issue or the problem, and not even just about coachees and their issues, or coachees and their organisations and *their* issues; it is actually mainly about the relationship. If the relationship itself is good, there is a better chance of change for the better – even if, for example, the question is not entirely addressed. So pay attention to your relationship and your working alliance with your coachee, and make it explicit if that helps to make it stronger. Be careful with interventions that jeopardise the working alliance.

7 *If you don't 'click', find a replacement coach*
There is little point in trying to achieve results in a working alliance that isn't functioning properly – in this case, one of the most important common factors is under pressure and there is a high risk that other important factors such as the personality of the coach (in the eyes of the coachee!) and the coachee's expectations will suffer as a result. In addition, in coaching as in psychotherapy we can expect the bulk of any achievements to be made in the first few sessions. If that part is already under pressure, it is better to 'regain' this and other factors by bringing in a different coach.

Luborsky (1976) agrees with this argument, and suggests trying out different combinations of patients and therapists even at a very early stage of treatment if the relationship is not ideal. Miller, Duncan, Brown, Sorrell & Chalk (2005) put this idea into practice and did achieve higher effect sizes in psychotherapy by constantly monitoring the working alliance, as perceived by the client, and suggesting a change of therapist to clients in the event of a working alliance that was less than ideal.

But also be aware that a referral itself always puts the relationship under pressure. A referral is always experienced in part as a rejection and a loss, however much the coachee understands rationally that it is better to move forward with someone else. So refer carefully and helpfully, and remain available to the coachee for any questions or further conversations.

8 *Look after yourself, to keep yourself as healthy as possible*
It is not even just about the issue, the coachee, the organisation *and* the relationship – it is also about your own personality, or in any case your personality as perceived by the coachee. It therefore helps to know how you are seen by others, and it helps to be seen as 'helping' in one way or another. How this is translated into personality traits is not very clear as yet, but it seems to make a difference in a positive sense if the coach comes across as attractive, competent, stable, healthy, happy, empathic, warm and trustworthy.

9 *Try to stay fresh and unbiased*
Applying pre-determined procedures and protocols, with often carefully considered and ingeniously devised interventions, appears to have little influence on the outcome. Indeed, it seems to have an adverse effect. It appears therefore to be the case that a coach who meets the coachee with a fresh, unbiased and sympathetic approach – and thus pays more attention to where the coachee is and to the relationship with the coachee – achieves better results.

10 *Don't worry too much about the specific things you are doing*
This follows from the meta-analyses: specific techniques and coaching interventions appear to make much less difference than the more general, common factors – and there are even strong indications that specific interventions make no difference at all. Even if clients are subsequently asked to name the most effective ingredients of their therapy journey, they very rarely mention specific discoveries and interventions, and much more often the personality of the therapist, or the opportunity to talk to someone who understands and supports them (see Tallman & Bohart, 1999, and our own results, reported in Chapter 5).

If you share the assumption that it is not about the specific things you say or do, you also become more relaxed as a coach about retaining and contributing recollections and suggestions. For example, it doesn't seem so terrible if you forget relevant (specific!) comments from previous sessions, or if you don't have any clear ideas for your coachee's future. You learn to pay more attention to what is actually going on here and now in this coaching relationship.

4.2 Effective coaching means relational coaching

The recent research findings in psychotherapy, as summarised in the previous chapter, are both sobering and instructive. If we accept them in relation to coaching as well, it is clear that we should place much less emphasis on ourselves as coaches during coaching, but should learn to put our relationships with our coachees and what is going on for coachees much more at the centre. Following my reading of the meta-analyses in psychotherapy I now find that many guides for coaches, including my own previous book on coaching, *Coaching with colleagues* (De Haan & Burger, 2005), place too much emphasis on the coach and on specific coaching techniques.

My view of coaching now is that coaching is predominantly an exercise in *self-understanding* and *self-changing* on the part of the coachee. This exercise takes place only partly in collaboration with an outside professional, the coach. The ability of the coachee to bring about the intended understanding and change is many times greater, however, than the ability of the coach to bring about change by means of a considered choice of interventions. Coachees do the actual work all by themselves, and the only thing that coaching can do is to help them find and activate their natural, inherent abilities. Coachees can and will use coaching in their own best interests, but it is and remains a change carried out for *and by* themselves. Even the amount of time that coachee and coach spend together, compared with the time that the coachee spends alone with his or her own issues, should give us cause for reflection. We know how important coaching can be for our client, and how effective coaching conversations are, but we should also realise who is doing the actual work: the coachee!

This is not unlike the vision advocated by Carl Rogers (see Rogers, 1961): the client-centred approach to coaching; though I here actually attribute a still greater power and ability to change to the coachee. What I have in mind is an approach that doesn't confine itself to facilitating, exploring and supportive interventions but can just as easily make use of more directive, suggestive and confronting interventions, precisely because I assume that the coachee can take it; or in fact that even the strongest confrontations, prescriptions and provocations are generally not powerful enough to unbalance the ability of coachees to change themselves, or to establish it if this is lacking. To put the cat among the pigeons: perhaps it is the case that coaching achieves such great effectiveness *despite* the interventions of the coach, whatever they may be.

In this perspective on coaching which, in line with existing literature in psychotherapy[2], I call *relational coaching*, we can trust the coachee fully to make use of and exploit contributions by the coach. The only thing the coach can actually influence, the only thing the coach can use to exert albeit an indirect influence on the outcome of coaching, is the *relationship* between coach and coachee. The effect of coaching is reminiscent of an *active placebo* in medicine (see, *inter alia*, Weil, 1995): a drug that has noticeable and measurable effects on the patient but does not demonstrably contribute towards the cure[3].

The following is a summary of what I mean by *relational coaching*.
1 An active effort by the coach to understand all of the subject matter contributed from the perspective of the *relationship*, i.e. current relationships that play a role in the subject matter, previous relationships and the present relationship in which the subject matter is being discussed here and now.
2 An active effort by the coach to make this relationship as strong and productive as possible, *as experienced by the coachee*. This means that the coach regularly explores with the coachee how the relationship is progressing:
   a) during the session, by making the relationship explicit where possible;
   b) at the beginning or end of sessions, when coach and coachee review the effects of their coaching journey together;

---

[2] *Relational coaching* has its origins in prominent schools of psychoanalysis such as the *object relations* school (see for example Fairbairn, 1952) and the *interpersonal* theory (Sullivan, 1953), which *relational psychoanalysis* (Mitchell & Aron, 1999) has further developed, and was also influenced by humanist and feminist views. For an excellent historical overview, see the first chapter of DeYoung (2003).

I would like to emphasise again that the results of research summarised in Chapter 3 and the ten commandments in this chapter still allow for many conclusions in terms of one's preferred approach to coaching. Duncan, Miller & Sparks (2004) for example arrive, on the basis of precisely the same results, at *client-directed therapy*, an approach that is essentially a combination of paradoxical and solution-focused psychotherapy.

[3] The organisational equivalent of the active placebo is the well-known *Hawthorne effect* (Baritz, 1960).

   c) by collecting supplementary data from the coachee and the latter's organisation, such as the regular use of rating instruments or (within the limits of the agreements specified in the contract:) by asking close colleagues of the coachee.

      If the relationship is productive and useful according to the coachee, the coach will make no attempt to end it. If the relationship is not ideal in the coachee's eyes, the coach will not hesitate to *refer* and to help the coachee enter into a relationship that will better meet the relational objectives.

3 No restriction on the specific interventions of the coach, either in terms of the nature of the contributions (styles of intervention) or in terms of the order of contributions (the phasing of conversations). The only limiting conditions which the coach himself lays down are:

   a) interventions should fit in with the specific *ideology* and basic assumptions of the coach concerning change, learning and development, i.e. the coach himself should genuinely believe in the interventions;

   b) interventions should be focused on supporting and reinforcing the relationship and thus the coachee's learning and development process;

   c) interventions should fit in with what relevant ethical codes (such as Appendix E) consider proper and permissible, and be sufficiently open to supervision by fellow coaches (for supervision, see Chapter 10).

4 The coach is aware of the common factors that, according to the latest studies, make a positive contribution to effective psychotherapy (Chapter 3), and attempts to exploit those factors to the utmost.

All of these aspects of relational coaching work together to make the coachee and the coaching relationship from moment to moment as central as possible in coaching conversations. The various coaching approaches as outlined in Chapter 1 of this book can be used, although the exact choice appears to be less important. As long as the coach feels that it suits his own personality, and he is truly behind it, the choice is justified. The various techniques can be used flexibly depending on how they seem to suit the coachee's issues and behaviour, and the competences of the coach.

All of this means that the relational coach observes from minute to minute what is going on in the relationship with his coachee. Casement (1985) calls this continuing reflective outlook *internal supervision*. I myself have called it *self-monitoring* elsewhere (De Haan, 2005). By constantly maintaining this exploring and questioning outlook on the relationship and the coach's own contribution to the relationship, the coach avoids the roles of adviser, 'smart ass', doctor – roles which make the relationship unduly asymmetrical. Internal supervision is maintained most critically by reviewing it regularly against supervision by others.

I consider it important to guard against the possibility that the research results from meta-analyses, as summarised in the previous chapter, may tempt us to adopt an eclectic, pluralistic or even nihilistic attitude (compare the concluding chapter of Smith, Glass & Miller, 1980). The research results tell us that any existing professional approach is as good as any other, but they don't tell us that we can exchange or combine approaches as we please, or that we can completely disregard the approaches themselves and their importance. The studies in question were carried out with professional therapists in their own practice – i.e. with individuals trained in one or more of those approaches, who apply the prescriptions and suggestions of those approaches more or less explicitly in their interventions. An important common factor is therefore the adoption and application of a *preferred approach*, something that eclectic, pluralistic or nihilistic coaches wouldn't do. The latter groups may feel all too free not to develop a coaching ideology that they truly believe in, or to pile intervention on intervention at random, without considering objectively how they fit in with their overall ideology or the objectives of the coaching.

The least we should do, in my opinion, is work with a *selective* eclectic approach, i.e. apply interventions from various traditions where we find genuine cause to use them and where, in our view, they fit in with the objectives and prerequisites of our coaching contract. Instead of setting aside the general idea of a dominant approach to coaching, we would do better to:

1 adopt one approach as fully as possible;
2 be aware of our own preferences;
3 work consistently;

4 use interventions and ideas from other approaches – i.e. insofar as
   they fit in with our preferences; and
5 pay attention to an integration at meta-level of the approaches that
   inspire us.

The window onto coaching in Chapter 1 is one example of an integration at meta-level of different approaches to coaching. Within this
model the coach can make a well-considered choice, opting either for
a particular quadrant or for an integrated application of more than one
quadrant. Using such a 'window', the coach can choose an approach
at meta-level without becoming eclectic or pluralistic, i.e. without
allowing his own ideology to become diluted.

In relational coaching the relationship is central. However, little is
known as yet about what precisely constitutes a relationship, how a
relationship can best be described, or how a relationship develops. In
Part II of this book, in Chapters 6 to 8, I attempt to gain a better idea
of what constitutes a coaching relationship by looking at the 'moments'
from which it is constructed.

4.3 The coaching relationship as a succession of critical moments

Coaching relationships can be seen as successions of 'critical' moments,
moments that define the relationship and make it the relationship that
it is (see Stern, 2004). The degree of 'criticalness' is on a sliding scale
from minor things noticed by coach or coachee to a situation so critical
that, for example, both partners experience a deep resonance or else
so much friction that they have to terminate the relationship. There
are a huge number of potential critical moments in a coaching relationship. Later in this book I will attempt a more systematic classification
of such moments.

Critical moments occur, for example, when the coachee recounts
something shared with very few others to date, or when a particular
vulnerability is examined together with the coach. Or when the
coachee appeals to the coach and asks explicitly for help. Or when
the coachee is unhappy with something the coach says. Or when the
'penny drops', and the coachee realises something not realised before.
A critical moment may be recognised as such by both parties, or it may

be felt by only one of them. For example, when the coach sees particular feedback about to be given to the coachee as a critical moment; or when the coach notices that there is something 'awkward' in the relationship that the coachee does not notice.

Appendices A and B of this book contain numerous examples of critical moments as experienced by coaches. These are the moments when tensions, uncertainties and anxieties arise. They are also the moments when the coaching relationship is really put to the test, and in my opinion it is often solely as the result of such moments that the coachee actually begins to learn and to change. In Chapters 7, 8 and 9 I go into more detail about such moments for coaches and how coaches can handle them. Here I would like first to look at the critical nature of such moments and how the coach might respond to them.

Simply due to the huge ability of a crisis to bring about radical change (see De Haan, 2003), it is vital that coaches should relate to their critical moments and remain effective even if the situation starts to become critical for them. In moments where fear of the new, uncertainty and doubt overcome coach and/or coachee, they are both closest to a breakthrough and to the possibility of real change through coaching. In his first Brazilian Lecture in 1973, Bion said that: 'Anyone who is going to see a patient tomorrow should, at some point, experience fear. In every consulting room there ought to be two rather frightened people: the patient and the psycho-analyst. If they are not, one wonders why they are bothering to find out what everyone knows' (Bion, 1973). This statement, and our own intuition that tells us that something new can be discovered only if the situation becomes 'palpable' or 'critical', are all the reasons we need to study critical moments further: what form do they take, how do they look different to coach and coachee, what is it that makes such moments critical, how are they resolved, etc.

Billow (2000) gives a detailed case study in which he monitors and analyses his own anxiety in working with one specific patient. Smith M. (2003) carried out qualitative research into the anxieties of ten counsellors and concludes, like Bion (1973), that anxiety is unavoidable and a condition for 'real' therapy. In his view, what is important is to experience enough anxiety to enhance discernment, concentration and attention, but not so much as to jeopardise clear-thinking.

I recognise this 'optimal experience of anxiety' as a condition for coaches to be able to handle their own critical moments. On the one hand, they want to be as sensitive as possible to such moments, in order to highlight them as early as possible and not allow them to pass unnoticed. But on the other hand, coaches also strive for a degree of strength, to remain in control of themselves and not be overcome by the critical nature of such moments. Coaches therefore strive to become simultaneously thinner- and thicker-skinned, in order to be well-prepared for their critical moments[4].

From these images of 'thin' and 'thick' skin we can infer two dimensions, which appear to be relevant when things become 'critical'.
- Thin skin refers to the degree to which critical moments, emotions or friction are perceived. In other words, how aware are coach and coachee of critical moments, i.e. how *sensitive* are they?
- Thick skin refers to the degree to which critical moments, emotions or friction can be handled. In other words, how deeply are coach and coachee affected by critical moments, i.e. how *robust* are they?

These two dimensions can be placed within a window, a window that is significant for both coachee and coach (see Figure 4.1). In fact, there is one such window that relates to the coach at every moment, and another – but with a different content – that relates to the coachee at every moment.

Individual tensions – such as anxieties and doubts – are shown in Figure 4.1 as dark blocks of different shapes and sizes. The shading in the window expresses how much grip the coach has on these tensions, with lighter areas showing more grip and darker ones less grip.

Just to take the window on the coach as an example: this window distinguishes between the following tensions/emotions/doubts etc.

---

[4] For more about this image of a thinner and thicker skin, and how supervision may help coaches to develop both simultaneously, see De Haan, 2008c. Other authors have used different imagery for these same dimensions which seem to many of us important to look after when it comes to personal learning. Harrison (1963) uses the images of 'castle' and 'battleground', and O'Neill (2000) speaks of 'heart' and 'backbone'.

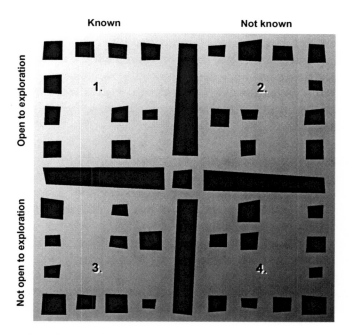

Figure 4.1 *A window onto the tensions experienced by coaches and coachees, which distinguishes between four different types or influences of tensions. The background colour gives an indication of how much 'grip' the coach or coachee has on these tensions, with lighter areas showing more grip and darker ones less grip.*

1   *Known and open to exploration.* These are tensions that the coach feels sufficiently comfortable with, so that they can be looked at and explored, and new insight can be derived from them. Ideally, coaches always work in this part of the window, where they can explore what is happening without feeling overwhelmed.

2   *Not known but open to exploration.* These are tensions that have not yet surfaced consciously, but that the coach can handle well. Examples are tensions of the coachee not yet intuited by the coach, or own tensions that have been laid to rest ('pre-conscious' tensions).

3   *Known but not open to exploration.* These are the tensions that overwhelm the coach, that make the situation critical, and that the coach does not quite know how to handle. Many of the tensions reported in Appendices A and B of this book meet this profile. They obstruct the coach and at the same time have the potential to be the start of new learning experiences for coach and coachee.

4 *Not known and not open to exploration.* We can only guess at the existence of these tensions – sometimes it becomes clear with hindsight that they did indeed exist, for example if the coach is left with an indefinable feeling. There are many possible candidates for this quadrant, including existential doubts that the coach has suppressed, artificially resolved, avoided, or completely failed to perceive.

Coachees are constantly discovering aspects of their own window during good coaching and, if things go well, their tensions become more perceptible and easier to use as a result of coaching, so they move towards the first quadrant, in the top left corner. In exactly the same way, *coaches* are constantly adapting and developing during good coaching. Their tensions equally end up in quadrant 1. They attempt to make their own tensions perceptible and usable, i.e. as available as possible and causing the minimum disruption for the coaching. This is an ongoing activity, both during every coaching relationship and throughout the career of the coach. Tensions that have spent some time in quadrant 1 become less tense through exploration and appreciation, while others – from quadrants 2 and 4 – give rise to new tensions and critical moments.

Tensions carry with them an emotional 'charge', such as anxious, uncertain, painful, expectant, enthusiastic, and they also have an emotional 'depth', which is expressed by precisely the same dimension that I used previously, in Chapter 1, for *intervention levels* (see Figure 1.2).

I distinguish three layers of 'depth' in relation to tensions.
1 *'Instrumental tensions'*, in which the coaching conversations are called into question by the coach and/or coachee, e.g. the content of the discussion, the process, the progress made, and what to do when. Typical considerations of the coach at this level of depth are 'What do I say now? How do I respond here? How do I structure this conversation?'.
2 *'Relational tensions'*, in which the nature of the relationship with the client and the boundaries of the coaching are called into question by the coach and/or coachee. Typical considerations of the coach at this depth are 'What is going on between us? What is being addressed here? What sort of appeal is being made to me?'.

3 '*Existential tensions*', in which coaching itself is called into question or a deeper intrapersonal issue is raised at this moment. Typical considerations of the coach at this level are 'Who am I to act as coach here? What sort of coach does this coachee need?'

This simple taxonomy is essentially a hierarchy: if the earlier, more profound tensions have not been resolved, we may experience difficulty adressing the more relational and instrumental tensions. Conversely, if we experience certain relational or instrumental tensions, we can assume that the deeper ones have been addressed at least to some extent, even if only temporarily and unsatisfactorily, unless those underlying tensions are now assuming the disguise of more superficial tensions[5].

Many tensions during coaching originate with the coachees, as it is they who come to the coaching with an array of tensions and queries, or 'issues', in the first place. Again, these issues may be different in nature: relatively instrumental, more relational or more existential, as expressed in Chapter 1 as the *scope* of coaching. Coaches then work with these tensions and issues, while also being exposed to their own tensions.

4.4 Relational coaching makes a difference at critical moments

Following this brief inventory of what may be critical in the moment between coach and coachee, it is possible to show something about the attitude of a *relational coach*. The conflicts inside the coach concerning a thinner or thicker skin exist over the full range of tensions, but a relational coach is able – even at critical moments! – to be particularly effective on the relational level, because that is the level where clients are met. This means that relational coaches have sufficient (self-)confidence in relation to their own more existential tensions, and have also gained some control over their own relational and

---

[5] We know that 'defences' work in this way: if we defend ourselves against certain anxieties and do not consider them, they can raise their heads again at a different 'intervention level'. For example, by not facing existential doubts we can run into relationship difficulties, or similarly we can 'somatise' mental anxieties, in other words translate them to physical anxieties on a literally more 'superficial' level, manifesting in the skin, voice, body temperature etc. (Freud, 1894). All of this happens without our having much to do with it, so sometimes it is only noticeable to someone else, such as a coach.

instrumental tensions while maintaining their vulnerability and sensitivity.

In Figure 4.2 I show what the tensions and anxieties in a relational coach might look like, a coach with a thick and a thin skin at the same time. This coach has relatively few tensions on an instrumental and existential level, and most of the remaining tensions on the instrumental level are open for exploration (so are located mainly in quadrant 3), and the remaining tensions on the existential level are usable (these are therefore located mainly in quadrant 2). Most of this coach's attention can be paid to the relational tensions, and thus to the anxieties and emotions present in the coachee at this moment.

'instrumental tensions'

'relational tensions'

'existential tensions'

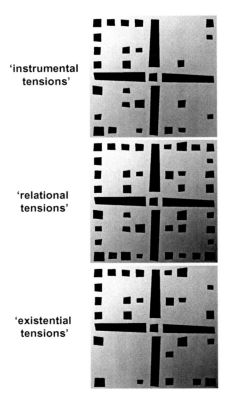

Figure 4.2 *A summary of the tensions of the coach at three levels of depth: instrumental, relational and existential. A 'good enough' coach has faced up to most of her existential tensions and has conquered most of her instrumental tensions so is able to focus primarily on her own relational tensions, where she meets her coachee.*

The tensions that concern a coach from moment to moment during coaching create a number of subtle but extremely relevant patterns. Bion may well have said (Bion, 1970) that the coach should work without memory or desire and, as far as possible, free from their own emotions and tensions. However, that is not as easy in practice as it sounds and doesn't prevent the ongoing creation of new memories, emotions, doubts and desires arising from the coaching relationship and from what the coachee contributes to it. In my opinion, a complete picture of the tensions of the coach, on various levels, remains important. Relational coaches have conquered most of their existential tensions, or in any case are not (or no longer) overcome by them (as indicated by the paler colour and emptier fields in Figure 4.2). They have also resolved most of their instrumental tensions; for example, through knowledge and experience of a range of methods, and through regular supervision (again indicated in the figure using paler and emptier fields). A relational coach consequently has more energy and attention to devote to anxieties and tensions in the relational area, where the focus is upon the relationship with this specific client at this specific moment. When coaches feel relatively secure in relation to many of their own tensions and anxieties, they are able to focus genuinely on the coachee and the coachee's issues, and what concerns the coachee at this specific moment. This is a unique combination of thin and thick skin, a balance between openmindedness, tension and certainty. A dynamic balance that is constantly changing and hence leads to a process of ongoing adjustment and indeed struggle for every coach, to which I devote most of the next part of this book.

Summary: from intervention to interaction

Ten commandments for executive coaches, based on what is known about **effectiveness** in therapy.
1 First, do no harm.
2 Have confidence.
3 Commit yourself heart and soul to your approach.
4 Feed the hope of your coachee.
5 Consider the coaching situation from your coachee's perspective.
6 Work on your coaching relationship.
7 If you don't 'click', find a replacement coach.
8 Look after yourself, to keep yourself as healthy as possible.

9   Try to stay fresh and unbiased.
10 Don't worry too much about the specific things you are doing.

Note: these commandments are based on the assumption that what is effective in therapy is also effective in coaching.

Building on that same assumption, we can conclude that effective coaching means **relational** coaching:
1   Good coaching is primarily an exercise in self-changing and self-understanding by the coachee, in which the coach helps by entering into and deepening a relationship.
2   The aim of the relationship is to make it as productive as possible in the eyes of the coachee, so the coach regularly investigates how the coachee views the productivity of the relationship.
3   The coach relates contributed subject-matter to this relationship but also to other relevant relationships of the coachee. All subject-matter is essentially taken to be relational.
4   Coaches do not impose any restrictions on themselves as regards specific interventions, but do make sure they fit in with the contract, their own ideology and their code of conduct.
5   Interventions are focused on supporting and reinforcing the relationship and thereby the coachee's learning and development process.
6   The coach is aware of and makes the maximim possible use of the **common factors** that improve effectiveness according to the latest research.

The coaching relationship can be seen as a succession of **critical moments**. Each of these moments gives rise to **tensions** in the form of anxiety, enthusiasm and other emotions. A coach tries to develop both a thinner and a thicker skin in relation to such tensions. Tensions vary in terms of the degree to which they can be perceived and used.

They also vary in terms of depth: **instrumental, relational and existential tensions.** A relational coach strives to make instrumental and existential tensions as manageable as possible, so that focus can be maintained primarily on the relational level.

Part II
The Ways of Research

Introduction: the paths towards research

I remember well how the work on Chapter 7 of this book progressed. We were on holiday on the Spanish coast, where the summer heat left us little option in the daytime but to take frequent dips in large volumes of cool water. A laid-back existence that imposed relaxation on a hectic lifestyle. Except that, to my amazement, this year the heat wasn't enough to keep me away from work completely.

Just before my holiday, I had received the last few critical moments of experienced coaches and I was now in possession of 78 brief accounts of what those colleagues found 'critical' in their work with clients. I noticed that, despite the summer heat, I kept going back to flick through the long list of accounts and make notes in the margins. Even during the siesta, when everything around us went quiet until the only sounds were the birds and the waves, I didn't give in to sleep but kept returning, time and again, to the list. I played about with the critical moments, rearranged them in different orders and started to think about encoding them in a way that would encompass the wide variety of ideas and emotions that they featured. For days and weeks I kept tinkering with the list and in the end came up with the first version of the longer article (De Haan, 2008b) during that same holiday.

What made working on this article, and also on the previous one (De Haan, 2008a), so enjoyable and fascinating? In the first place, the unique opportunity to look over the shoulders of a broad group of fellow coaches and read about their experiences with coachees. I recognised many aspects of the accounts and was frequently surprised, in the form of 'Oh, right. So that's how you tackle that? Now there's another way to do it!' But it wasn't just that feeling of recognition that kept drawing me back to these descriptions time and again. It was also the activity of exploring, mapping, cataloguing and, as it were, searching for ways to gain access to their critical moments and, indirectly, to those of their coachees.

Later, I realised that I was exploring critical moments without really finding them genuinely critical myself. Without an explicit contract, I had started to coach without noticing it, in a way that was completely safe for myself. 'Coaching without clients', that was what preserved my holiday mood and gave me so much satisfaction. I experienced none of the anxiety about the unknown that I normally feel during coaching conversations, but I was nevertheless able to give my full attention to genuine coaching issues. It was as if the 'work' aspect of the coaching had simply fallen away!

More generally, the work on this part of the book made me realise that 'research' is more relevant to coaching than I had previously thought. I have been saying for years that coaching is in fact nothing more than 'observing' and 'saying what you see'. But I hadn't realised how close the activity of coaching is to that of research.

In this part of the book I wish to report on four research studies in the field of executive coaching. First, in Chapter 5, I give an example of a traditional effectiveness study similar to those that have been taking place for decades in psychotherapy and medicine. This is a study in which we derive one figure, or a series of figures, from an entire coaching relationship and attempt to reach objective conclusions on the basis of large numbers of such figures. Instead of deriving a single figure from each entire coaching relationship, the other chapters in this part of the book look at a diametrically opposed method which explores an entire account on the basis of a single moment of coaching. This is a method of research which focuses on more personal and relational aspects of coaching, namely on the processes of personal change as they occur from moment to moment.

Chapter 3 gave a brief summary of the research into helping conversations that has been carried out within psychotherapy. Chapter 5 contains an overview of similar research that has taken place recently, on a much smaller scale, within the younger discipline of executive coaching.

It is understandable that there should be less interest nowadays in traditional effectiveness research in coaching, because so much has already been achieved with such research in psychotherapy, where the numbers and objectivity of the measurements have reached a level that would be inconceivable in the much smaller field of executive coaching. Moreover, effectiveness research cannot tell us very much about *how* the effect is achieved, only *that* a certain effect is achieved under certain circumstances. Consequently, a lot of useful research remains to be done into the moments of coaching itself, and into the changes taking place in the hearts and minds of coach and coachee during coaching.

Psychotherapy too has seen increasing interest over recent years in this type of research into the process of change itself (Carlberg, 1997; Stern *et al.*, 1998; Stern, 2004). In Chapters 6, 7 and 8 I apply the same method of exploration to executive coaching: in Chapters 6 and 7 with the aid of written case studies by the coaches participating in the research, and in Chapter 8 by means of in-depth interviews with a new group of fellow coaches.

There is ample evidence that coach and coachee have very different perspectives on the coaching (Horvath & Marx, 1990; Tallman & Bohart, 1999). It therefore appears important to explore both perspectives. In relational coaching, where the quality of the relationship from the perspective of the coachee is at the centre, the perspective of the coachee obviously takes precedence. But that of the coach is also relevant, if only because it is the only one that coaches can influence directly. In Chapter 5 the perspective of the coachee is central; in Chapters 6, 7 and 8 it is that of the coach. Follow-up research into critical moments from the perspective of the coachee is underway at present. (see De Haan, Bertie, Day, and Sills, 2008).

Chapter 5
Coachees Have Their Say: Which Interventions Work for Us?[1]

5.1 Introduction

In executive coaching, leaders and managers submit issues from their practice to conversation, to explore and bring those issues forward with the help of an executive coach. The promise of executive coaching is not so much to offer instant, ready-made solutions, but rather to foster learning and change by employing a range of interventions, such as listening, summarising, paraphrasing, interpreting and discovering links with other themes and the present coaching interaction itself.

This study sets out to examine which are the aspects of the executive coaching intervention that coachees find most helpful in bringing their issues forward.
- Which qualities in their coach?
- Which coaching behaviours by their coach?
- Under which conditions are they most helped, i.e. in terms of their own preferred learning styles and in terms of their objectives with the coaching?

The questions are explored by means of a study that is largely quantitative but also contains some qualitative questions, involving a large web-based questionnaire (163 closed and 3 open questions), 71 executive coaching clients, and two measurement points in time: shortly after the beginning of the coaching journey and approximately six months later (after the end of their coaching journey for the majority).

---

[1] For an extended version of this chapter with a more detailed overview of the data and more analysis, see De Haan, Culpin & Curd (2008). My thanks to Judy Curd for the statistical analyses that went into this chapter.

Because of constraints in the set-up of this research, we are only focusing on the coachees as clients and recipients of coaching. But it is important to realise that we can discover only some of the effects of coaching via the coachee, because coaching is essentially an *organisational* intervention. The chosen set-up cannot be translated easily to the rest of the coachee's organisation, however, because the latter generally has no direct contact with the coach. For the same reason, it is not possible to work with a control group of executives not engaged in coaching, as all of the questions on the coaching experience would be pointless for them. However, I believe that this is nevertheless an important starting point for effectiveness research in coaching, if only because the chosen set-up allows us to inquire about the impact of *specific* coaching interventions.

I did not wish to study the effectiveness of the entire coaching intervention, because that has already been done (see the summaries with seven research articles in Kampa-Kokesch & Anderson, 2001, and ten articles in Feldman & Lankau, 2005). Moreover, in my view the very convincing demonstrations in psychotherapy that were discussed in Chapter 3 are also valid for coaching – if only because the differences between the practices of therapy and coaching are probably smaller than those within those two professions.

If we consider the existing literature in the field of coaching outcomes more closely, we note that most empirical research into executive coaching is concerned, like ours, with the value of coaching from the perspective of the coachee. Those articles are often written by the coaches themselves and serve partly to justify their own work. Usually, the research takes the form of an extensive evaluation among the coachees. Occasionally, coachees are asked to estimate how much their coaching journey has contributed to the bottom line of their organisation in financial terms. For example, McGovern, Lindemann, Vergara, Murphy, Barker & Warrenfeltz (2001) evaluated a group of 100 managers in 67 organisations who were coached for between six and twelve months. They found that the vast majority of participants were very satisfied with the coaching: their estimate was that the coaching returned, on average, 5.7 times the original investment. The dominant paradigm of existing research in executive coaching is therefore *quantitative outcome research*: the systematic exploration of clients' perceived effectiveness or return on investment (ROI) of their experience.

I know of only five quantitative studies that explore the effectiveness of coaching by looking at effects other than coachee satisfaction, which I will describe in more detail here. Two studies without a control group are those of Olivero, Bane & Kopelman (1997), and of Thach (2002), who studied 31 managers from the healthcare sector and 281 managers from a telecoms multinational respectively. In the case of Olivero et al. (1997) the managers took part in a three-day training course, followed by eight weeks of coaching. They found that both the training and the coaching increased productivity considerably, with the bulk of the increase attributable to the coaching (average 22% increase due to training and 88% due to training and coaching). In the case of Thach (2002) the managers underwent a 360° feedback process before and after their coaching. They found an average increase in 'leadership effectiveness' in the eyes of others of 55–60% and in their own eyes of 52–56%, i.e. a result comparable to that of Olivero et al. (1997). Thach (2002) also realised that part of the large effect obtained may be due to the 360° feedback process itself (which would then apply to Olivero et al. 1997 as well), so part of this large improvement may be due to a so-called *Hawthorne effect* (Baritz, 1960), a consequence of having the research apparatus and not so much of the coaching intervention.

Ragins, Cotton & Miller (2000) studied a group of 1162 professionals from many organisations and looked at the effect of formal or informal mentoring relationships on a range of work and career attitudes. 44% of the respondents had an informal mentor, 9% a formal mentor as part of a mentoring programme and 47% no mentor (control group). Their results show that the crucial factor that determines the outcome of mentoring was the *mentee's satisfaction with the mentoring relationship* (as is also demonstrated by research in psychotherapy, as summarised in Chapter 3; see also Horvath & Symonds, 1991): in the absence of that satisfaction, there were no demonstrable differences between professionals who were mentored and those who were not. If the satisfaction is there, however, the professionals clearly demonstrate more positive attitudes towards themselves (self-confidence), their work, promotion prospects, organisation and career

– with no significant differences between formal and informal mentoring[2].

Evers, Brouwers & Tomic (2006) measured self-efficacy beliefs and outcome expectancies on three dimensions each. Their study compared a pre-intervention and post-intervention measurement, and also involved a control group. Whilst their numbers were not very large (30 managers in both the experimental and the control group) but they do find some objective evidence for a positive outcome of the coaching intervention. They found a significant ($p < 0.05$) increment for the coached group over the control group for one of the three dimensions in both self-efficacy beliefs and outcome expectancies (not the same dimension).

One of the most thorough studies into the effects of executive coaching was undertaken by Smither, London, Flautt, Vargas & Kucine (2003). They worked with a control group and their measure of outcome was evaluations by independent researchers and by the coachees' superiors, colleagues and staff (360° feedback). The research was conducted among 1202 senior managers of the same multinational organisation and involved 360° feedback results from two consecutive years. The researchers found that managers who work with an executive coach are significantly more likely than other managers to:
- set specific goals;
- solicit for ideas for improvements from superiors; and
- obtain higher ratings from direct-reports and superiors.

In summary, there are good indications that executive coaching as an intervention is effective and yields a modest but quantifiable outcome.

---

[2] As the authors themselves concede, they cannot rule out the possibility in this study that the professionals with a more positive mentoring relationship are more satisfied in general, and so more satisfied with themselves, their organisation and their career. As regards the differences between formal and informal mentoring programmes (as between assigned and chosen mentor relationships), it is interesting that Ragins et al. (2001) can demonstrate slightly negative effects for formal mentoring programmes – where the mentees are not able to choose their mentor – when (1) the mentor works in the same department as the mentee and (2) female mentees are assigned to a male mentor.

In the small but growing body of research literature on coaching I have found only one article exploring the question of *what sort* of coaching is effective or, in other words, which coaching models, qualities of coaches or coaching behaviours make a difference to coachees? Scoular & Linley (2006) have looked at

1. How a 'goal-setting' intervention at the beginning of the conversation impacts perceived helpfulness;
2. Personality (dis-)similarities between coach and coachee and their impact on perceived effectiveness.

In 117 one-off 30-minute coaching conversations (random) conditions with and without goal-setting were compared and both coach and coachee completed two personality questionnaires (MBTI and NEO). Outcome measurements at 2 and 8 weeks after the session showed

1. No difference between 'goal-setting' and 'no goal-setting';
2. When coach and coachee differed more on the personality instruments the outcome scores were significantly higher.

This chapter operates from a similar paradigm to Scoular & Linley (2006), with a larger range of aspects of the executive coaching intervention measured. Judging from the plethora of training programmes focusing on specific coaching techniques (e.g. regarding step-methods such as the GROW method, solution-focused coaching, or systemic coaching), it is thought by many that *specific behaviours* make all the difference in executive coaching. In this study, I wanted to explore the differences in technique that coachees report, and look particularly at which techniques or behaviours they find more or less helpful in their coaching journey.

From the previous research literature it can be seen that over-all helpfulness from the perspective of the client of coaching has been sufficiently established. Here the focus is therefore on *what particular aspects of coaching* make up this general impression of helpfulness. I examine two main areas that have been suggested in the literature: behaviours of the coach and learning styles of the coachee. Essentially the questions are "what does the coach *do* to make the experience (more) helpful?" and "How does the coachee *receive* or *work with* the coaching to make the experience (more) helpful?"

5.2 Description of the study

In order to explore the matter of specific helpfulness, we chose 'Helpfulness' as our main independent variable, and as many different coaching behaviours as possible as the main dependent variables. Our central question was the following:

What is it that makes the coaching journey worthwhile/effective/helpful to participants: how is it that they themselves feel that they learn or change through executive coaching?

5.2.1 Participants

The recipients of individual executive coaching who participated in this study were selected from four different sources: coachees of Ashridge Consulting's accredited coaches (9%), clients of the Ashridge Centre for Leadership's executive coaches (3%), clients of our colleagues at i-coachacademy (18%), and participants in the *Ashridge Leadership Process* who as part of that process receive at least four sessions of executive coaching by an Ashridge accredited coach (70%). We invited 257 coachees to participate and complete our web-based questionnaires, and the number of responses was 71 (response rate 28%) for the first questionnaire and 31 (response rate 43%) for the second questionnaire. The profiles of participants who completed the questionnaires are in Figure 5.1.

5.2.2 Questionnaires

We designed a web-based questionnaire covering all aspects of the research question, which could be completed in less than 30 minutes. We made sure that participants received the questionnaire early in their coaching relationship, after at least one coaching conversation, and in most cases after two conversations with their coach. A follow-up invitation was sent after about six months (at least after three months, with an interval of up to nine months) which, for most participants, was after the completion of their coaching journey.

The questionnaire contained 163 closed questions (usually on a 5-point Likert scale) and three open questions, grouped as follows.
- Background information about the participant: four items.
- Information about the coaching relationship: seven items.
- Behaviours of the coach: 70 items, which were scored twice, for 'Frequency' and 'Impact', so 140 items in total.

Descriptor	Range	Questionnaire 1		Questionnaire 2	
		Frequency	%	Frequency	%
Sex	Male	45	63.4	23	74.2
	Female	26	36.6	8	25.8
Age	26-30	3	4.3	1	3.2
	31-35	13	18.6	3	9.7
	36-40	16	22.9	9	29.0
	41-45	19	27.1	11	35.5
	46-50	10	14.3	5	16.1
	51-55	7	10.0	2	6.5
	56 and over	2	2.9	0	0.0
Professional role	Director	26	36.6	12	38.7
	Manager	29	40.8	11	35.5
	Consultant	5	7.0	2	6.5
	Project leader	5	7.0	2	6.5
	Other	6	8.5	4	12.9

Figure 5.1 *Characteristics of the participants in the study.*

- Kolb's Learning Style Inventory (Kolb, 1984): 12 items.
- Three open questions, about the coach, the outcomes and more generally, the coaching experience.

In the next section I present the structure of the questionnaire in more detail.

Dependent variables

The dependent variables were coach behaviour and learning style of the coachee, measured using the following well-known questionnaires:

- The *Coaching Behaviours Questionnaire* originally devised by Richard Phillips (and published as Appendix E of De Haan & Burger, 2005) to measure the six categories of coaching intervention proposed by Heron (1975).
- The *Learning Style Inventory (LSI IIa)* originally devised by David Kolb (1984).

The main advantage of using these questionnaires is that they cover a wide range of aspects that many professionals consider relevant to the area they measure: coaching behaviours and learning styles, respectively. In our book on executive coaching (De Haan & Burger, 2005), we have shown that Heron's model covers a full range of behaviours which are used in very distinct approaches to executive coaching. Kolb (1984) likewise demonstrates that his model covers a wide range of approaches to and experiences of learning.

The *Coaching Behaviours Questionnaire* yields scores on six independent categories of coaching intervention (see Chapter 9, section 9.1.5).

1 *Directing* or providing guidance, advice and recommendations.
2 *Informing* or providing information, knowledge and summaries.
3 *Challenging* or increasing (self-)understanding and exploring preconceptions.
4 *Discovering* or deepening understanding by facilitating self-exploration.
5 *Supporting* or building self-confidence and self-esteem.
6 *Releasing* or exploring emotions causing internal barriers.

These categories were measured twice in each measurement by all participants in the study, once for the frequency or quantity of that type of behaviour of their coach, and once for the impact or influence of the behaviours.

The *Learning Style Inventory* yields two independent dimensions (see Kolb, 1984).
- An individual's preference for abstractness over concreteness ('AC-CE').
- An individual's preference for action over reflection ('AE-RO').

Another advantage in working with these existing questionnaires is that after extensive use they have been validated and found reliable and internally consistent. The Cronbach Alphas for the *Coaching Behaviours Questionnaire* have been computed for a group of 292 managers (see Curd, 2006) and they were 0.86 (directing); 0.83 (informing); 0.88 (challenging); 0.93 (releasing); 0.89 (discovering); 0.86 (supporting); whilst the Cronbach Alphas for the *Learning Style Inventory* have been computed for a group of 5023 on-line users (see Kolb & Kolb, 2006), and they were 0.82 (AC – CE) and 0.82 (AE – RO).

I added ten other coaching behaviour items which were not linked to the Heron model but are deemed relevant in other specific coaching approaches (De Haan & Burger, 2005; see Figure 5.3 for the ten items).

In total, therefore, there were $(2 \times 6) + 2 + (2 \times 10) = 34$ dependent variables. The coaching behaviours were measured on a 5-point Likert scale ranging from 'Not at all' to 'Very high', while the particants, in order to measure their own learning styles, were requested to rank four statements from 'Most like you' to 'Least like you'.

Independent variables
In order to check the starting position of a participant, we included several filter questions, and a measurement of the degree of helpfulness the participant experienced in the coaching. This resulted in the following independent variables:
1 Participation in the coaching. Who took the initiative to participate: you yourself, your employer, the Ashridge programme you participated in, or someone else?
2 Executive coaching experience, expressed by two questions: 'How many coaching sessions have you received to date from your coach?'

and 'What is the expected length of your coaching (total number of sessions)?'

3 Aim of the coaching journey, where the participant was requested to select one or two of the following:
- I would like to learn something new;
- I would like to strengthen myself, become more resilient;
- I would like to change my behaviour or approach;
- I would like to stop doing certain things;
- I would like to reflect on my practice;
- other: . . . (max. five words).

4 Evaluation of the *helpfulness* of the coaching journey, on a scale from 1 to 10 where 1 is low and 10 is high.

5 Evaluation of appreciated qualities of the coach. Here, the coachee was presented twice with a list of 20 qualities and requested to select:
- 'Three qualities that you really appreciate in your coach', and
- 'Three qualities that you have perceived but are less relevant for the coaching'.

For more information on the answers to these questions, see De Haan, Culpin & Curd (2008). Also, the answers to question 3 are summarised briefly in Chapter 2 of this book.

Additional qualitative data: the open-ended questions
At the end of the closed questions the participant was given the option of answering three open-ended questions:
1 Would you like to mention any contributions from your coach that made the coaching particularly helpful to you?
2 Could you name three specific outcomes that you ascribe to the coaching: (1) . . . (2) . . . (3) . . .
3 Is there anything you would like to add regarding your experience with coaching?

75% of the participants took up the option and answered at least one of the three questions.

5.2.3 Procedure
Because of the exclusive, confidential and personal nature of any coaching relationship, it was important for us to approach the partici-pants gently and always to involve their executive coaches. For this

reason we informed the network of Ashridge executive coaches through e-mail and conversations about this research, and made it as easy as possible for them to 'submit' their clients to us: we asked them to send us only the e-mail addresses of their clients. With those addresses we invited the coachee to our web-based questionnaire in an e-mail, in which we stressed the confidential nature of the research and the fact that we would only report general patterns and never specific facts from their particular coaching relationship. We also invited some of our wider networks of coaches to do the same.

Because we were always dependent on both parties to open up their confidential coaching relationships to our research, the data collection was spread out over a relatively long period, from December 2004 to April 2007. We analysed the data with the help of SPSS, a statistical software programme.

5.3 Quantitative results: helpfulness appears to be a generic experience

The 'Helpfulness scores' of the participants ranged from 2 or 3 to 10 for both questionnaires, which is a good spread with some scope for the computation of dependencies. The average Helpfulness was 7.21 (first questionnaire) and 7.87 (second questionnaire), a rising figure that persists if we compare the same group of 31 that completed both questionnaires (7.30 and 7.87, respectively). A t-test has shown that this is a significant difference at $p < 0.05$ and that it is a large effect ($\eta^2 = 0.18$; see Figure 5.4). Despite this clear increase in the evaluation of the coaching, we cannot conclude definitely that coaching is valued increasingly over time by this group. There may be an element of self-selection: perhaps more of those who experience such an increase are prepared to fill in the second questionnaire. A similar increase in scores with increasing experience was found in our earlier study into learning experiences with peer consultation (De Haan & De Ridder, 2006).

In Figures 5.2 and 5.3 all the correlations between Helpfulness and the dependent variables are shown. There seems to be a small but significant relation between Learning styles and Helpfulness. We can make this relationship clearer if we rotate the independent learning style dimensions to two new independent dimensions (correlation $r = 0.02$):

AC − CE + AE − RO and AC − CE − AE + RO. The former does not correlate at all with Helpfulness ($r = 0.04$) but the latter correlates significantly ($r = 0.27$ and $p < 0.05$). These rotated dimensions correspond to the diagonals in Kolb's matrix (Kolb, 1984), i.e. AC − CE + AE − RO with the Converging versus Diverging dimension and AC − CE − AE + RO with the Assimilating versus Accommodating dimension. In other words, assimilators ('theorists') seem to value the coaching significantly more than accommodators ('activists').

We also looked at the correlation between the Aims of the coaching (question 3, above) and Helpfulness. One or more of the five aims that we proposed turned out to apply for more than 95% of the participants, because the final open option was used only by 3 participants. The aim that went together with the highest score for Helpfulness was 'I would like to strengthen myself, become more resilient' with 7.43 and the lowest was 'I would like to stop doing certain things' with 6.80, but the difference in scores was not significant.

If we correlate Helpfulness with Coaching behaviours, and also the Coaching behaviours among themselves, the surprising finding is that all of the variables actually display a consistent and significant positive correlation.

- All correlations between Coaching behaviours and Helpfulness were positive and significant at the $p < 0.01$ level (see Figure 5.2 for the results of the Impact questions for the first measurement).
- Different Coaching behaviours all correlate at the $p < 0.01$ level, with correlations between 0.37 and 0.84 (see Figure 5.2 again for the Impact questions and the first measurement).
- Frequency and Impact results for the various Coaching behaviours also correlated significantly ($p < 0.01$), with coefficients between 0.27 and 0.73 for different categories and between 0.86 and 0.92 for the same categories. In fact, t-tests demonstrated that there were no significant differences between the scores on Frequency and Impact. For this reason I will confine myself to the Impact results in this chapter, with the footnote that my conclusions also apply to the Frequency results.
- If we compare the score for Coaching behaviours between the first and second measurements, we again note correlations with significance at $p < 0.01$ level and coefficients between 0.46 and 0.66.

Scales		N	M	SD	α	Correlation coefficients with							
						1 Helpfulness	2 Directing	3 Informing	4 Challenging	5 Releasing	6 Discovering	7 Supporting	8 AC-CE
Heron categories of coaching behaviour – Impact	1 Helpfulness	70	7.21	1.61		-							
	2 Directing	70	26.71	9.10	0.90	0.31**	-						
	3 Informing	70	30.11	8.38	0.87	0.46**	0.66**	-					
	4 Challenging	70	29.56	8.05	0.84	0.40**	0.61**	0.68**	-				
	5 Releasing	70	28.76	8.85	0.87	0.46**	0.59**	0.56**	0.72**	-			
	6 Discovering	70	35.91	7.43	0.84	0.40**	0.37**	0.53**	0.52**	0.60**	-		
	7 Supporting	70	30.61	7.79	0.81	0.48**	0.65**	0.65**	0.60**	0.70**	0.64**	-	
Learning styles	8 AC-CE	71	-3.23	12.10		0.22	0.00	0.05	0.13	0.23	0.00	0.24*	-
	9 AE-RO	70	-5.51	11.92		-0.18	0.29*	0.15	0.13	0.15	-0.01	0.08	-0.14

Figure 5.2 *Mean values, Standard deviations, Internal consistencies (Cronbach Alphas) and Correlation coefficients of the scales used (data from Questionnaire 1).*

However, the t-tests show that there is one significant difference, to which I will return later.

The ten questions with added Coaching behaviours also correlate demonstrably with Helpfulness (see Figure 5.3). They also correlate with each other, largely with a significance of $p < 0.05$. Because these are not composite variables but individual questions on the questionnaire, the correlations are lower as expected. Only numbers 5, 6 and 8 appear not to correlate with Helpfulness, perhaps because they have a low Mean score and little spread (particularly question 8), or because they are less seen as coaching behaviours by coachees (5 and 6 being very challenging).

To summarise, we find that almost all 17 incremental scales that measure the experience of coaching (1 Helpfulness, 6 × Heron categories of Coaching behaviours, 10 × additional Coaching behaviours) correlate significantly with each other. This is remarkable since these variables cover the widest possible range of coaching behaviour. Although they are theoretically very distinct and coachees also measure them very differently (see the standard deviations and Alphas in Figure 5.2), coachees fail to distinguish between the variables when it comes to helpfulness.

In earlier research into the learning experiences of participants in peer consultation we came to the same conclusion (see Table 3 in De Haan & De Ridder, 2006). Coachees and participants in learning groups appear to experience helpfulness in a *generic* way: if they find the coaching or action learning helpful, they will score higher on a wide range of aspects of the learning experience. So, even if they are able to distinguish carefully between those aspects, they will assign all of the aspects a higher value if they value the learning experience more highly.

This appears to lead to the conclusion that coachees value the helpfulness of their coach *almost irrespective of* the specific behaviours of the coach or the specific occurrences in the coaching. In other words, coachees look much more at generic aspects such as the quality of the relationship or the person of the coach. Indirectly, this offers clear support for the idea that it is primarily 'common factors' which determine the effectiveness of coaching (see Chapter 4).

Additional coaching behaviour	M	SD	Correlation coefficient with Helpfulness
1. Respond to some of the things I say with lightness and humour	3.56	3.65	0.27*
2. Manage my expectations explicitly	3.18	2.85	0.28*
3. Rephrase or paraphrase what I have just said	3.30	3.25	0.28*
4. Draw attention to specific words or metaphors that I use	3.32	3.50	0.35**
5. Play the devil's advocate bringing out the inconsistency of what I've just said	2.89	3.45	− 0.00
6. Convert my objections into opportunities	2.86	3.10	0.22
7. Suggest and review 'homework' for between the sessions	2.78	3.00	0.36**
8. Engage in 'live' exercises such as role-play, mind-mapping etc.	2.07	2.45	0.23
9. Approach concerns that I raise from a very different and new perspective	3.27	3.55	0.47**
10. Make explicit the patterns of be haviours that I seem to engage in	3.29	3.55	0.31**

Figure 5.3 *Mean values, Standard deviations and correlation coefficients of the additional Coaching behaviours with Helpfulness (data from Questionnaire 1).*

Paired T-test	t	Significance (2-sided)	η^2
Pair 1: Helpfulness Questionnaire 1 & 2	-2.538	0.02	0.18
Pair 2: Directing Questionnaire 1 & 2	0.044	0.97	-
Pair 3: Informing Questionnaire 1 & 2	0.0150	0.88	-
Pair 4: Challenging Questionnaire 1 & 2	-1.274	0.21	-
Pair 5: Releasing Questionnaire 1 & 2	-2.093	0.04	0.13
Pair 6: Discovering Questionnaire 1 & 2	-0.302	0.76	-
Pair 7: Supporting Questionnaire 1 & 2	-0.552	0.58	-

Figure 5.4 *Paired T-test comparing the answers to Questionnaires 1 and 2, for the Helpful-ness and Impact of Coaching behaviour dimensions. Frequency of Coaching behaviour gives the same picture, while all other comparisons between the two questionnaires yield non-significant differences. Cohen (1988) refers to* η^2 *values under 0.06 as a moderate effect and over 0.14 as a large effect.*

Listening, understanding and encouragement from the coach are deemed most helpful

If we look at the qualities that were most appreciated in a coach, then there are clearly three that stood out in that they were ticked by over 30% of respondents: Listening, Understanding and Encouragement. They were followed by Knowledge and then Empathy, Authenticity and Involvement. Other qualities that were observed but deemed less relevant to the coaching (the second question about coach's qualities) were Calmness, Humour and Warmth. However, there was a much larger spread in the responses to this question so it seems those answers are more about the individual traits of the coach.

Participants with different learning styles respond differently to the coaching

In Figure 5.2 we find two other correlations, with significance level $p < 0.05$, namely correlations between Learning styles of the coachee and Coaching behaviours of the coach.

1   A correlation of $r = 0.24$ between the coachee's Preference for abstractness over concreteness (AC-CE) and Supporting coaching behaviour.
2   A correlation of $r = 0.29$ between the coachee's Preference for action over reflection (AE-RO) and Directing coaching behaviour.

In other words, we find that coachees who have a more 'abstract' (theoretical) learning style value the supportive style more, whilst coachees with a more extravert learning style value the directive style of coaching more. Intuitively, we can understand that coachees who are more extraverted might appreciate a more 'interventionist' coach, with more suggestions and feedback. Also, we can imagine that more abstract 'theorists' value some support for the often more lonely work that they do. Moreover, these correlations tally with the differences previously found in the valuation of coaching by these two groups, because the directing style is often seen as less of a coaching behaviour whilst supporting is seen by many as the 'most' coaching behaviour (Heron, 1975).

Coachees gain in appreciation for the 'releasing' aspect of coaching

If we compare the results of measurement early in the coaching rela-tionship (Questionnaire 1) and measurement late in the relationship or after the end of coaching (Questionnaire 2), we find two significant ($p < 0.05$) differences between the distributions (see Figure 5.4): for Helpfulness and for the Releasing dimension of coach behaviour – in both Impact and Frequency. The η^2 effect sizes are shown in Figure 5.4. There is a large effect for Helpfulness and a moderate effect for the Releasing dimension (Cohen, 1988). The intriguing conclusion is that it appears that our participants begin to perceive or value releasing interventions more as the coaching relationship develops. Releasing takes place at a deeper intervention level than the other styles in Heron's model, so it is understandable that it takes time to permit, handle and value interventions of that type.

5.4 Qualitative results: evaluating the importance of the coaching relationship

In the first questionnaire 38 participants provided 73 responses to the first qualitative question, regarding contributions from the coach that made the coaching helpful. Through content analysis of this data, we were able to assign all of the responses to one of the following ten categories: Insight/Awareness, Knowledge & Experience, Coach Attributes, Challenge, Support, Listening, Space & Balance, Planning, Role Modelling and Courage & Confidence (see Figure 5.5). The top-scoring categories were as follows.

1 Insight into and awareness of the coachee's issues and behaviour.
2 The coach's knowledge and experience.
3 The coach's support, availability and being attuned to the needs of the coachee.

Here are some direct quotes from the participants as examples of the type of reflections that occurred frequently and which we allocated to the most frequently used categories.

1. Insight into and awareness of the coachee's issues and behaviour
- 'It has made me more aware of things that I do and it has helped me to live in the moment and to act.'
- 'Recognising what has gone on – and what is going on.'
- 'Honesty to myself made me aware of "deeper" underlying feelings and reasons for my behaviour.'

Response categories:	Were there any contributions of the coach that made the coaching particularly helpful for you?		Can you name three specific outcomes that you ascribe to the coaching?	
	Questionnaire 1	Questionnaire 2	Questionnaire 1	Questionnaire 2
	Frequency	Frequency	Frequency	Frequency
Insight & Awareness	16	2	19	16
Knowledge & Experience	10	6		
Coach Attributes	7			
Challenge	4			
Support	9	1		
Listening	2			
Space & Balance	6		2	2
Planning	5	2	6	3
Role Modelling	5			
Courage & Confidence	7	1	25	13
Relationships			13	5
Skills			22	19
Change			8	1

Figure 5.5 *Results of analysis of the responses to the first two open questions at the end of the questionnaires. All of the responses to the first open question could be classified in no more than ten categories. Only three additional categories were needed for the responses to the second open question.*

2. The coach's knowledge and experience

- 'Understanding about my work situation and offering sound, practical and inspirational advice.'
- 'My coach started with a psychometric questionnaire which set a common language for our communications and also encouraged depth of thought in terms of motivations.'
- 'Sharing some material on different types of leaders.'

3. The coach's support, availability, and being attuned to the needs of the coachee

- 'Very focused on my needs for development.'
- 'Having the opportunity to discuss "stuck" issues in an unthreatening environment.'
- 'Using the coach as a sounding board to test my thinking.'
- 'Helpful to go through what I had worked out in my own mind with someone removed from the situation.'

Next, the personal attributes of the coaches that the participants found helpful were mostly to do with personal qualities and the way that they conducted the relationship between the coach and the coachee. Some of the attributes that were emphasised were how kind and courteous the coach was, how interested they seemed to be in the life of the coachee and how open and available they were for the coachee. An example of feedback received is:

- 'Always found my coach to be very approachable, quick to respond to my mails and proffering timely and very useful feedback.'

Interestingly, all those who commented on attributes of their coach also rated the helpfulness of their coaching experience highly: the average helpfulness score for those who commented on their coach attributes is 8.25, significantly higher than over-all average. It appears again that the better the coaching relationship from the perspective of the coachee, the higher the helpfulness of the coaching process is rated (see also the conclusions in psychotherapy in Chapter 3).

The second open question related to specific outcomes that participants ascribe to the coaching. 65% of participants were able to list one or more outcomes from their coaching and we needed only three new categories in order to classify their answers: Relationships, Skills and Change (see Figure 5.5 again). The three outcomes emphasised most were:

1 Courage and (self-)confidence.
2 A set of skills and tools to take away.
3 Insight into and awareness of their own behaviour or issues.

Here are some direct quotes from the participants as examples of the type of reflections that occurred frequently and which we allocated to the most frequently used categories:

1. Increased courage and self-confidence

- 'Given myself confidence to tackle projects that would not have come across my radar screen.'
- 'Ability to face my fears and by doing so become more comfortable showing my vulnerability.'
- 'I have raised concerns with my boss that I would have otherwise kept to myself.'

2. Development of new skills

- 'I now have a structured way of attacking any problem that comes my way.'
- 'Better performance in management meetings.'
- 'Helped me create more cohesive management and team.'

3. Insight into and awareness of their own behaviours and issues

- 'I can better see how my behaviour is perceived by others.'
- 'Higher levels of self-awareness.'
- 'I have learnt to recognise the good things in me; previously I was only aware of the negative things.'

Participants used the third open question ('Is there anything you would like to add?') mainly to communicate that they have found the coaching to be a very valuable experience, which confirms other research using mainly open questions (see for example McGovern *et al.*, 2001, or Blackman, 2006). The results of the open questions in the second questionnaire confirmed the same picture as the first (see Figure 5.5).

5.5 Conclusion

The results of this study have shown that these clients of executive coaching interventions appreciate *all* the behaviours of their coaches more if they find the coaching more helpful. This was not demonstrated for three very specific behaviours only: 'playing the devil's advocate'; 'converting objections into opportunities' and 'engaging in live exercises such as role-play, mind-mapping, etc.' (see Figure 5.3). The fact that coachees appear not to differentiate between specific behaviours of their coach can be seen as additional support for a *relational* perspective on executive coaching, where the crucial predictor of the outcome of coaching is the 'coaching relationship, as perceived by the coachee'. More support for a relational perspective is found in:

- the fact that coachees most value coach qualities that benefit the relationship, such as listening, understanding and encouragement; and
- the fact that coachees who attribute qualities such as friendly, courteous, approachable, available, attentive and responsive to their coach generally experienced a significantly better outcome.

From all these results we can conclude that most coachees first try to establish a strong working relationship or working alliance, and then mostly focus on their own issues without worrying very much about the specific behaviours of their coach. A similar picture also emerges from psychotherapeutical research that concludes that clients report fewer changes in the working alliance than their therapist (Martin, Garske & Davis, 2000). The following were other findings.

1 Coachees with different learning styles attribute different value to (aspects of) coaching. The assimilating learning style appears to correlate most positively with a positive outcome, while (a) coachees who prefer 'action' in their learning style value a *directing* coaching style more highly, and (b) coachees who are more focused on 'abstractness' than 'concreteness' value a *supporting* coaching style more highly.
2 The follow-up measurement shows that coachees not only start to value their experiences of coaching significantly higher later on in the journey, but that they also appreciate the *releasing* style of coaching more.

Looking in detail at all these responses of coachees to their coaching experience, we find strong corroboration for the existence of generic, common factors at work (see Chapter 3), and we also find some support for Carl Rogers' (1957) idea that what they appreciate most in their coach is support, encouragement, listening and understanding. At the same time, we find evidence that coachees start to value the more challenging releasing interventions more later in the course of their coaching relationship.

If we take a step back from these findings, we find that we have confirmed another conclusion from research in psychotherapy, namely that the perspectives of clients and their therapists are very different (Horvath & Marx, 1990 and Tallman & Bohart, 1999). We know that coaches are strongly aware of their specific coaching model, their specific approaches and their specific behaviours, and that they they find models of specific coaching interventions like that of Heron (1975) relevant and distinctive. On the other hand, such specific aspects of their coaching relationship appear to interest the client much less. The fact that some of the language we coaches use appears to be much less relevant for our coachees teaches us that we perhaps still have to find a meaningful vocabulary for our clients' experiences.

There is certainly more research to do into what specific aspects of the coaching relationship – if it is not specific behaviours of the coach – are crucial and decisive for the impact on most of our coachees. I hypothesise that the categories that emerged in the analysis of responses to the first open question, such as Insight, Knowledge, Support and Courage, or the coach qualities that our participants mentioned, such as Friendliness, Courtesy and Responsiveness, may provide a good initial starting point for formulating relevant and effective discriminators. This list should be extended with the term Working Alliance: not studied in these questionnaires but certainly identified elsewhere as a relevant measure of success in the eyes of the client (see for example Horvath & Symonds, 1991).

Summary: coachees have their say

This chapter describes **quantitative research into the helpfulness of coaching,** using the following research question: What is it that makes the coaching journey worthwhile/effective/helpful to participants: how is it that they themselves feel that they learn or change through executive coaching?

In the first place, our research confirms that coaching is generally regarded as a helpful intervention by coachees. As is also clear from the summary of research by others, **coaching appears to make a demonstrable, positive difference time after time**.

In a nutshell, coachees' answers to the question of which interventions work for them boil down to: '**All interventions work for us**'. Coachees appear to consider aspects other than specific interventions when they evaluate their own experiences of coaching.

This is exactly what we would predict from a radical **relational perspective**.

Other patterns in the responses also point to a relational perspective of the coachee:
- They mainly value qualities of the coach which benefit the **coaching relationship**, such as listening, understanding and encouragement.
- They mention spontaneously qualities that point to the **building of a relationship**, such as friendly, courteous, approachable, available, attentive and responsive.

This study therefore confirms other research (as cited in Chapter 3) showing that the working alliance from the perspective of the client is the best predictor of outcome.

It is also clear that we need to look for a **new vocabulary** for the specific aspects that clients themselves value and look for in their coaching. An initial proposal in this respect is made at the end of the chapter.

Other findings are that:
- Coachees with different learning styles assign different values to (aspects of) coaching: **coachees with the assimilating learning style have the highest appreciation** for coaching, while coachees who prefer action in their learning appreciate the **directing style** more, and coachees who are more focused on abstractness value the **supporting style** more highly.
- At the time of their follow-up questionnaire – i.e. much later in their experience with the same coach – coachees give a significantly **higher score** for **helpfulness** on average, but also for the **releasing style** of coaching.

Chapter 6
'I Doubt therefore I Coach': Critical Moments of Less Experienced Coaches[1]

6.1 Introduction

Since November 2002, a colleague and I have been running a five-day *Coaching!* module in the Netherlands, for management consultants and executives who already have experience of conducting individual coaching conversations and want to develop their coaching skills further. The module invites participants to compare alternative coaching approaches, to gain a better understanding of their own preferred styles and to develop a more distinctive, unique coaching style. The final preparatory assignment for the module is:

Describe briefly one **critical moment** (an exciting, tense or significant moment) with one of your coachees. Think about what was critical in the coaching journey, or a moment when you did not quite know what to do.

In the course of the module, participants learn on the basis of their own critical moments and coaching issues, by means of a variety of exercises in the form of coaching conversations.

Around three-quarters of the participants are professionals who have recently completed a full year of training to become management consultants, while a quarter are independent coaches. None hold a diploma or are accredited as a coach or therapist and very few have completed longer-term training in this field. The module has now been run seven times and 72 of the 79 participants have sent in detailed preparatory assignments (a 91% response rate), leaving us with a treasure trove of accounts of 'critical moments' as experienced by aspiring

---

[1] An earlier version of this chapter, with 56 critical moments, appears in De Haan (2008a).

coaches, numbering 101 to be precise. 21 of the 101 were discarded at an early stage because they did not take place in a 'pure' coaching relationship but within a hierarchical relationship or between immediate colleagues. The 80 remaining moments proved to be very recognisable, even for more experienced coaches, and appear to complement each other rather than point in different directions. All former participants in the module gave permission for their critical moments to be published. In this chapter, I attempt to identify recurring patterns within the sample and investigate how coaches can handle these critical moments.

6.2 Initial classification of the 80 moments

I initially placed the 80 real-life critical moments in a particular order, arranging them under summarising headings (see Appendix A). The moments fall naturally under headings that describe aspects of the coaching process, but they could also have been classified differently, and many critical moments can be categorised under a number of different headings in principle. I have already carried out an initial *interpretation*, therefore, by choosing both order and headings. The following is a list of the headings and the number of moments under each heading.

1   All moments are critical (two moments)
2   The very beginning – acquisition (four moments)
3   The very beginning – the first conversation (four moments)
4   The very beginning – building a relationship (three moments)
5   Am I good enough? (two moments)
6   Am I doing it well enough? (nine moments)
7   There's something there . . . (four moments)
8   There's nothing there . . . (four moments)
9   What do I unleash? (two moments)
10 The coachee's emotions (four moments)
11 My own emotions (three moments)
12 My own doubts (five moments)
13 Deferring my judgement (seven moments)
14 Breakthroughs (three moments)
15 Directing the conversation (seven moments)
16 Matching coach to coachee (five moments)
17 Limits of coaching (nine moments)
18 Impact of the organisation (two moments)
19 Team coaching (one moment).

6.3 Summary in the form of a 'doubtful' story

As the next step in listening to these coaches and interpreting their critical moments, all 80 critical moments were summarised as follows.

'Who am I to think I can do this work?', is the first question asked by every coach. Presuming that you can coach someone else, and at the same time finding that presumption very presumptuous. That makes it so difficult to recommend yourself, or to explain your own contribution to a potential new client. Even after that, this doubt remains anxiety-provoking: 'when does it start, how does it start, what is going to happen, and will I be capable of saying something back?' And then, *when* something happens, when the coaching relationship is entered into, when something is said or something is contributed within that relationship, new doubts immediately set in: 'Do I understand, how do I respond, and is it good enough?'. Then, the question 'What should I offer?' at the same time as the question 'Do I have to offer something?'[2]. Sometimes, you even start to have doubts about your own doubts, for example, in the form of the question 'Should I contribute my doubts, or not?'[3]. Doubts can also extend to the activity of coaching itself, as in 'is this or that still coaching?', a different expression of 'am I doing it right?'.

Difficult confrontations with your own doubts are the moments when your coachee asks you what to do, or when you yourself take the initiative to advise the coachee. But there are also more subtle confrontations with those doubts, when the coachee takes them away, for example by putting you on a pedestal, flattering you or 'learning an awful lot from you'. That turns out to feel so good that you want that good feeling more often and start to say things that stand you a greater chance of attracting such compliments.

But there are also times when the doubts are relieved, and coaches actively seek out those critical moments: when the 'penny drops' or the 'breakthrough takes place'; that is, when your coachee starts to feel, think or act differently.

---

[2] As described in critical moment lvii (see Appendix A).
[3] As described in critical moment xxix (see Appendix A).

The coach who is aware of this frequently realises the extent to which coaching is in fact a single, long succession of critical moments, often in the form of doubts: 'do I have something to offer as a coach, am I good enough, am I doing it right, what is going to happen, and if it happens will the coachee and I be able to handle it, where are the boundaries and can we avoid overstepping them?' These questions follow each other in many different variants. There is the oppressive feeling that something may happen at any time, something that will have important consequences, but we don't know what, which consequences, when or to what extent we will be involved ourselves.

When all of the doubts about coaching as a conversational form fade into the background a little, more specific doubts arise about the situation, e.g., the doubt whether the coach will be able to handle this specific coachee. 'Difficult' coachees appear to be those who have false expectations, shirk responsibility, or are quiet and introverted.

And if the doubts about the coaching situation turn out to be manageable, there are still external influences to contend with. Internal coaches in particular often feel pressure from the coachee's manager or others within the organisation to achieve results or to take action in a particular direction. Results and actions which are often either outside the scope of the contract or cannot be guaranteed. Team coaching is a special case, in which the various options and dilemmas are more visible as they are personified by the various people around the table.

All in all, a story full of doubts, doubts about yourself, your professional interventions and the boundaries of your profession[4]. To summarise even more concisely, these new coaches are mainly feeling two things in their critical situations: 'what is going on?' and 'do I have an answer to it?', or: 'what do I see?' and 'how do I respond?'.

---

[4] Only 11 of the 80 critical moments do not refer directly to doubts of the coach.

One coherent story emerges clearly from this summary, a story I will call the 'critical story of the new coach and her coachee'. However different all of these coaches may be, it appears on further examination that they experience very similar tensions in their work. It is also noticeable that experience and training as a coach does not lead to different tensions in their coaching work: when I ask more experienced coaches about their critical moments, very similar aspects come to light[5]. This brings to mind Rogers' famous pronouncement 'The most personal is the most universal' (Rogers, 1961): in other words, the critical moments in coaching point strongly to a general human experience with a certain form of conversation, namely a 'helping conversation'. This is an experience familiar even to children, without them being aware that they are coaching or being coached.

6.4 How to handle these critical moments and doubts?

6.4.1 Analysis

The following contains a transcript of all 80 critical moments in 67 doubts, worded as concise questions, in accordance with the 'critical incidents' technique (Flanagan, 1954). The original critical moments often lead to more than one of the doubts[6]. I take the process of interpretation a step further here, by proposing brief essentials that I see recurring in different critical moments. As in real coaching conversations, I reformulate the critical moments 'contributed' above and provide them with summarising headings. To each of the resulting groups of similar doubts, I also give a short personal response.

The concise questions below, however, are not strictly doubts in themselves. The doubt arises only if they cannot be answered straightforwardly – if the coach cannot or does not dare to ask the question openly, or if the answer is ambivalent. Doubts and tensions always go hand-in-hand in this material.

---

[5] Compare with the moments in Appendix B: similar themes but in general less doubtful.

[6] For the translated text of all of the critical moments (with Roman numerals), see Appendix A.

1. Doubts about every coaching conversation, and every moment in a coaching conversation

1	What is going to happen now? (i, v, vii, xxxvii, xlvi, lvii, lxii)
2	How is the coachee coming across? (viii, xii)
3	How can I get an idea of the coachee's way of thinking? (xi, xii, xx, xxv)
4	What will I be able to say about this? (vii, xliii, xlv, xlvi, lxii)
5	Can I ask this? (iv, xiii, xvii)
6	What is going on in my coachee? (lxiv)
7	How is the coachee going to interpret this? (v, vii, x, xxi, lx, lxiv)
8	Do I understand enough of this? (xviii, xx, xli, lxiv)
9	Can I keep my coachee's issues central? (xvi, xvii, xlii, lviii, lxii)
10	How do I find tools to use: after all, coaching is more than 'just talking'? (ii)
11	Is this the actual/real problem? (xi, xxv, xxxiv, lxii)
12	Is this coachee willing? (v, vii, ix, xxviii, xxxii, lxii)
13	How can I get my coachee to take more responsibility for his/her own issues? (ix, xx, xxviii, xxxii, liii, xxxix, lxii, lxvii, lxxviii)
14	Does my coachee want to change? (xxviii, lxvii, lxviii)
15	What will come out of this conversation? (ix, xxxi, xlvi, lvii)

If these doubts don't run through the coach's head in every conversation, how can they be a good coach? These doubts indicate that the coach is interested in the coachee, in the coachee's issue, in the coaching, and in the results of the coaching, so they must be vital to good coaching. Annoyingly, of course, these doubts and the lack of a definitive answer also make the coach uncertain, and permanently unfulfilled. This first set of doubts already shows clearly how important something like 'containment' (Bion, 1963) is for the coach: remaining calm, open and authentic even in a situation of pregnant, even existential questions and doubts.

2. Doubts about the coaching relationship and transference[7]

16	Finding my role, and that of the coachee . . . (i, ii. xix, xxxiv, lxxvi)
17	Am I entering the other person's territory if I bring up the question of behaviour? (xxvi, xxvii, xxxiii, lx)
18	How do I recommend myself? (iii, iv, v, vi, liii)

---

[7] Transference is the phenomenon whereby relationship patterns from outside the coaching relationship influence that relationship itself, where something can be learned from those patterns. The concept was introduced by Freud.

19   Will I be accepted? (iv, vi, xi, xiv, xv, xxiv, xli, liii, lxviii)
20   What does the coachee think about me and my interventions? (vii, viii, xiii, xli, lxvi)
21   Does the coachee have confidence in me, and how do I develop that confidence? (vi, xi, xiii, xiv, xv, xxiv, lx)
22   Does the coachee have confidence in the coaching? (vi, xxxvi, liii)
23   What to do if the coachee becomes emotional about the coaching? (xxxvi)
24   How do I handle undermining of the coaching by the coachee? (ix, xxviii, xxxvi, xlv, lxvii, lxxi)
25   How do I handle denial (especially of summaries) by the coachee? (xii, xxviii, lxvii)
26   Am I being seduced by my coachee? (xi, xliv, lxxii)
27   What to do if my coachee puts me on a pedestal? (xliv)
28   What to do if my coachee tempts me to 'join in the grumbling'? (lii)
29   What to do if I myself become emotional about the coaching? (xxxviii, xxxviv, xli)
30   What if I doubt my coachee's abilities? (li, lxviii)
31   What to do if my coachee irritates me? (xl, liii, lxii)
32   How do I handle introverted coachees? (lxiv, lxv, lxvi)
33   How do I handle awkward or egocentric coachees? (lxviii)
34   How do I bring up the relationship itself? (ix, xxiii, xxvi, liii)
35   When to call it a day? (xii, xl, lxii, lxxvii, lxxix)

It is difficult to underestimate the importance of the relationship between coach and coachee. First of all, the coachee needs a minimum of confidence in and acceptance of the coach in order to work with him or her (18–22). This leads to confidence in the results and hope of improvement, a 'placebo effect' which, as we saw in Chapter 3, has been demonstrated to account for a substantial proportion of the effectiveness of therapy – entirely independent of the actual therapeutic work. Second, in 23–28 we see the enormous importance of *transference* and in 29–33 the equal importance of *counter-transference* to the results of coaching. Friction in the relationship between coach and coachee provides insight into the coachee's other relationships. Quite rightly, the coaches contributing to this research point out that the people who are not open to coaching interventions are often precisely the ones who need coaching (see moment v), and that these critical moments between coach and coachee are precisely the ones that are seen as turning points in retrospect (see for example moment xxxvi).

An important and daring task of the coach is to raise the subject of the coaching relationship itself and the possibility of transference (34).

3. Doubts about guiding the coaching conversations

36	What to do if there is no issue? (xxix, xxx)
37	What to do if the issue is entirely open? (xxix)
38	How to raise the fact that there is 'something' wrong, an uncomfortable reaction from the coachee? (xxv, xxvi, lxiii)
39	What to do when I come across deeper layers and stronger emotions? (xxxiii, xxxiv, xxxv, xxxvi, xxxvii, xxxviii, lxxix)
40	How to 'press on' if the coachee is not open to reflection? (ix, xvi, xxviii, xlvi, lxiii, lxviii)
41	How to handle a 'breakthrough', and the subsequent feeling of satisfaction? (xxxiii, xxxvi, liv, lv, lvi)
42	What to do with my *esprit de l'escalier*? (xxv)
43	Is listening and summarising enough? (xvii, lviii)
44	Can I offer my own interpretation (without being asked)? (x, xvi, xvii, xxvii, lx, lxi, lxxii, lxxiii, lxxv)
45	How can I give my more critical interpretation? (xvi, xxi, xxii, xxvii, xlix)
46	How to voice my opinion? (xlvii, xlviii)
47	Can I offer advice (without being asked)? (x, xxii, xxxiii, xlvii, xlviii, l, li, lx, lxi, lxxiii)
48	What to do if my coachee asks my advice? (xxi, xliii, xliv, xlv, xlix, li)
49	Can I ask for feedback about my approach? (xvii)
50	Do I have to structure the conversation or guide it and, if so, how? (ix, xvii, xxxi, xxxviii, lvii, lviii, lix, lxv)
51	Team coaching: how to involve and coordinate different interests? (xviii, lvi)
52	How do I find a balance between objective and personal themes? (lix, lxvi)
53	How do I find a balance between my objectivity and joint responsibility? (ix, xxxiii, lxii)
54	How do I find a balance in terms of timing, i.e. when and how to say something? (lxiii, lxv, lxviii)

Dealing with emotions and the suspicion that 'something' is going on in the coachee is high on the list of a coach's critical moments. You never know for sure: is there 'nothing' there or is there 'something' there? And how do you bring 'it' up in a way that is not too controlling and does not put the relationship under unnecessary pressure from your side? In coaching, the coachee should be central, so coaches do not wish to over-direct the conversation. However, they notice that a summary has a certain directing effect, as does the question of whether there is 'something' going on here, or an interpretation, or feedback, or giving advice.

In many of the doubts above, we can see that coaches feel very responsible for direction, for the balance between different topics during the conversation and for when something is said. Although this is understandable, in my view it is primarily the coachee who should be responsible for those things: coaches should reconcile themselves to the fact that quite fundamentally they cannot direct or plan their coaching conversations. Direction is an illusion, sometimes on the part of the coach, sometimes on the part of the coachee, and often both. The illusion of being able to direct coaching is one of our defences against the presence of unpleasant uncertainties and doubts. Coaches may indeed ask what aim or result the coachee has in mind, but they cannot derive certainty from that question about what will happen next. Indeed, objectives set by coachees often mask underlying, more essential needs.

4. Doubts about the boundaries of coaching conversations

55	Where is the boundary with therapy; when to refer? (xx, xxxiv, xxxv)
56	How to work without an explicit contract? (xix, lxix)
57	How to work without the explicit label coaching? (lxix)
58	What if my coachee has 'feelings' for me? (lxxi)
59	What if I myself become attached to the coaching? (lxxvii)
60	How to coach if a result is demanded by a third party? (xix)
61	What if I also have other roles with respect to the coachee, such as colleague, adviser, or manager within the same organisation? (lxx – lxxvi, for example)
62	What if I want to 'tip off' the coachee's manager? (lxx, lxxvi)
63	What if the coachee's manager 'tips me off'? (xix, lxxii, lxxiii, lxxv)
64	What if my coachee starts talking about a common colleague? (lxxiv, lxxvi)
65	What to do with information that I have from elsewhere in the organisation? (lxxiii, lxxv, lxxvi)

> 66 What if I myself want to use information from the coaching elsewhere in the organisation? (lxxiv, lxxv, lxxvii)
> 67 What to do if the organisation has a negative impact on the coaching? (lxxviii, lxxix)

Doubts 55–60 show the importance of explicit coaching contracts and codes of conduct to which coaches not only adhere and refer, but of which they themselves are conscious during the coaching itself. With the aid of ethical rules (such as those described in the code of conduct in Appendix E), these doubts can be answered with relative ease. Other doubts concern examples of transference, such as strong feelings for the coach on the part of the coachee, and vice versa. These are times when, provided it is used properly, the coaching itself can achieve a lot. Doubts 61–67 have as much to do with ethics as with the boundaries of the coach's role, especially as they apply to internal coaches. It appears to be even more critical for internal coaches than for external coaches to agree explicitly that everything said in coaching sessions is completely confidential and will not go any further. The coach's answers to doubts 62–67 should therefore be quite clear in my view: respect the boundaries!

6.4.2 Synthesis
How can coaches learn from their own critical moments? How can they better handle these tensions and doubts, and perhaps even make use of the most critical moments in their practice? Here are some suggestions and ideas that follow on from the analysis above.

1. The critical moment says something about the coach, and about the coaching
The tension of coaches at any moment in the coaching process says something about the moments they experience as critical, i.e., the most sensitive aspects of their own activities as a coach. The key question in identifying one's own tensions and doubts is 'what comes from whom?', i.e. what part of these tensions comes from me and what originates from the coachee? Tensions arise partly due to a specific sensitivity and/or susceptibility on the part of the coach, partly due to what the coachee does in the conversations with the coach. A good coach tries to distinguish carefully between the transference brought

in by the coachee and the transference that they themself contribute to the coaching situation. This enables the coach to use his or her own counter-transference as an antenna alerting him or her to what the coachee triggers in the coach (see Heimann, 1950).

2. Critical moments are breakthrough moments

Coaches themselves often describe their critical moments in retrospect as breakthrough moments (consider, for example, moment xxxvi, or liv – lvi, in Appendix A). Critical moments are very often a blessing for the coaching process, because they are moments where deeper layers and ways of viewing and assessing things differently are found. Take, for example, the moment when an awkward silence descends because the coach is still pondering what to do, or the moment when the coachee suddenly comes out with something delicate that he or she didn't dare to mention before.

3. The more critical moments, the better the coaching

It would be lovely if coaches could seek out their own blessings. Although critical moments are potential breakthrough moments, this does not mean that all the coach needs to do is create as many critical moments as possible in order to generate an equal number of break-throughs. The only coaches who might well subscribe to this assertion are those who work provocatively (see, for example, Farrelly & Brandsma, 1974). They use their coaching conversations to 'deliver' critical moments to the coachee, although this may mean that the critical moments can become more those of the coach than those of the coachee. The coach may learn something from them, but in most cases the coachee learns very little. The more critical moments the better, therefore, but only if they come from the coachee.

Coaching is about getting coachees to share and (re)experience their own critical moments. For the coach, this means being available, asking questions, listening, exploring, and building up a relationship in which critical things can be expressed and critical transitions can be experienced. Most of all, it means not avoiding or repressing critical moments when they occur. Our coachees do enough of that them-selves. The art is to use those moments in the coaching process itself, by contemplating them and asking questions about them, together with the coachee.

To this end, coaches need a unique combination of readiness[8] and daring, warmth and an awareness of boundaries. The best short description of these two almost diametrically opposed characteristics that I have found is in the title of the book by O'Neill (2000): *Coaching with backbone and heart*. Strength, daring and containment (*backbone*) to examine the critical moment, and acceptance, readiness and warmth (*heart*) to welcome and support it. This leads us back to the vital 'common factors' that have been shown to account for over 70% of the outcome of therapy (see Chapter 3 or Wampold, 2001).

4. Coaches can only continue to learn thanks to their critical moments

We all have the tendency to want to eliminate our doubts and anxieties. This applies to our coachees but equally to ourselves as coaches. Before we know it, we are skirting around or ignoring our tensions, or pinning them down with a firm interpretation. And the more we coach, the more we ourselves build up long-term defences against our tensions and existential doubts without realising it. This is perhaps the main reason why inexperienced therapists often appear to perform better than experienced ones. They set to work with more enthusiasm, involvement and vulnerability (see Dumont, 1991).

I was not able to examine the differences between more and less experienced coaches in this study. However, it suggests that the relatively inexperienced coaches in our sample do already cover a full range of critical aspects of coaching. What are the actual benefits of experience in coaching? The following are possible differences between experienced and less experienced coaches.

1 It is evident that more experienced coaches become both calmer and more sensitive as a result of training and practice. However, they may also become more jaded and lose their edge at the same time.

---

[8] Also referred to as *containment* (Bion, 1963), and *negative capability* (Bion, 1970).

2 I can imagine that experienced coaches may sense critical moments sooner, and develop a 'suspicious' antenna that alerts them to such moments. However, critical moments are always most critical for those encountering them for the first time!

3 A process of self-selection probably takes place: the coaches who remain receptive and continue to ask questions about their coachees and themselves will stay in the profession while others will seek a change of career. However, it may also be the very people who are susceptible to flattery or suffer from a 'helper's syndrome' (Stroeken, 1988) who tend to stay in the profession.

All in all, therefore, the value of experience in the coaching profession is not unambiguous. Only by very careful experiential learning, ongoing supervision and undergoing coaching themselves can coaches translate experience into more professional action. What is more, in the 80 critical moments described here, a number of subtle forms of transference remain implicit or are lacking, forms that more experienced coaches would probably identify more explicitly, such as working hard for the coach, competition with the coach or 'using' the coach for non-learning purposes or 'flights into health' during the coaching where a coachee's problems suddenly and miraculously 'fix' themselves.

Due to the phenomenon of transference, everything a coachee does during coaching conversations is relevant to the coaching. Equally, everything the coach feels is relevant to the coachee. Critical moments for the coach are therefore of the utmost importance for their coachees. What is the situation, then, with the critical moments described in this book? Do they also tell us something about the coachees of these coaches? My experience of facilitating and participating in supervision groups of external coaches (see also Hawkins & Shohet, 1989) tells me that they do. Time after time, a critical moment as reported by the coach says something about the contribution made by that coach's client. As in the supervision of coaches, the purpose of the coaching for the coachee is often not to repress, deny or avoid that tension – or whatever defence the coachee wants to apply to it. The main question in the coaching of critical situations is 'how do I keep this tension in the room?', or, in other words, 'how do I keep my coachee in doubt?', or 'how can I extend the time to examine this doubt as a doubt, so that we can continue to learn from it?'

6.5 Conclusion

As other research confirms (see, for example, Miller, 1979, and Stroeken, 1988), good coaches are greatly impacted by the experiences of helping conversations gained early in life. In a sense, everyone experienced such conversations, so everyone is ready to coach other people. But only if those experiences have made them receptive, sensitive and slightly suspicious (but not paranoid) do they stand a chance of becoming excellent coaches.

My analysis of 80 real-life critical moments of coaches led to the following conclusions.
- Critical moments go hand-in-hand with doubts.
- Those doubts usually come down to 'what is going on?' and 'do I have an answer to it?', or: 'what do I see?' and 'how do I respond?'.
- Doubts and critical moments, provided they are handled properly, form a starting point for significant learning experiences ('breakthroughs') on the part of coachees.
- It helps when coaches have more critical moments, entertain more doubts and are more suspicious, although it is probably better if they do not generate the critical moments themselves.
- Preparing oneself for critical moments implies coaching with 'backbone and heart'.

In conclusion, the quality of coaches seems determined primarily by their ability to doubt, not to know what is coming next, and to greet what comes next with questions. Like Descartes in his famous *Meditations*, they experience a significant turning point when they shift their own attention away from the many doubts and uncertainties that assail them during the coaching and towards the activity of doubting itself, which can be regarded as the starting point and *raison d'être* of their own professional behaviour. Descartes' famous saying *cogito ergo sum* can therefore be rephrased for coaches as 'I doubt therefore I coach', and I encourage coaches to coach with that ongoing and deliberately maintained doubt as their only certainty.

Summary: I doubt therefore I coach

In the first phase of the study of critical moments in coaching, we asked 72 relatively inexperienced coaches to answer the following question:

'Describe briefly one **critical moment** (an exciting, tense or significant moment) with one of your coachees. Think about what was critical in the coaching journey, or a moment when you did not quite know what to do.'

Analysis of their 80 descriptions of critical moments yields the following results.
- Critical moments appear to be moments when something unusual happens or the coach is put to the test more than usual.
- Some coaches report that all moments in coaching are in fact critical moments.
- Critical moments of inexperienced coaches appear to be primarily associated with **doubts**.
- These doubts relate to the relationship, the direction and limits of coaching.

The 67 specific doubts identified were grouped as follows.
- Doubts about every coaching conversation, and every moment in coaching.
- Doubts about the coaching relationship and transference.
- Doubts about the direction of coaching conversations.
- Doubts about the boundaries of coaching conversations.

The 67 specific doubts identified also appear to hold the following lessons for coaches.
1   The critical moment says something about the coach, and about the coaching relationship.
2   Critical moments are potential **breakthough moments**.
3   The more critical moments, the better the coaching.
4   Coaches can only continue to **learn** thanks to their critical moments.
5   Preparing oneself for critical moments implies coaching with **backbone and heart,** or a thin and a thick skin at the same time.

Chapter 7
'I Struggle and Emerge': Critical Moments of Experienced Coaches

7.1 Introduction

Following the study of critical moments of relatively inexperienced coaches, a study which was carried out among 72 coaches, the majority of whom were in their first year of formal coaching activities (see the previous chapter), and which yielded interesting new perspectives on the doubts and dilemmas faced by coaches during their coaching conversations, it seemed a worthwhile exercise to embark upon a similar study among more experienced coaches.

The central research question appears to be suitable for repeating with more experienced coaches, and for an approach using e-mail, which would lower the barrier to participation as much as possible and make sending out a reminder less of a nuisance to the recipient. The question asked in the study reported in Chapter 6 was:

Describe briefly one *critical moment* (an exciting, tense or significant moment) with one of your coachees. Think about what was critical in the coaching journey, or a moment when you did not quite know what to do.

This question was posed to 110 experienced coaches from my own network (61 women, 49 men), that of the Ashridge Business School and that of my colleague Yvonne Burger. The criterion stipulated in the e-mail was that coaches should have at least eight years' coaching practice behind them after completing their formal training or accreditation. Many of them were not formally accredited, however, because such accreditation was not common practice a decade or more ago. The reminder e-mail was sent out three weeks later. Five respondents replied that they did not meet the criteria and 47 coaches responded (43%), communicating a total of 78 moments.

The coaches who responded are among the best and most experienced coaches I know. To be precise, the group of 47 experienced coaches consists predominantly of external coaches. More than 30 of these are independent coaches, the next largest cohort consists of seven coaches accredited and working at Ashridge, and two are internal coaches. 25 of the 47 coaches are based in the Netherlands, 18 in the United Kingdom, two in Germany, one in the United States, and one in South Africa. 28 women and 19 men responded; 26 replied in Dutch and 21 in English. Even though the e-mail left open the possibility of asking others ('If you know anyone else who might be interested . . .'), only one of the 47 respondents was not contacted by myself directly.

The aim of the study is to obtain a greater understanding of the processes that lead to change as a result of coaching. Change through coaching is usually investigated by means of outcome studies (for a summary of most of the outcome studies before 2007, see Chapter 5), which make it possible to determine the degree of effectiveness, and sometimes – in very balanced and well thought-out meta-studies; see Wampold, 2001 – the conditions under which greater effectiveness can be achieved. What is not possible with outcome studies, however, is to gain any understanding of the complex processes of coaching that often extend over several sessions and are influenced by countless factors both internal and external to the coaching itself. As a result it seems impossible, using these measurements of effectiveness, ever to gain an insight into the exact factors that lead to specific coaching results; in other words, into the (multiple) causality of coaching.

This is why I opted in this case for a method that, rather than collating large numbers of very general and discrete comments on coaching (usually consisting of ratings on a Likert scale), studies the personal side of coaching and focuses on critical moments in coaching: 'turning points' and 'dilemmas' as perceived by the coach himself. In so doing, I followed the exhortation of Rice and Greenberg, who wrote as long ago as 1984 in their book *Patterns of Change* that 'What is needed is a research method that can tap the rich clinical experience of skilled therapists in a way that will also push them to explicate what they know, yielding a rigorous description of the important regularities they have observed' (cited in Carlberg, 1997).

The type of study to which this article belongs is *narrative* and *qualitative* in nature (see Smith J.A., 2003), so what I am primarily looking for here is *meaning*, in an *inductive* manner. The researcher is not an objective observer in such research, but participates as a subjective 'colleague' in the material (in this case the critical moments), by imposing a sequence, identifying patterns, and inferring interpretations[1]. By asking respondents to describe a moment, we are in fact choosing the 'unit' of coaching to be studied: the moment, the event, the ultra-short time period. However, the descriptions given by the participants in the study clearly show that those moments are always linked to a whole conversation, to a coaching relationship, and sometimes to many years of personal coaching journey. The contributions differ in many respects, though: some cite the most critical moment of their career, dating back ten years or more, while others simply mention the 'critical moment that happened yesterday, and another one from today'.

All of the coaches gave consent for the anonymous use of their critical moment, and took steps themselves to ensure that their incidents were untraceable. I did not select further, so all of the moments contributed are reported here. The only (minor) changes I made were to edit every moment into a single paragraph, to remove spelling and stylistic errors and to translate the Dutch contributions into English as literally as possible. In some cases I also deleted some of the background information that was not directly relevant to the moment but related to the background of the coach or to my study, for example. I did not contribute a 'critical moment' myself because I did not wish to influence the study material.

The coaches who took part in the study also offered the researcher some unsolicited advice, such as:
- 'Are you sure you get the "tough cases" as well, this way?'
- 'Taking stock of the results of critical moments for the person being coached can also yield interesting information. As a coach, you are

---

[1] The very choice of moments as the study material stems from my personal experience of coaching: it is often moments that somehow leave an impression with me, that make a difference to me, and that I refer to many times subsequently.

keen to record the positive effect of a critical moment, but what is ultimately important is whether the person being coached experiences it.'

Before moving on to the overview and analysis of all 78 critical moments, I would like to start with some more of the valuable comments made by the participants in their e-mail responses.

- 'Even though I've been doing this work for years and notice I'm becoming more and more skilful at handling these moments . . . I still find it exciting.'
- 'I certainly do know moments like that, and I have to say I like them.'
- 'I realise of course that it's not about breakthroughs on the part of the coach, but nevertheless . . .'
- 'A critical moment can occur at any stage.'
- 'Apparently I find difficult situations hard to think about or remember! I've never had a situation where I broke out in a sweat or was completely stumped. No-one ever says anything aggressive, no-one ever walks out, there are never any awkward silences or a total energy drain.'
- 'My impression is that there must have been more critical moments, but I think they often occur in your first few years as a coach; as time goes by you find yourself at a loss for words less and less often.'
- 'I don't usually experience much excitement in the coaching although, as a teacher of other coaches, I admit to saying: if it's not exciting, there's nothing happening.'

7.2 Initial classification of the 78 moments

I initially placed the 78 real-life critical moments in a particular order, and arranged them under summarising headings (see Appendix B). The moments fall naturally under headings that describe aspects of the coaching process, but they could also have been classified differently, and many critical moments can be categorised under a number of different headings in principle. The headings have been chosen in such a way that more than one moment comes under each heading. I have already carried out an initial *interpretation*, therefore, by choosing both order and headings.

In the overview, the moments under headings 1, 5, 8, 15, 16 and 17 were in Dutch only and those under heading 12 in English only. The moments are therefore reasonably well mixed and different national cultures contribute to most of the headings. Interestingly, the Dutch have much more to say about counter-transference (headings 15, 16 and 17). This might be due to the more direct and candid nature of Dutch culture. After all, counter-transference is something very personal and intimate, which perhaps not everyone writes about easily. I should add that it was a Dutch person (myself) who chose the headings.

There are in fact only three main themes in the list of headings:
1 managing key conditions (headings 1–3);
2 deepening the coaching conversation and the coaching relationship (headings 4–11); and
3 handling what happens in the coaching conversation and the coaching relationship (headings 12–18).

The following is a list of all of the headings and the number of moments under each heading.
1 Managing key conditions: context of the coaching conversation (three moments)
2 Managing key conditions: triangular contracts (seven moments)
3 Managing key conditions: 'reading' the coachee (four moments)
4 Deepening by exploring (three moments)
5 Deepening by continuing to ask questions (two moments)
6 Deepening by summarising and mirroring (six moments)
7 Deepening by giving feedback (four moments)
8 Deepening by contributing something oneself (two moments)
9 Deepening by means of transposition (homework, role-play, psychodrama, etc.) (eight moments)
10 Deepening by bringing up the transference here and now (four moments)
11 Deepening by bringing up the coaching relationship (five moments)
12 Handling surprises as a result of exploring (three moments)
13 Handling surprising transference phenomena (five moments)
14 Handling counter-transference phenomena: 'can I actually help the coachee?' (two moments)
15 Handling counter-transference phenomena: 'I feel responsible for the coaching' (five moments)

16 Handling counter-transference phenomena: 'I want to drop out myself' (three moments)
17 Handling counter-transference phenomena: the coach's own emotions (eight moments)
18 Handling questions and suggestions from the coachee (four moments).

7.3 Summary in the form of a 'doubtful' story

As the next step in listening to these coaches and interpreting their critical moments, I have summarised the main themes of all 78 critical moments as follows.

Experienced coaches appear to have distinctly fewer doubts than coaches who are just starting out (see the previous chapter). They approach their field of work, the coaching conversation and the coaching relationship, with more confidence than the relatively new coach, usually with an attitude of 'I struggle and emerge'. They are aware that they will have to monitor a lot of things closely if they are to achieve a genuine coaching conversation, and that they will have to keep connecting and deepening during every coaching conversation in order to safeguard the coaching from moment to moment. They also realise that there will be surprises, unsought discoveries[2], unintended learning effects and unforeseen setbacks. They know that they may meet strong emotions, in both their coachee and themselves, and that it is worth their while – however difficult that may be – to grasp hold of those surprises and emotions and to exploit the opportunity presented by the surprises to deepen the contact.

More generally, these coaches experience coaching as something that cannot be taken for granted, that has to be earned and protected, and that, due to a wide range of factors beyond the coach's control, may sometimes have to be abandoned or on other occasions may bear exceptional fruits. Coaching is therefore a constant struggle, but one that can be faced with confidence, because, in one way or another, it does usually end in some positive benefits for the coachee, and hence also for the coach. The struggle begins right at the start of the coaching relationship, and the accompanying psychological contract, when all

---

[2] Unsought discoveries that are reminiscent of the old Sri Lankan story of the three Princes of Serendip (Merton & Barber, 2003).

of the potential environmental factors, uncertainties and emotions already play a role. It continues later, during the coaching conversations, when the coach feels he owes it to his profession to embark upon a 'risky' intervention, for example when:

- directing or otherwise influencing the process and the method of working;
- making explicit and reacting to what is happening here and now;
- extending the conversation to other, similar experiences of the coachee;
- making connections with the same behaviours displayed elsewhere by the coachee (transference); and
- identifying or making use of counter-transference.

7.4 How to handle these critical moments?

7.4.1 Analysis

The following contains a transcript of all 78 critical moments in just under ninety concisely worded anxieties. The original critical moments can often be reduced to one or more anxieties[3]. I am taking the interpretation a step further, by proposing distilled essences that I see recurring in various critical moments. As in real coaching conversations, I reformulate the critical moments contributed above and give them summarising headings. To each of the resulting groups of similar anxieties, I also give a brief response. Unlike the critical moments of less experienced coaches, not all of the anxieties and anxiety signals that coaches experience here can be reworded in the form of doubts or dilemmas: they are often *facts*, facts of which the coach is absolutely certain but which pose an obstacle or cause positive anxieties.

In this list I have, as far as possible, resisted the temptation to discuss all anxieties in terms of the coachee (with attributions as defences, projections, resistance, difficult behaviour, progress, relapse, etc.). It would have been easy to give in to that temptation. Equally, it would be entirely feasible to view the anxieties from the coach's perspective only. However, since they always arise in a *relationship* between coach and coachee, with other people and organisations more in the background, I consider the best description to be that where the relationship remains as central as possible.

---

[3] For the verbatim text of all of the critical moments (with Roman numerals), see Appendix B.

1. Anxiety about the boundaries of coaching (contracting, triangulation, etc.)

1	Key conditions are not right for coaching (ii)
2	Conversation unhealthy for both parties (lv)
3	Trust comes under pressure (l, lxxii, lxxviii)
4	The coach's options are limited by confidentiality agreements (viii, ix, x, lxxvii)
5	Pre-conditions (iii)
6	What will fellow coaches think about me and my methods? (vi, xxxvi)
7	Awkwardness because coachees meet in the waiting room (i)
8	Different expectations or needs within the triangular contract (v, vi, vii, viii, ix, x, xli)

It is clear that, for experienced coaches, coaching – and hence critical moments – begins before the conversations themselves, even before the first meeting. Many anxieties were highlighted on the fringes of coaching: before the start, between sessions, vis-à-vis other interested parties, and after the coaching under the scrutiny of fellow coaches or supervisors. Coaches learn how important it is to manage such key conditions and boundaries properly, and have them under control first, before embarking on the coaching per se. Many anxieties about the boundaries of coaching occur at the start, when those boundaries are being laid down jointly, during both formal and informal contracting. However, it is noticable that these boundaries also cause anxiety later on, at the start and end of every meeting for example, and in relation to other parties not actually present during the coaching conversations.

2. Anxiety due to satisfaction

9	Relief, enthusiasm, or relaxation as the result of cooperation (xii, xvi, xix, xxi, xxix, liii, lvi, lviii, lxvii, lxxviii)
10	Breakthroughs and turning points (xv, xvii, xviii, xxii, xxxiii, xxxiv, xxxv, xxxix, xlii, li)
11	Confident expectation that things will turn out well (xiv, xlix)
12	Considerable vulnerability achieved in the conversation (xix, lv)
13	Different elements come together and are expressed in the way the coachee handles the session itself (li)
14	Pleasantly surprised: the coachee corrects me (xii)
15	Pleasantly surprised: the coachee wants to continue (lvi)

Many reported anxieties are connected with satisfaction and success, with a welcome initiative from the coachee, a breakthrough, or a deeper level of collaboration. These are very positive anxieties in a sense, therefore, even though they are also anxieties in a more worrying sense for many experienced coaches, because they are aware of the pitfalls of success: loss of concentration, being seduced, being 'taken in' by the coachee's positive feedback, loss of sense of reality in attributing the coachee's successes to oneself, later undoings or reversals – to name but a few. Some coaches are therefore cautious in claiming a successful change (see, for example, moment xlii in Appendix B), although others ascribe a lot to themselves (see, for example, xxix or xxxiii in Appendix B).

The phrase 'turning point' was mentioned three times in the critical moments, and there were also three occurrences of 'breakthrough' or 'shift'. Critical moments are often associated with periods of radical change in the coaching. Coachees appear to come back often to such moments, which run like a sort of thread through the coaching process (see, for example, xxxiii or xxxix).

3. Anxiety about the coach's own role

16 Anxiety related to the coach's own uncertainty about what to do (ix, xi, xxxviii, xliii, xlvii, lii, lxxvii)

17 In conjunction with the coachee, not knowing what to do . . . (viii, xxxiii, lii)

18 Uncertainty about what will enter the coachee's consciousness (xxxii)

19 Uncertainty about what I am getting into (xix)

20 Uncertainty: am I being inviting enough? (lxxv)

21 Uncertainty: what now? Is it going quickly enough? Is it exciting enough? (xliii, lix, lxi)

22 Uncertainty: what will best serve the coachee? (vii, xlix, lxxiv)

23 Uncertainty: can I keep up with the coachee and understand what his/her issue is about? (lvii, lxi)

24 Uncertainty: can I help the other person, am I failing him/her, am I doing enough? (xviii, xxiii, xliii, liii, lviii)

25 Uncertainty: does the coachee need me? (xlix, lviii)

26 Uncertainty: is this in fact (professional) coaching, am I the right coach? (vi, x, xxv, xlvii, liv)

27 Anxiety about my own motives in coaching (lx)

28 Worry about failing to fill the allotted time with coaching (liii)
29 Anxiety about the coach's view of his/her role: knowing better than
    or 'rescuing' the coachee (lii, lx)
30 Sense of responsibility in being taken into someone's confidence,
    especially when significant consequences are anticipated (lxii,
    lxvii)
31 Sense of responsibility in a tragedy (lii, lxxiv)

Even experienced coaches are sometimes very uncertain. They may be uncertain about what is happening in this conversation (anxieties 16–21), what this coachee needs (anxieties 22–25), or what is and is not part of their own role and contribution as a coach (anxieties 26–29). It is touching to note that even experienced colleagues have doubts, ranging from doubts about what they should do or whether they are doing it well, to major doubts about themselves. Perhaps this uncertainty typifies the experienced coach who has managed to avoid becoming jaded despite repeating situations and events. Research has shown that there is a risk of coaches, or at least psychotherapists, becoming less effective as they gain in experience (Dumont, 1991).

A feeling of being responsible can increase the uncertainty even further – for example, when coachees take you into their confidence, or share their 'improper conduct' with you, or when affected by a major and traumatic event, or take important, irreversible decisions as a result of the coaching (anxieties 30 and 31).

4. Anxiety about the coach's own intuition

32 At the outset: difficult to assess a new coachee (xi, xii)
33 At the outset: can I make a connection? Have we established trust?
    (iv)
34 Can I trust my feeling, inspiration or intuition? (xiii, xx, xxvi, xxxiii,
    xl, xlix)
35 There is more going on here, and do I dare to take a guess at it? (xix,
    xlvi)
36 Searching for something new that will shed new light (xvi)
37 Can I have confidence that 'internal' changes are sometimes the most
    important result of coaching? (xxi, lviii)

The coach's own intuition is mentioned so frequently by the participants in this study that it merits separate examination. What we are

talking about here are hunches or thoughts (compare Freud's *freie Einfälle* or free associations) relating to the material contributed by the coachee, but also to suggestions or methods that may help the coachee, i.e. interventions which may benefit the coachee. In fact, all of the critical moments demonstrate that coaches work very intuitively, because they rarely if ever give a rationale for the great diversity of ways in which they coach; and if they refer to a foundation in specific types of approach (such as solution-focused coaching in xxxix and xlviii and person-centred counselling in lvi), this appears to be more a reference to the coach's toolkit than to an approach specifically tailored to this coachee or this conversation. In short, coaching will remain a largely intuitive area of work until it can be demonstrated conclusively what works in what circumstances.

5. Anxiety about what coaches contribute, or do not contribute, themselves

38	Gathering courage to help the coachee to gather courage (xxxii, xl)
39	Can I refrain from judging despite having opinions? (xx)
40	Anxiety about really facilitating decision-making and not taking part in it (lxiii)
41	Having the nerve to explore further, by listening or by asking a personal question (xviii, xx, xxi, xl, lxxi)
42	Am I being too controlling, am I not disempowering the coachee? (xii, xiii, xxxviii, lxviii)
43	Is this a step too far? (xxxii)
44	Does it help if I start to talk about myself? (lxxiv, xxx)
45	The anxiety of stagnation, impasse, emptiness, silence, breathless anticipation (vii, xiv, xxxii, xxxiv, xxxviii, xlix, lii)
46	Anxiety (including uncertainty, anticipation) about making a suggestion (ii, xxxii, xxxiii, xxxiv, xxxv, xxxvi, xxxviii, xxxix)
47	Anxiety about saying what I think and feel about the coachee (or their story) (xxiv, xxvi, xxix, liv)
48	Anxiety about reflecting back what the coachee has said (xx, xxii)
49	Anxiety about challenging the coachee by stating their merits (xxii)
50	Anxiety about bringing up patterns displayed by the coachee, here and now with me (xxiii, xxv, xli, xlii, xliii)
51	Anxiety about asking about a parallel between this conversation and other situations the coachee has experienced (xxv, xliii)
52	Anxiety about laying down the coach's own conditions in a nonnegotiable way (iii)

> 53 Anxiety about placing my coachee and the coaching relationship itself under pressure (iii, xxviii, xl, xlv)
> 54 Anxiety about referring (or taking the decision to refer) a coachee (iii, xxv, xlvi, xlvii, xlviii, liv, lxxiv)

Many specific coaching interventions are described as causing anxiety. In the same order as the anxieties identified above, these are: withholding opinions or control, exploring, talking about yourself, doing nothing (tolerating the silence), making a suggestion or proposing a way of working, practising directness and openness (including supportive feedback, patterns here and now with the coach, parallels with other situations experienced by the coachee), laying down key conditions, placing the coachee and the coaching relationship under pressure, and referring – more or less the entire spectrum of coaching skills.

6. Anxiety due to specific behaviour of the coachee

> 55 What to do if the coachee has already achieved everything? (lviii)
> 56 Difficult to establish and maintain contact (iii, xxvi, xxviii, xlviii)
> 57 Flogging a dead horse (vii, xli)
> 58 Torrent of words and rationalisations from the coachee (xxv, xxxiv, xxxix, xl, xli, xlviii)
> 59 Standing by speechless while the coachee drops a bombshell in team coaching (xliv, lxxvi)
> 60 The feeling of being manipulated (lxxvii)
> 61 Team coaching: coachees don't want to take the path that I think is the right one (lxxvi)
> 62 It is suddenly about me, the tables are turned (lxx, lxxi)
> 63 Unsettled by sexual advances from the coachee (lxx)
> 64 Feeling guilty because the coachee criticises me or makes a special effort for the meeting (xliii, lv)
> 65 My advice is not taken up (xxxi)
> 66 The coachee asks for something I am unable to offer (lxxvii, lxxviii)
> 67 Anxiety due to a coachee who starts to control proceedings (xii, xxxvii)
> 68 Intense emotions and surprises (xxi, xlix, lii)
> 69 Intense emotion, distress or a cry for help and comfort (xlix, liv, lvi)
> 70 The coachee is angry or critical (xviii, xl, xliii, l, lv, lxxi)
> 71 Being corrected by the coachee (xii)

Here we are entering the territory of transference: all behaviour displayed by the coachee during the coaching for which it is worthwhile at least investigating the hypothesis that it comes from elsewhere or also occurs elsewhere, i.e. outside this situation with this coach. The participants in this study report a wide variety of transference phenomena, ranging from the entirely innocent (such as 65) to the hugely unsettling (for example, 63). I myself would in any case typify anxieties 55–64 as resistance, i.e. as largely unconscious defences against the coaching itself, but I realise that this holds the coachee entirely responsible for that behaviour, even though it occurred in the relationship with the coach, and that I am being overly quick to voice an opinion about what is going on in the coachee.

7. Anxiety stemming mainly from the coach

72	My ability to put things into perspective appears to be deficient (lxix)
73	My opinion, my ethics are an obstacle (lxxii)
74	I am enticed by my own suggestion (xxxi)
75	Doubts about the qualities of my coachee (xxvii, lxxvii)
76	Mistrust of the coachee (l)
77	Mistrust of the coachee's manager (v)
78	I am enticed by the pressure on the coachee (xvii)
79	My own anxiety is an obstacle (xxxvii)
80	My own emotions are influencing the coaching situation, e.g. because they chime with what the coachee is saying (lxxiii, lxxiv)
81	My own subconscious is sending out the wrong signal (lxxiv)
82	I need positive feedback (lxi)
83	The situation is not exciting enough for me (lix)
84	I observe too little response or signs of a learning effect (lxi)
85	My discomfort is an obstacle (lix)
86	My distractedness is an obstacle (lxiv, lxv)
87	My inability to comply with the contract is an obstacle (lxvi)
88	My possible competition with my coachee is an obstacle (lvii)

Virtually all anxieties rooted in counter-transference are unique and individual, specific to this coach and to this situation. They are not easily generalised, even though the phenomenon whereby the coach's own agenda or emotions play a role in the coaching is a relatively universal one. It is fascinating to note that, precisely when factors inherent to the coach are truly an obstacle, when there is a good chance that relevant information will emerge in the counter-transference (see Heimann, 1950), we often lose the ability to practise the necessary openness about our own observations. This is reminiscent of Bion's prescription to work 'without memories or desires' (Bion, 1970). Reading through the critical moments, many of them show how difficult that is in practice.

In the light of Bion's pronouncement one might say that the coach's own memories (own opinions and doubts, and own emotions resulting from what has happened to the coach) play a role in some way in anxieties 72–81, and his own desires play a role in anxieties 82–88. In fact, as one coach writes, each of these cases concerns the failure of the coach's own ability to put things into perspective, the loss of the 'evenly hovering attention' (Freud, 1912) which is so essential to effective coaching.

7.4.2 Synthesis

What insight can we derive from this study of critical moments? What are the mechanisms that lead to such moments, and what are their consequences? What can these moments teach us about the processes of change through coaching? And how can coaches better handle tensions of this kind and so make better use of critical moments in their practice? We have certainly not heard the last word on this but, in the meanwhile, we *can* present a number of suggestions and ideas on the basis of the above analysis. Each of the four sections below opens with a quote from one of the experienced coaches in this study. Since these are recurring challenges that experienced coaches cannot avoid but need to handle as well as possible, time after time, I refer to them here as 'struggles'.

1. The struggle to stay 'fresh and receptive'

'I also have a belief that things will work through to a positive conclusion which helps me if I'm feeling a bit stuck or unsure.' (xlix)

Developing and using their own intuition is certainly an important theme for experienced coaches. Can we perceive, feel, sense something we are not yet aware of, perhaps even something that the coachee is not yet aware of, something that summarises the coachee's issues at a deeper level?

The participants in this study often associate intuition with confidence, the confidence that allows them to bide their time until something presents itself or until something sheds new light on the issue. They describe how they can increase their confidence by being quiet, creating a safe situation and approaching the coachee with an open mind. They contrast that situation, full of confidence, where intuition can thrive, with moments of stagnation and uncertainty. There is a clear association between confidence and flexibility, having options and trust, and between lack of confidence and rigidity, stagnation and uncertainty.

I believe that, for experienced coaches, confidence will entail staying fresh and receptive, with the same keen anticipation and unbiased outlook they had when they started their coaching career. It means not following fixed patterns and certainly not holding preconceptions 'acquired' in earlier coaching assignments. This applies to their attitude to every coachee and every conversation, but equally to every moment of coaching. Conversely, if they can remain attentive, fresh and receptive, confidence will automatically follow.

2. The struggle to retain and increase the coach's ability to put things into perspective
'Surpassing my own frame of thinking and ability to put things into perspective.' (lxix)

Tensions can permeate the coaching conversations by many different routes: they may stem from the material contributed by the coachee, the coachee's presentation, the moment itself, or from 'memories and desires' of the coach. All of these tensions form both a basis or opening for new insight, and an obstacle to or diversion from the gaining of that insight. Tensions can point to the right emotion and the elusive insight, but they may also inhibit intuition and the ability to think clearly. One problem with this study is that it only provides evidence of the tensions of which coaches were aware, not of those that went unrecorded by the coach. It is likely that many more tensions arise during coaching, tensions that coaches are simply not aware of – or are only partly aware of, due to vague irritations, fatigue, and distractions. The earlier study (see Chapter 6) also showed how important it is to be sensitive to these half-perceived tensions, in order then to use them in a way that will benefit the coaching.

In my view, *external* tensions (stemming from the coachee's material and presentation) obstruct the coach only if they give rise to *internal* tensions, i.e. if they influence the coach's ability to put things into perspective, his detachment and his patience. It is therefore vitally important for the coach to learn how to handle his own internal tensions – to allow those internal tensions to exist, to note their presence but at the same time to reserve some attention for perceptions, hunches, making connections and other coaching interventions. This enables us to broaden our frame of thinking and our ability to put things into perspective, which is vital because coachees are more different from ourselves as coaches than we think. Our powers of logic have a strong tendency to lead us to regard everyone as similar, and to assume that others are similar to ourselves, that they feel and react just as we do. However, we are often wrong about that, not to mention the (many) situations in which we coach someone from a different culture or a completely different background and profession than ourselves, where the differences in outlook are even more prominent.

3. The struggle to contribute 'containment' to the relationship
'You set the tone, you lay down your key conditions in a non-negotiable way: you can get off to a flying start or you can pack up and clear off.' (iii)

Many participants in this study write about managing the relationship that they offer their coachees, about managing the boundaries of the relationship through contracting and the continuing 'psychological contract': the unanimity and trust that coach and coachee share, in other words the 'alliance' that coach and coachee attempt to forge with each other. They write about the tensions that arise when this working alliance is tested, such as when the basic conditions are disputed, their mutual trust comes under stress, or the coaching begins to resemble a game of chess with arguments and rationalisations.

I believe that the term 'containment' is a good summary of what is needed for a trusting working alliance. Bion (1963) employed this term to signify remaining calm, receptive and authentic even in a situation of terse, even existential tensions and doubts, which is in keeping with what participants in this study seem to be striving to achieve. Participants describe:

- on the one hand, the need to invite, to remain sympathetic and to give unconditional support, even in the case of problematic issues and strong emotions; and
- on the other hand, the need to define a stable context, to have firm boundaries and to persevere with their openness, even if the coachee would prefer not to hear certain things.

This is precisely the dual meaning of 'containment': setting boundaries on the one hand but, on the other hand, within those boundaries, creating space for development and change.

4. The struggle to contribute the coach's own observations
'Touching a chord that makes the coachee open up rather than clam up.' (xxvi)

The need for fresh observations and intuitions has already been mentioned, but perceiving and identifying does not seem to be the hardest part: actually *saying*, i.e. expressing observations appears to be much more difficult for experienced coaches. Indeed, it is often the simplest and most striking things, such as the predominant emotion in a story, a lack of eye contact or a downturn to the mouth, or the quality of the rapport between coach and coachee, that are the riskiest things to mention. Clearly, the coaches who write about this find that as many as possible of their own observations need to be communicated, but in such a way that the coachee can listen to and consider them. As many of the critical moments illustrate, with some coachees this is a tall order.

I believe this is where the boundary lies between real coaching and an 'ordinary' good conversation: it is so much easier not to mention some things we have observed, and instead just to keep to friendly and welcoming words. A professional coach does not shy away from actually creating critical moments in the coaching process, and tries to bring tensions to light as far as possible if they remain implicit. Moreover, I believe that this is an outstanding example of an area where experience helps, because once we have successfully attempted to communicate observations to coachees, we strengthen our nerve to keep doing it in future.

7.5 Conclusion

My analysis of 78 critical moments of experienced coaches appears to indicate that positive changes occur through coaching mainly when:

- The coaches have sufficient confidence to allow intuition to do its work.
- The coaches' intuition can come up with fresh observations.
- The coaches develop their ability to put things into perspective.
- The coaches (have the courage to) reflect their observations back in such a way that the coachee can hear them.
- The coaches can develop a relationship with the coachee that is well-defined yet allows both parties space.
- Which results in more confidence to allow intuition to do its work (*da capo*).

If this is successful, the coach generates a self-fulfilling, iterative process of increasingly sensitive and in-depth coaching.

Most of us – whether we are coaches or not – have a personal relationship with 'moments of change' or 'turning points': moments when our lives and/or careers changed course and we learned how to function on a new level. Carlberg (1997) defines 'turning point moments' as those moments when the therapist notes something qualitatively new in relation to the client's behaviour or to the relationship between therapist and client. Carlberg reports how he has identified two common threads in all of the turning points that he has studied:

1 Experienced therapists appear to relate turning points to unpredictable and unusual incidents in an otherwise fairly predictable therapeutic relationship. After these incidents they need to step outside the system to review the situation.
2 Experienced therapists always experience a deeper 'emotional meeting' at these moments, an 'intersubjective phenomenon between two subjects, each influencing the other, which prepares the way for change to take place'.

Carlberg here follows Daniel Stern's 'process of change study group' (see for example Stern, Sander, Nahum, Harrison, Lyons-Ruth, Morgan, Bruschwiler-Stern & Tronick, 1998; Stern, 2004) which calls such moments 'now-moments', 'weird moments' and 'moments of meeting'. Although I am not able to investigate Carlberg's suggestion directly here, it *is* possible to go back to the critical moments and compare. Among the 78 critical moments in Appendix B I can identify 26 major and minor breakthroughs, 20 of which (77%) display explicit evidence of both unpredictability and a deeper emotional meeting, either positive or negative. This appears to support Carlberg's conclusions, especially because 'unpredictability' and 'deeper emotional meetings' always go hand in hand.

However, the other six breakthroughs (vi, xx, xl, xliii, xlv and lxi) contain neither demonstrable unpredictability nor a demonstrably deeper emotional meeting. In addition, I actually found one example of a critical moment that did not contain a breakthough but did contain both unpredictability and a deeper emotional meeting (lxxviii).

Let us compare the two groups studied once again: 72 coaches early in their career (Chapter 6) and 47 coaches with more than eight years' experience (this chapter). Differences that emerge straight away from a reading of all 158 collected 'critical moments' are the following.
- Less experienced coaches appear to have more doubts during coaching, some of them about their own suitability for the role of coach.
- More experienced coaches still struggle with their critical moments, but do so with more self-confidence, sometimes giving the impression that some major drama is required before the experienced coach in question perceives a true critical moment.
- More experienced coaches appear to have a different sort of self-awareness that seems more linked to a desire to show that they are doing things right. While the critical moments of the less experienced coaches were more often 'egodocuments', some of those of experienced coaches appear to be more a case of 'demonstrating accountability'. This may of course be partly due to the context of the study, which was different for each group.
- At the end of Chapter 6 I predicted that experienced coaches would write more about:
  - a sense of being seduced by the coachee working hard for the coach;
  - competition with the coach; or
  - 'using' the coach for non-learning purposes or 'flights into health' during the coaching.

- This material does indeed show that experienced coaches more often mention such forms of more subtle (counter-) transference.

Two of the moments reported here by experienced coaches come explicitly from the start of their coaching careers (xii, lxii) and a third participant writes that, in his view, critical moments occur primarily in a coach's first few years.

There remains much to discover about change through coaching in the moment itself, though this list of critical moments gives an indication of the type of moments that coaches experience as critical. It would seem that the quality of coaches is determined primarily by their ability to tolerate tension and to tackle the ongoing struggle with new tensions and uncertainties. Like the Zeeland resistance fighters in their battle against the elements and the Spaniards, the coach experiences a significant turning point moment when he shifts his own attention from the many struggles that occupy him during the coaching, to the struggle itself, which can be viewed as the starting point and *raison d'être* of his own professional activity. On behalf of coaches, therefore, I adopt the well-known motto of the province of Zeeland, 'I struggle and emerge' (*luctor et emergo*[4]), and encourage coaches to coach with devoted attention to that ongoing and deliberately maintained struggle.

Summary: I struggle and emerge

In the second phase of the study of critical moments in coaching, we asked 47 coaches with at least 8 years' experience to answer the following question:

'Describe briefly one **critical moment** (an exciting, tense or significant moment) with one of your coachees. Think about what was critical in the coaching journey, or a moment when you did not quite know what to do.'

---

[4] In the middle of the 80-year war between Holland and Spain, Elizabeth I of England supported the Zeeland fighters (Treaty of Nonesuch, 1585), after which they wrote on their banners *Autore Deo, favente regina, luctor et emergo*. The motto has remained on the Zeeland coat-of-arms ever since.

Analysis of their 78 descriptions of critical moments yielded 88 specific **anxieties**, grouped as follows.

- Anxiety about the boundaries of coaching.
- Anxiety due to satisfaction.
- Anxiety about the coach's own role.
- Anxiety about the coach's own intuition.
- Anxiety about what coaches contribute, or do not contribute, themselves.
- Anxiety due to specific behaviour of the coachee.
- Anxiety stemming mainly from the coach.

The 88 specific anxieties identified appear to indicate that positive changes occur as a result of coaching mainly when:

1 There is sufficient **confidence** to allow intuition to do its work.
2 The intuition of the coaches can lead to **unbiased** observations.
3 Coaches also develop the maximum possible **ability to put things into perspective**.
4 Coaches (have the nerve to) put forward their observations in such a way that the coachee can hear them.
5 Coaches can develop a **well-defined** relationship with the coachee, yet one that offers **space**.
6 Which results in more confidence to allow intuition to do its work (*da capo*).

Differences emerging from a comparison of the critical moments of inexperienced and experienced coaches:

- Less experienced coaches appear to have more doubts during coaching, including doubts about their own suitability for the role of coach.
- More experienced coaches still struggle with their critical moments, but do so with more self-confidence.
- Most experienced coaches appear to have a different sort of self-awareness that is more linked to the desire to show that they are doing a good job.
- Experienced coaches are more likely to highlight more subtle forms of (counter-)transference.

Chapter 8
Coaches Have Their Say: How to Handle Critical Moments?[1]

with Andrew Day, Eddie Blass, Charlotte Sills & Colin Bertie

8.1 Introduction

The analysis of real-life critical moments that coaches encounter in their practice, as reported in the previous chapters, made us curious about the generative processes and dynamics around these moments. The next phase of this research consisted of a more in-depth analysis of the emergence of the moments and the processes that ensue as a consequence. In particular, we were interested in the *handling* of these moments, and how coaches make use of external support such as supervision in their handling of critical moments.

Having had the coaches identify and relate critical moments in their coaching relationships in the previous chapters, this study goes on to explore similar critical moments through in-depth interviews and to look at the role that supervision and other ongoing professional development activities may play in supporting experienced coaches through critical incidents.

We hypothesised that the process of supervision might be important in helping coaches to reflect on and make sense of critical moments within the coaching process and in exploring how to respond to them. For this reason, we asked explicitly whether critical moments were taken to supervision and what came out of their handling through supervisory activities. We are not aware of any existing literature that has explored how coaching supervision supports coaches in working with critical moments.

---

[1] For an extended version of this chapter, with a more detailed overview of the data and more analysis, see Day, De Haan, Blass, Sills & Bertie (2007).

Much of the counselling and therapy literature suggests that ongoing professional development for the practitioner is essential to protect both client and counsellor. However, there does not appear to be any hard evidence that this is indeed the case (see McLennan, 1999) and there is even some research highlighting counterproductive examples of supervision (see for example Gray, Ladany, Walker & Ancis, 2001; or Lawton, 2000). A similar pattern is emerging in the literature with regard to coaches (see for example Stevens, 2004): supervision is rapidly gaining in popularity, while at the same time there is no real evidence that it is beneficial.

The purpose of this research is, therefore, twofold:
1   to investigate the *dynamics* and impact of critical moments within the coaching relationship; and
2   to explore how experienced coaches use supervision and other continuous professional development activities to help them to work with critical moments.

We will look at the coaching relationship from the perspective of a 'working alliance', a term coined by Greenson (1965), which is usually understood as:
1   the coachee's experience of the coach being supportive and empathic; and
2   a sense of working together towards the goals of the coaching (compare various definitions of the working alliance in Luborsky, 1976).

8.2 Description of the study

Telephone interviews of 1–2 hours were carried out with 28 very experienced coaches (mean coaching experience was 11.3 years), exploring between 1 and 3 critical moments that they had experienced in their coaching work during the previous 12 months. A total of 51 critical moments were produced. Only 5 of these moments overlap with those in Chapter 7, stemming from some of the 7 experienced coaches who were also in that earlier sample. Permission was obtained from all coaches who participated in this research for their responses to be used in the study and published with identifying details changed or removed. All the coaches interviewed had had some form of psychological, organisational development, counselling or psychotherapy training, and ranged in their employment from being predominantly internal coaches employed by organisations to external coaches employed on a consulting basis. The gender split was equal male to female. 25 of the 28 had regular supervision, 19 with a paid supervisor and 6 in peer consultation groups. Only 3 did not have any form of supervision; however, those 3 were planning to go to supervision or had some form of peer support. For a comprehensive overview of the various moments that were recorded, see Day, De Haan, Blass, Sills & Bertie (2007).

The primary methodology adopted for this study was again that of the critical incident technique (Flanagan, 1954). The starting question about the critical moment was the same as in the earlier research (see Chapters 6 and 7):

Describe briefly one critical moment (an exciting, tense or significant moment) with one of your coachees. Think about what was critical in the coaching journey, or a moment when you did not quite know what to do.

This time the interviewer asked the participant four follow-up questions relating to each critical moment, concerning the context, what happened, what they did at the time, and their perspective on the outcome. They were then asked whether they took the moment to supervision, and if not, why not; if so, what happened at supervision, what were the results and what was learned.

8.2.1 Comparison with previous study of critical moments of experienced coaches

Our first analysis comprised a detailed comparison with the analysis in Chapter 7 of 78 critical moments of equally experienced coaches. We were satisfied that the 51 new moments in this research largely replicated the same anxieties, and covered all seven groupings of anxieties distinguished in Chapter 7. Here is a detailed comparison, reporting most of the new anxieties found in the present study:

1. Anxiety about the boundaries of coaching (contracting, triangulation, etc.)

10 of the 51 moments reproduced specific anxieties in this category. The anxiety that was replicated most was (3): 'trust comes under pressure' (twice). Here are some new anxieties in this category.

- A request to share notes. (twice)
- What information to share with whom in a triangular contract? (twice)
- Triangular contracts: new boss 'sees no need for coaching'.
- Re-contracting, from coaching to psychotherapy, and then regrets from coachee.
- Anxiety around taking a personal history of the coachee.
- A coachee's anxiety about limits of coaching.

2. Anxiety around satisfying outcomes

8 of the 51 moments reproduced specific anxieties in this category. The anxiety that was replicated most was (9): 'relief, enthusiasm, or relaxation as the result of cooperation' (three times). Some new anxieties in this category were:

- Coach pleasantly surprised about the great progress coachee has undertaken.
- Strengths of coachee become more apparent.
- A rise in self-worth and self-belief.

3. Anxiety about the coach's own role

4 of the 51 moments reproduced specific anxieties in this category. A new anxiety in this category was:

- Is the coachee really making the choice himself, or am I pushing the choice?

4. Anxiety about the coach's own intuition

4 of the 51 moments reproduced specific anxieties in this category.

5. Anxiety about what coaches contribute, or do not contribute, themselves

21 of the 51 moments reproduced specific anxieties in this category. Interestingly, two anxieties were found 7 times in the new data set,

(47): 'Anxiety about saying what I think and feel about the coachee (or his story)' and (50): 'Anxiety about bringing up patterns displayed by the coachee, here and now with me'. Some new anxieties in this category were:
- Being very directive – e.g. when my coachee is at a very low point, when teaching emotional distance and resilience, when a push is 'what she really needed'. (three times)
- Reflecting back what the coachee does, here with me.

6. Anxiety due to specific behaviour of the coachee
19 of the 51 moments reproduced specific anxieties in this category. Interestingly, one anxiety was replicated 5 times in the new data set, (70): 'The coachee is angry or critical', and another anxiety (66): 'The coachee asks for something I am unable to offer' occurred 3 times. Some new anxieties in this category were:
- The coachee is physically threatening. (twice)
- The coaching becomes very personal and this upsets the coachee. (twice)
- The coachee tells me what to do.
- The coachee flatters me.
- The coachee pulls me into criticising him (to become a 'wicked stepmother').
- I am concerned for the coachee's overall health.
- The coachee is ambivalent, sends out mixed messages, which 'de-skills' me.

7. Anxiety stemming mainly from the coach
6 of the 51 moments reproduced specific anxieties in this category. Some new anxieties in this category were:
- How to say this helpfully, without triggering a defensive response?
- I cry, and that sets the coachee off.
- Endings are an issue for me which led me in this case to prolong the coaching.

8.2.2 Study method: the temporal process and supervision
After finding this confirmation that the conclusions from Chapter 7 are also applicable to this new selection of critical moments, we

undertook a thematic analysis of the new material resulting from the in-depth interviews.

- What made these moments 'critical' for the coaches?
- What were the coach's anxieties and emotions before, during and after the critical moments?
- What was therefore the temporal pattern of each moment reported?

The last two items on this list are new analyses. The temporal pattern of each moment was investigated by breaking each incident down into codified phases or stages in the developing relationship between coach and coachee. The purpose of this analysis was to investigate the temporal process of the unfolding relationship, for each incident. We therefore looked for distinct phases in the stories that were told, and we characterised those phases in terms of the coaching relationship. The only aspect of the stories that we could not put into relational terms was the 'interior dialogue' of the coach that comes through, which we have identified as being in a state of 'unshared' or 'private' reflection.

The use of continuing professional development by these coaches was investigated by categorising:

1 the different forms of professional development (compare the ones listed in Chapter 10);
2 the reason or reasons given for discussing critical moments during development activities;
3 their experience of working through the moment in development activities; and
4 what happened as a result of discussing the moment in development activities.

It is important to be aware of the limitations of this methodology, which stem from the fact that these are self-reported critical moments given from the view of the coaches themselves, which inevitably creates biases. We hear only one side of the story, the side that selected the moments. We don't know what the coachees in those critical moments would have said. Another bias may result from the effect of 'everyday memory' which tends to yield distorted reports of critical events in ways which create a more positive self-image (see, for example, Goodman, Magnussen, Andersson, Endes-tad, Løkke & Mostue, 2006). We are aware of these shortcomings in this type of qualitative research, but as coaching always takes place within a confidential and exclusive relationship between two people, they seem to be impossible to avoid without creating a 'laboratory environment', which in turn would have a significant (negative) impact on the outcome of the coaching relationship[2], so 'pure research' without distorting real-life critical moments appears to be fundamentally impossible here.

8.3 The temporal patterns of the critical moments

In the process of analysing aspects such as context, events, actions and outcomes associated with the critical moment we became aware that the dynamics of the unfolding relationship between coach and coachee seem to be significant for the outcome.

On the basis of the stories and outcomes reported, therefore, we devised relational codes for the different phases of the coaching relationship. Nine codes covered all the various occurrences in the 51 stories. We should point out that it would be difficult and in many cases impossible to identify the individual contributions made by the different parties in the relationship (including third parties, e.g. within the organisation of the coachee). In many instances, it was impossible to determine 'who did what' in the detailed descriptions: who was responsible for a breakthrough, distance or final breakdown within the coaching relationship. Coaching therefore turns out time and again to be a joint process, and it is better to focus on the relationship per se in the description.

---

[2] Wampold (2001) argues convincingly that a laboratory environment, which would be more geared towards the research outcomes and less towards the interest of the outcomes of the client journey, would not be the same process and would yield overall lower effectiveness.

The nine codes that describe all of the different phases of the relationship are:

AE: *Action, issue, or (raw) emotion.* All moments start with some action, emotion or (presenting) issue, so all moments start with AE. This code only occurred at the beginning of each critical moment.

CA: *Counteraction,* sometimes technically called 'defence'. This is some action taken as an immediate, unprocessed response to a previous action or emotion. Coachee or coach, or coachee and coach, could be undertaking this counteraction, and the result for the relationship is the same: essentially an ongoing state of action/issue/emotion.

IM: *Interior monologue* or internal (and sometimes ethical) dilemma. This is something coaches convey only about themselves. Indeed, we only have this data in the form of thinking-after-the-fact, so we don't know what state the coaching relationship was in. However, we usually found hints of 'distancing' (see DI below) or 'unshared reflection' in the relationship together with IM.

DI: Explicit *distancing* in the relationship, sometimes expressed as the coachee not turning up, or the contract being discontinued, or the request for another coach.

RE: Shared *reflection*, where coach and coachee explore the actions, issues and emotions, and/or the state of their own relationship.

DE: *Deepening* of the relationship between coachee and coach, sometimes expressed as 'new issues were shared', sometimes as re-contracting, often as more calmness and dissipation of conflict.

CH: Satisfactory *change* for the coachee, sometimes expressed as new insight, sometimes as a new way of working together, a breakthrough, a promotion, or a decision taken.

BR: *Breakdown* of the relationship, which is also the end of coaching.

UF: *Unknown future.* We used this code not to signify any question marks about the future of the relationship (as there are always multiple question marks for coachee and coach, and even more for us as researchers), but rather to indicate a certain type of outcome which is unresolved and ongoing. This code therefore occurred only at the end of the relationship.

Using this method, the 51 critical moments generated 51 strings of codes, e.g. 'AE – CA – BR' or 'AE – CA – RE – DE' or even 'AE – RE – CH – AE – RE – UF', the shortest string containing 3 codes and the longest 6. These strings illustrate a range of recognisable temporal patterns within coaching relationships and make those relationships amenable to comparison, even though they are of course very different.

Each incident had an opening phase, with Action, issue, or (raw) emotion (AE) and often Counteraction (CA), and sometimes distancing (DI); then an intermediate phase which could contain Shared reflection (RE) or more Counteraction (CA), and sometimes Distancing in the relationship (DI), and then an ending which was found only to be of three types:

1 a positive outcome: Deepening of the relationship between coachee and coach (DE) and/or Satisfactory change for the coachee (CH),
2 a negative outcome: Breakdown of the relationship (BR) and/or Distancing in the relationship (DI), or
3 an Unknown outcome (UF), because the critical moment is still fresh and still moving towards some form of resolution.

Explicit Distancing in the relationship (DI) only occurred as an outcome in two cases, as it usually led to a Breakdown (BR) or would be ongoing (UF).

When we distinguished the critical incidents which had some Reflection (RE) towards the end from those that did not, we noticed that reflection was connected to a fundamental difference in the outcome of the critical moment (see Figure 8.1). The completed sequences (i.e. those that did not end in UF) on the whole fell into two categories. The first category contained a pattern of responses that contained no reflection. These patterns of interaction followed the following pattern: Action, Issue or emotion (AE) followed by Counteraction (CA) and then a distancing in the relationship or a breakdown in the relationship. The second category contained a point of Reflection in the relationship (RE) initiated by either the coach or coachee. Here the pattern consisted of Actions, Issues and Emotions (AE), followed by a

Outcome: final phases of the temporal process	Number of critical moments with this outcome
AE / DI / CA → DI	1
AE / DI / CA → BR	10
AE / DI / CA → DE/CH	None
AE / DI / CA → UF	6
AE / DI / CA → RE → DI	None
AE / DI / CA → RE → BR	1
AE / DI / CA → RE → DE/CH	28
AE / DI / CA → RE → UF	5

Figure 8.1 *The final phases of all the temporal patterns in the 51 critical moments, as an indication of the outcome of the temporal process.*

range of other phases leading up to Shared Reflection (RE), then a Deepening of the Relationship (DE) and/or a positive Change for the coachee (CH).

There is only one critical moment where reflection (RE) leads to breakdown (BR), and even in that case the breakdown (BR) is a con-sensual process of referral to another coach, with whom work is now proceeding very well. On the other hand, there are as many as 11 moments in which ongoing AE/DI/CA (presenting of issues, acting out, experiencing emotions and distancing) without reflection (RE) has led to a breakdown (BR) and in which the issues and problems, emotions, actions and counter-actions and new emotions, and finally distancing, continue to dominate. Moreover, Figure 8.1 shows that none of the moments that lead up to change (CH) and deepening (DE) of the relationship can do so without shared reflection (RE) preceding that positive outcome.

Our data suggests that in many of the critical moments there was a point of rupture (AE, CA) in the relationship between the coach and their coachee. This took the form of an emotional disturbance in or suspension of their working alliance. At these points, our participants reported that they were anxious and full of doubts. If they responded to the coachee's emotional state by being aggressive or avoiding the 'here-and-now' emotional reality, this resulted in distancing or break-down in the relationship. In these moments the coach's response to the coachee's emotional reaction paralleled or reversely paralleled the coachee's response. For instance, irritation is met with (counter-) irritation or reversely, with feeling intimidated, rather than with interest or curiosity.

In a number of incidents, for example, the coach reported that she responded to the coachee's irritation by becoming irritated herself or by blaming the coachee. This pattern of responses in the relationship seemed to amplify the levels of emotion in the relationship. In these instances, we observed how this increase in the level of (unprocessed) emotion resulted in a loss of trust and in some cases in the end of the coaching session or even the relationship. Where the relationship broke down, both coach and coachee were left with feelings of frustra-tion or even hostility. The level of emotion and anxiety becomes so overwhelming that neither coach nor coachee are able to generate sufficient *containment* (Bion, 1963) to handle the anxieties within their relationship.

If, however, the coach was able to reflect on his or her emotional state and respond in a manner that 'contained' (Bion, 1963) the coachee's emotion then the result tended to be a deepening of the relationship or evidence of change on the part of the coachee (and possibly the coach). Regardless of the source of the rupture, analysis of the critical moments suggests that the key to whether the relationship broke down or was strengthened seems to lie with the coach and coachee's ability to reflect and thereby to manage their relational space. In these moments, the possibility was created for generative learning, a moment of insight or growth for the coachee. The coachees heightened their awareness and/or developed insight into themselves, the coaching relationship was strengthened and deepened, and there was a shift in the coachees' behaviour or state of mind (compare Greenson, 1965).

Specific interventions of coaches who were able to overcome the rupture in the coaching relationship were very diverse, and included:

- confronting or challenging the coachee with interest and acceptance;
- providing feedback to the coachee in the 'here and now' about what they are noticing or observing;
- sharing their own feelings with the coachee and reflecting on the possible link to the coachee's issues and feelings;
- helping the coachee to clarify their thinking, and
- proposing a future conversation to discuss the rupture and the relationship.

An example of a containing response from a coach is as follows: 'I started working with an executive client who was quite resistant and aggressive. Almost belligerently, he asked "So what are your qualifications?". I knew this would be a key moment and my response mattered. I said: 'It must be quite frightening to be here. I'm not even sure if you want to be here. Let's spend a bit of time to look at why it seems to be difficult'. He kept on repeating his challenge, until he said, 'I really don't want to be here'. I think giving those professional qualifications would have been missing the point, really. We had 10 successful sessions. He was actually quite depressed. He told me later he didn't like this at all, it shocked him (he used the word 'frightening'). It was important for me to hold my own. It was critical in terms of the way we related'.

Reflection between the coach and the coachee on critical moments is therefore very influential on whether points of heightened emotion are used generatively in the coaching process or lead to a breakdown or distancing in the coaching relationship. This seems to confirm Bion's (1965) general idea that what clients try to achieve is to transform their emotional experience through thinking into new opportunities for action, so in the coaching relationship they may move from:

1 raw 'Emotion' (including raising an issue, or 'acting out'); through
2 'Thinking' (helpful reflection); to
3 'Change' (a new way of seeing things, or, developing new, better-considered actions).

8.4 How to handle these critical moments: the use of supervision

8.4.1 Analysis

After exploring the participants' experience of critical moments in coaching we asked them whether they had taken their experience to supervision (or whatever form of continuing professional development they undertook) and what their experiences had been. Of the 51 moments described by the sample, 47 were recounted by coaches who had supervisors (or peer supervisors) and 34 of those moments were taken to supervision. The majority of the sample undertook supervision at least once a month.

Participants' motivation for using supervision

When asked why they chose to take the moments to supervision, the most common responses from participants were:

1 to seek reassurance, guidance and a way forward (11 moments);
2 to examine their response to the challenge (9 moments); and
3 to understand themselves better (6 moments).

The participants seemed therefore to be using supervision to work through their anxieties and doubts about their work and to understand their emotional responses to the critical moments. For critical moments that had emerged suddenly, supervision took on a role of helping the individual to make sense of their experience and their reaction, perhaps to gain reassurance that they had handled the moment competently. For those moments that had evolved over a longer period of time (i.e. a number of sessions), supervision provided an opportunity for coaches to plan a strategy for working with the coachee. One participant for instance gave the following account of their motivation for using supervision:

'I was at a loss about what to do. We explored my need to be more assertive about his engagement in the coaching process. His attitude and approach was not personal towards me but was part of a pattern or phenomenon for the client.'

Thirteen moments which could have been taken to supervision or continuing professional development activities, were not. We were surprised to find that the participants described many additional forms of support to formal supervision. These alternative forms of support included action learning, informal consultation with colleagues, talking to partners or colleagues, and self–reflection. We found that coaches used these forms of support to help them make sense of a critical moment when practical and timing constraints prevented them from meeting with their supervisor.

When asked why they had not taken the moment to supervision, the most frequent response from the participant was that they were 'okay with the outcome' (8 moments). This reinforces the finding from above that a trigger for a coach to take a moment to supervision is their own anxiety and doubt about their work with a coachee. However, three participants did acknowledge that they had avoided taking a moment to supervision because they were not good at asking for help or were concerned about being criticised by their supervisor (see Lawton, 2000). That barrier is much lower if coaches feel good about their own attitude or response during a critical moment. Here are some typical

Summary of supervision by the coach	Number of coaches with this experience
1. Reassurance received	11
2. Management of the client relationship explored	9
3. Instructions or advice received	5
4. Scope for clarification found	4
5. New interpretations found	4
6. Self-understanding increased	3
7. Understanding of the coachee's situation increased	1
8. No noticeable outcome	1

Figure 8.2 *What happened at supervision according to the coaches interviewed.*

examples of moments that were taken to supervision – critical, but not *too* critical.

- 'Because of the positive nature of the meeting I was left asking myself "what am I missing?"'
- 'I wanted to "go round the loop" and check if what I had done was right. Raised it as an area in my mind which causes me more anxiety than it apparently caused my client.'
- 'It felt extremely risky. Somewhere I felt I had done well, but it still felt risky. I think I looked for affirmation.'

The motivations of these experienced coaches for using supervision to respond to a critical moment, therefore, are to help them to deal with their doubts and anxieties that arise from the moment, even when the outcome, for them, was positive. Many of the participants also tell us that they were looking for reassurance from the process of supervision. Supervision may therefore provide important 'containment' for the coach in helping them to contain a coachee's anxiety and heightened emotion.

In view of these findings, we subsequently had to ask ourselves whether participants had in fact shared their most critical moments with us . . . ?

How supervision helped participants to respond to critical moments

The importance of receiving reassurance is further highlighted when coaches describe how supervision helped them to respond to critical moments. The management of the client relationship was also a common theme that was explored at supervision. Figure 8.2 below highlights the responses participants gave to the question of what happened during supervision.

The approaches during supervision most commonly mentioned were as follows.

1 The coaches talk about their own experiences and receive feedback, support and advice.
2 The coaches attempt to make sense of their own experiences.
3 The coaches put into words what they took away or learned from the supervision session.

Learning outcome for coach due to supervision	Number of coaches with this outcome
1. More about coaching relationships	15
2. More about myself	8
3. The value of reassurance	6
4. To trust myself	6
5. Ethical considerations	4
6. Personal values	3
7. Boundaries of the role of coach	2
8. Clarity of argument	2
9. Motivation	1

Figure 8.3 *What did the coaches learn during supervision, in their own estimation.*

The coaches also felt they were provided with the space to reflect and to become aware of different aspects of the moment that they perhaps had not considered previously. They report that they usually get the reassurance and support that they were looking for from supervision. For example:

- 'Supervision helped highlight the role of religion and spirituality. This had a big impact. It really changed our line of inquiry.'
- 'Supervision gave advice about how to attend to her and leave my own opinion out of it.'
- 'I presented, others listened, asked questions, went to the roots of things, both internal (therapeutically) and external (organisationally). They gave me confirmation. They carried me through (just like I carried her).'

It is clear therefore that coaches use supervision for reassurance, confidence building, and benchmarking their practice. Supervision also raises their awareness and adds perspective, whether this is self-awareness, context awareness or process awareness.

What did participants learn from supervision?
Figure 8.3 presents an overview of the learning outcomes described by the participants in this study as a result of their discussion of critical moments during supervision or other continuing professional development activities.

Interestingly, if this is compared with the range of issues that the coaches take to supervision we can see that learning about coaching relationships occurs more often than the coach expects, as they do not always identify the issue as being a relationship management issue when they raise it at supervision. For example:
- 'There is a big gulp when you're going to say something and going to massively reframe something. Unless you have the courage, they will not have it.'
- 'Take time to build a relationship. Stay with the process of the relationship and the work gets done.'

Participants also described that reviewing critical moments in supervision helped them to learn something about themselves.
- 'To be still more cautious. Don't take it personally. That is very difficult. My personal confidence was shocked.'
- 'That I must be careful not to think everything is my fault.'
- 'About holding, containing when someone is in survival mode as opposed to competency mode. You can ask too much when they are in survival mode. Try and trust my intuition on this. I realise I do work more intuitively than I thought.'

The data points to a process of 'internalisation' for some of the coaches in our sample who internalised the responsibility for any tensions or difficulties in the work. More coaches identified issues as 'personal' than as relationship management issues, suggesting that they perhaps internalise their relationship management issues as 'their problem' rather than a problem with the management of the relationship as a whole. This goes some way to explaining the high rating of gaining reassurance in terms of outcomes of supervision, as coaches might find it reassuring in itself that the problem is not of their 'doing' alone.

This research suggests therefore that supervision is important for two reasons. Firstly, the process maintains the psychological health of the coach in the context of difficult emotional material; and, secondly it helps the coach to identify what 'material' belongs to them and what belongs to the coachee, thereby identifying their contribution to the coaching relationship.

The question remains whether formal supervision differs in effectiveness and quality from other forms of support, or whether different forms of continuing professional development are equally valuable. Our participants tell us in any case that we should not underestimate the importance of informal support, given its immediate availability and the large degree of confidence and trust involved.

8.4.2 Synthesis

The critical moments outlined by the participants confirm that the key point in the coaching relationship that is challenging to them as coaches is when they arrive at that point of *rupture* in the coaching relationship, where there is anxiety and doubt on the part of the coachee and/or the coach. As described in Chapter 6, such moments are often moments when the coachee is about to enter new territory, be it seeing something in a different light, interpreting something differently, or coming to a realisation about themselves in the situation they are considering. Usually, it is important that the coach does not back away from these moments of rupture. In fact, this is essentially what differentiates a coaching conversation from any other good conversation (see Chapter 7). Coaches stay with moments of tension and anxiety in the relationship and use them as opportunities for generative learning despite the real or perceived risk of a breakdown of the relationship. The importance of reflective skills and practice (Reason, 1994) on the part of the coach is also demonstrated by this study.

Our analysis of the 51 critical moments conveyed by our participants seems to confirm earlier research into the development of the working alliance (e.g. Horvath & Marx, 1990; Safran, Crocker, McMain & Murray, 1990; and Safran, Muran & Wallner Samstag, 1993), which provided evidence for the existence of a rupture-repair cycle in successful counselling and therapy. We have to add here that meta-analysis has shown that coachees tend to find the working alliance more stable than therapists and observers (Martin, Garske & Davis, 2000). It is therefore important to study critical moments from the perspective of the coachee as well, and we have now embarked on research in that area (De Haan, Bertie, Day, & Sills, 2008).

At supervision, the coach will express his anxieties and doubts in terms of questions such as 'What is going on?', 'What is going on for my coachee?', and 'How can I help my coachee?' There are no right or wrong answers to these questions, and no set formulae or solutions. Supervision affords the coach the space to explore these doubts and anxieties. If supervision is not available, coaches seek alternative support mechanisms such as trusted colleagues, peer consultation sets, and partners.

This research clearly shows that critical moments in the coaching relationship are challenging both to coaches and their coachees, and that even experienced coaches may feel uncertain about the impact they are having on the coachee and the relationship. This insecurity is partly overcome through getting the reassurance of friends and colleagues, but may be most effectively addressed through the process of supervision. The level of emotion involved, and the diversity of the critical moments reported, which often show a clear connection with transference and countertransference, is a strong argument for the importance of 'formal' supervision as a better delineated and more professional form of reflection.

Supervision would appear to be most useful to coaches if it occurs within the time frame of a critical moment or rupture in the working alliance. If the experience is still fresh, coaches gain both reflection and increasing insight but also a way of responding, of generating containment for themselves and their coachees, and of preventing their own defensive behaviour. If more time elapses and the 'incident' has developed into a breakthrough or the end of the relationship, there appears to be less of a need to take the experience to supervision, although a coach may of course still have much to learn from it.

Supervision can help coaches explore their management of the coaching relationship, and to understand themselves within the context of that relationship, their own needs and wants within that relationship, and their own motivations. This can increase their self-confidence because they are comforted by finding:

- that they react just as others would in the same situation; or
- that they can convert their intuitions and emotions into helpful interventions; or simply
- that they can trust their own anxieties and emotions as guides to their intuition.

In addition, supervision can help identify those situations which are not suitable for further coaching interventions and where the coach should refer the coachee on, and can help resolve and give guidance on ethical dilemmas that may be troubling the coach. Supervision is therefore a mechanism for providing 'containment' for the coach which can enable the coach in turn to provide 'containment' for the coachee.

8.5 Conclusion

Critical moments, leading to ruptures in the coach/coachee relationship are potential opportunities for insight and change, firstly within the coaching relationship and secondly for the coachees themselves. The coach's containment of the coachee's anxiety at these moments seems to be critical for the outcome. By definition, these moments are difficult, emotionally laden and high-risk for coaches to manage, and hence coaches and coachees may seek many different forms of support in dealing with these moments. It may be reassuring for less experienced coaches to know that even very experienced coaches still feel anxiety and doubt in these situations, and they still struggle with finding resolution and their own role in that process.

The heightened emotion in the 'here and now' of the coaching relationship at the point when a critical moment arises seems to be important for facilitating the learning of the coachee. We can argue therefore that learning through coaching is as much an emotional process as a cognitive process (Maroda, 1998). When the coaching relationship is able to 'contain' these heightened emotions (i.e. anger, fear, sadness, etc.) then the moment can be reflected upon by coach and coachee, raising the possibility for the coachee to explore new options, both in this relationship, in other relationships generally, and in the workplace. This confirms what Safran *et al.* wrote in 1990: 'the successful resolution of an alliance rupture can be a powerful means of disconfirming the client's dysfunctional interpersonal schema'. This finding demonstrates that it is critical for coaches to be aware of their own 'internal script' (Berne, 1972; Lapworth, Sills, and Fish, 2001), so that they are able to contain a coachee's emotional material.

Supervision affords coaches the space to work through moments that they find difficult in their coaching work. Supervision succeeds or fails on its ability to provide that space, or 'containment'. The fact that many moments were taken to supervision even after a positive outcome is an indication that coaches (and probably their coachees as well) still felt they needed reassurance after the anxiety had drained away, in order to feel competent and to find confirmation of their methods. It also suggests that managing these critical moments is not part of the coach's everyday repertoire of skills or competencies. They require the coach to have confidence in the process at a deeper level and to stay in the coaching relationship even when confronted with new, unknown and uncomfortable experiences. In order to find that confidence and that presence, having another forum for discussion and another person to discuss those moments with, i.e. a relationship outside the coaching relationship, is sometimes a sine qua non.

Summary: coaches have their say

In the third phase of the study of critical moments in coaching, we asked a largely new group of 28 very experienced coaches to answer the same question:

'Describe briefly one **critical moment** (an exciting, tense or significant moment) with one of your coachees. Think about what was critical in the coaching journey, or a moment when you did not quite know what to do.'

In this phase we used **in-depth interviews**, which revealed more about the context and outcome of the 51 critical moments reported, and allowed us to ask questions about:

- how the coaches handled those critical moments;
- the extent to which they used professional development activities; and
- their experiences during those development activities.

Only 5 of the critical moments overlapped with the sample in the previous chapter. However, the anxieties reported showed a large overlap with the patterns described in that chapter.

Critical moments generally coincided with major or minor **ruptures** in the **working alliance** within the coaching relationship.

It was possible to describe all of the extended accounts of critical moments in just nine **relational phases**, which kept recurring in different orders: action, counteraction, interior monologue of the coach, distancing, shared reflection, deepening, change, breakdown and unknown future.

It also emerged that **all** moments with a favourable outcome, a deepening and/or a change, contained a phase of shared reflection prior to that outcome. Moreover, almost all of the moments that ended in a breakdown lacked such a stage of shared reflection.

Participants' **motivations** for taking these critical moments to supervision were:
1   to seek reassurance, guidance and a way forward (11 moments);
2   to examine their response to the challenge (9 moments);
3   to understand themselves better (6 moments).

The reported **outcomes** of discussion during supervision mainly have to do with increased understanding, of the coaching relationship and of themselves, and greater self-confidence.

Supervision appears particularly important in order to contribute the necessary **containment**:
- after which coaches themselves can offer more containment to their coachees in turn;
- after which the necessary **shared reflection** can be re-established within the coaching process;
- with which the rupture in the coaching relationship may be repaired.

Part III
The Ways of Excellence

Introduction: the paths towards excellence

Recently I had cause to revisit a classical path to excellence of which I have previous experience: insight meditation (Nanamoli, 1991). My elder daughter has always displayed an overabundance of energy, and little interest in sleep. At eight o'clock each evening the two-year-old is still bubbling over with plans, questions and ideas, but it is time to start her long, slow ritual of winding down and disengaging, which I am now able to parallel by my own. I close the curtains to darken her room, read yet another bed-time story and give her a bottle of milk on which to lavish her last reserves of attention, eagerness and affection while I myself quietly withdraw from her life. The process usually takes between half an hour and an hour. Time stands still for me. I can't play with her or talk to her any more because that will bring her back to wakefulness but, equally, I can't leave the room or do something else because that will make her feel insecure or alone, which will also make her more awake.

A perfect time to fetch my meditation cushion from the cupboard. My daughter fidgeting, chattering and occasionally crying beside me, and my own internal desires to get up, go off and do something 'useful' are ideal temptations from which to disengage. Her little noises and requests are relatively minor distractions. Sometimes I do have to attend to her, but most of the time my silent presence is enough. My own internal process is a much greater distraction, stemming from irrepressible desires to, for example, change position or leave the room in order to get on with the remainder of the evening that we adults have to ourselves.

As soon as she settles, lies down and begins to chatter more to herself, I adopt a half lotus posture and try to concentrate on my breathing. The primary task in vipassana meditation is very similar to the primary task in relational coaching: 'be aware of what is happening in this moment and try to focus on every moment as it comes'. This instruction to experience every moment consciously seems easy to follow, and is anything but in practice, either here or during coaching. Usually, I start off by managing less than ten seconds of noticing what is happening in me: my breathing, listening to my daughter, the feeling of my foot resting on my thigh. Then my thoughts soon start to drift: 'Is she asleep yet?', 'What's for supper?' or 'How many e-mails do I still have to answer?' If such questions arise and I can immediately register the fact that I have started thinking, there is no problem and I can continue to focus on every moment. But thinking is insidious; it is not only the question that arises, but often the germ of an answer as well, or the desire to keep thinking and distract myself. This gradually becomes harder to register; in fact, the thoughts sap my ability to register and I become lost, distracted, no longer present in the moment. Later, when my foot starts to protest and really make its presence felt, I give in to the pain, change position, and again am distracted from the moment itself. Strange how a task that sounds so straightforward can turn out to be so difficult.

Insight meditation is a genuine path to excellence – even though thinking about it during the process diverts one from that path. Remaining present and attentive during anxieties and doubts, while exploring any reactions that arise, is the path that was once followed and described by the Buddha (Nanamoli, 1991). It is also the precise combination of two activities that I described at the start of the first two sections of this book: dealing with anxiety about the unknown (see the introduction to Part I) and *careful examination of* what corefully examing happens in the here and now (see the introduction to Part II).

Excellence in coaching is therefore in keeping with the Buddhist understanding of excellence. Excellence in Buddhism is a path of exploration into the true nature of things, gaining insight first into the omnipresent nature of suffering, then into the cause of that suffering, then into the possibility of escaping that suffering and finally into the achievement of a state of peace and composure (Nanamoli, 1991). The achievement of insight and peace by means of exploration. This is primarily an exploration of the here-and-now and of how one's own distractions, desires, irritations and other impulses make this moment a moment of suffering, in which we are slaves to those impulses. The dawning of insight is inextricably bound up with the conscious awareness of those impulses and *at the same time* registering our own reactions to them, without giving in to them. This is an ongoing process of exploration of one's own here-and-now, without allowing ourselves to be dragged down into our here-and-now.

In my view, excellence in coaching means exactly the same thing and is just as transient and unachievable an ideal as reaching excellence in insight meditation. It is the bringing together of the existential, immediate anxiety about the unknown that was discussed in Part I of this book and the detached, unbiased exploration or research dealt with in Part II, i.e. studying ourselves while we coach.

Achieving excellence according to a more Western tradition, which, since classical antiquity, has consisted in having a sense of moderation and finding the right balance between two extremes, is also largely relevant to coaching. Excellence in coaching means conquering an impossible dilemma and even reconciling a paradox, namely the fundamental dilemma between being consciously anxious and exploring that anxiety, two activities that *cannot* in fact be combined by their very nature:

- being engrossed in the client's frame of reference, *and at the same time* in our own;
- being engrossed in the relationship, participating fully in it, *and at the same time* examining, commenting upon and asking questions about the relationship;
- experiencing transference, *and at the same time* putting it into words;
- experiencing the moment, *and at the same time*, in thinking or speaking or writing, recording what is happening in that moment.

What we *can* do is keep a dynamic balance between these two extremes. In practice, this is possible only by steering an unstable and fluctuating course. In my view, therefore, mastery involves keeping to that course as tightly as possible, while enduring the fact that you are never truly on course.

The next three chapters are about the education of coaches, their continuing professional development, and the sources of inspiration of (some) coaches. Chapter 9 discusses coach education in terms of possible development programmes and accreditation processes. This chapter gives an outline of what it means to *become* a professional coach. Chapter 10 gives a summary of professional development activities for coaches, and therefore describes what it means to *remain* a professional coach. In Chapter 11 I give an introduction to 12 books that I personally found valuable as sources of inspiration in coaching, and I explain why. Finally, Chapter 12 makes a prediction concerning the research and development that may await the coaching profession in the future.

Development activities such as training and accreditation and forms of continuing professional development such as co-coaching and supervision are as education and consultancy are to other professional groups. Taking part in a training programme is mainly a question of appropriating and practising models and behaviours, while consultancy mainly offers opportunities for reflection and practice on the basis of a coach's own current work with clients.

Chapter 9
Training and Accreditation of the Executive Coach

9.1 Areas of competence of the coach

There is a wide range of literature on the competences of the coach, but much of it is written on the basis of a specific perspective or preferred style. Extensive research in psychotherapy, using meta-analyses (see Chapter 3), shows that there is no single best method of coaching and that different coaching styles are equally effective, although effectiveness does depend to a large extent on common factors such as the coaching situation, the presenting issue, the coach and the coachee. Experienced coaches are aware of their own preferred approach or approaches, and are able to deviate from them if a different approach appears to be more effective. *Flexibility* in choosing a personal coaching approach is perhaps the most important skill a coach can have.

However, in a general sense, there are many things to be said about the attitudes and values, knowledge, methodical skills and behavioural techniques displayed by 'excellent' coaches. The following pages contain some suggestions regarding these competences of the coach, based on different layers of the 'coach personality'. Ideally, those different layers should fit together well and support each other, resulting in a fully congruent and well-integrated coach. This model of personality starts with a relatively stable core and moves towards a more changeable outside: from convictions, values and ethics, to attitudes, knowledge, relational skills and specific styles, and lastly, to specific behaviours (see Figure 9.1).

9.1.1 Convictions and values of the coach
The convictions and values of coaches can be as diverse as those in their different family backgrounds and cultures. However, I do often

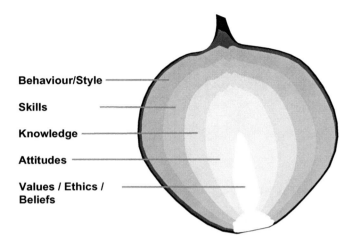

Behaviour/Style

Skills

Knowledge

Attitudes

Values / Ethics / Beliefs

Figure 9.1 *The coach as 'onion': structure of the personality of the coach in five nested layers*

find that coaches have a high regard for personal or cultural achievements and a certain openness to convictions other than their own.

Downey (1999) challenges coaches to consider the following basic convictions, which can underpin their effectiveness and which they can hang onto even when they are in doubt whether they fully hold.

1   Coachees have huge untapped potential.
2   Coachees have a unique map of reality – not to be confused with reality itself.
3   Coachees have good intentions, for themselves and for others.
4   Coachees achieve their own objectives – perfectly – at all times!

Good coaches are well aware of the impact that coaching can have on their coachees, and weigh their words and gestures carefully. They are continually aware that the coaching is for the coachees' benefit, not for the greater glory of the coach, and should therefore focus exclusively on the interests of the coachees. Coaches therefore refer their coachees elsewhere if they feel unable to help further, and have a reliable referral network of fellow coaches and therapists.

Good coaches' values also inspire them to act in accordance with the relevant codes of conduct (see, for example, the code in Appendix E) and provide them with a natural 'compass' with which to navigate their way through ethical dilemmas and conflicts.

9.1.2 Attitude of the coach

In my view, the attitude of a coach is characterised by:

- empathy, respect, warmth and authenticity in relation to the coachee;
- tolerance and openness to different values and opinions;
- availability: calm and space for the coachee;
- an appropriate balance between detachment and involvement;
- an encouraging and gentle approach towards the coachee;
- readiness to let the other person take initiative and responsibility;
- an attitude of service towards their coachees, helping them to (learn how to) progress themselves;
- an inclination to give as little advice as possible (even if that is requested), based on the conviction that giving advice is often an insult to the other person, who has already spent a long time thinking about the issue and can give the best advice himself or herself;
- a confrontational approach only if the coachee can take it and will benefit from it, otherwise a preference for supportive interventions;
- humour and an ability to put things into perspective.

9.1.3 Knowledge of the coach

What knowledge does a good coach have? This depends partly on the coachee's presenting issues (see also Chapter 1). Where the coaching concerns issues that revolve around content and specialist knowledge ('what' and 'how' questions) the coach could benefit from that specialist knowledge. Yet many issues asked by coachees are more personal in nature, linking their person and their work ('who' questions). For example, these are issues about how coachees hold their own in the organisation, how they work with others or act with respect to their managers. When addressing this type of issue specialist knowledge is less important, and can even be an impediment (the coach might switch from coaching to giving expert advice). What knowledge, then, is relevant to addressing these 'who' questions?

- In the first place, *self-knowledge:* you as coach are aware of the way in which you tend to view problems, and are able to look at the coachee from multiple perspectives. You know the patterns and traps lying in wait for the unwary coach (for example, being quick to give advice, asking leading questions, or only taking in the positive in the coachee's account); and are aware of the emotions you experience during sessions and how to manage them professionally. You are also aware of your main qualities, which are relevant because one's biggest pitfalls are often associated precisely with these.
- Good coaches have knowledge about the *development of individuals and groups.* You know which problems are associated with particular life stages and what patterns may emerge in them.
- Because coaching is always work-related, you also have knowledge about the *development of organisations,* often including a sound understanding of management and change.
- Coaching is not therapy. Nevertheless, a basic knowledge of *psychodynamics and psychotherapy* is necessary to enable the coach to choose the right interventions, to keep a watchful eye on the boundary between coaching and psychotherapy, and to make timely referrals.
- Knowledge of different *approaches to coaching, interventions and levels of intervention,* as well as of your own preferred styles and interventions, is necessary in order to be able to tailor your approach to the coachee in his or her context. It is also necessary in order for you to remain aware what your own contribution is at any moment in the coaching conversation.
- Coaches have extensive knowledge of *communication techniques* (conversational techniques, influencing styles, etc.), in order to be effective in directing the conversation and to make coachees aware of their effectiveness in communication and in using influence.

9.1.4 Strategic skills of the coach

Coaches need a number of skills in order to mould their approach consistently over a longer period and so create a context for constructive interventions within coaching sessions:

- Coaches are able to maintain *relationships:* they have the ability to build up and wind down relationships with a wide range of coachees, to create the *working alliances* that create the possibility of coaching. It helps in this respect to be clear, unambiguous and consistent, and to be able to tolerate a wide range of feelings, both within oneself and in others.

- An effective coach is able to use the different areas of knowledge outlined above effectively in the coaching context. This starts with effective *management of expectations*, an issue that comes up afresh in every session (see also the sections about contracting in Appendix F). The coach is transparent and checks regularly that the goals of the coaching are clear and attainable.
- An effective coach *can work consistently with different approaches* – such as insight-focused, coachee-focused, problem-focused and solution-focused approaches – and makes a considered choice, depending on the issue, the coachee and their context.
- Irrespective of the approach adopted, a coach is good at *recognising patterns and mental models*. The coach is on the lookout during the sessions for possible links between the coachee's issues and relationships, and also between the 'here and now' in the coaching relationship and other work relationships.
- Perhaps most importantly, coaches are able to manage their own many painful experiences in coaching conversations, as in the case of:
  - ambiguity, 'not understanding' and 'not knowing';
  - managing their own emerging 'stuff', in the form of personal judgements, recollections and expectations;
  - handling criticism, unrealistic expectations and transference.

The coach would do well to develop a *buffer* between 'stimulus' and 'response': staying calm and attentive in a situation marked by surprising or painful stimuli.

9.1.5 Specific interventions of the coach

A useful model for the different specific skills that the coach can use at any moment in a coaching conversation has been provided by John Heron (1975). The six styles proposed by Heron can be represented effectively in our 'window onto the coach'[1] from Chapter 1, see Figure 9.2.

Three of these styles are relatively directive (challenging, directing and informing) and three are more facilitative (releasing, discovering,

---

[1] I have renamed Heron's *six categories of counselling intervention* as follows: *prescriptive* – directing, *catalytic* – discovering, *confronting* – challenging, *supportive* – supporting, *informative* – informing, *cathartic* – releasing.

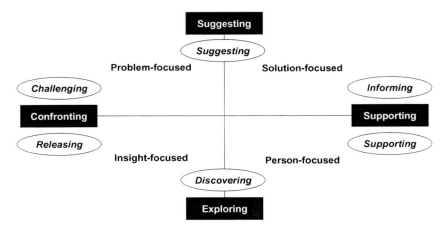

Figure 9.2 *The window onto the coach: six specific behavioural styles of coaches*

supporting). The styles can also be viewed in complementary pairs, as follows:

1 *Discovering* and *directing* are both strongly directional, one with the coachee in the lead and the other with the coach in the lead.
2 *Releasing* and *challenging* are both confrontational, although the former is much less critical of the coachee than the latter.
3 *Supporting* and *informing* are both supportive, the former on the basis of feelings and the latter on the basis of content.

There is more on Heron's model of coaching styles in Chapter 11, section 11.4.1; specific examples of the various styles and a question-naire for self-scoring on the styles can be found in *Coaching with colleagues* (De Haan & Burger, 2005).

9.2 Coach education

The question, of course, is whether you actually need specific educational programmes in order to become a coach. After all, you learn most in practice, so perhaps an apprenticeship to a 'master' (an experienced coach) is better than education. The master coach will make occasional suggestions about areas of study and training, with the design of the learning path shared by the 'master coach' and the 'apprentice'.

A coach training programme can be designed in numerous ways, and there are major differences between the many existing programmes as a result. Important differences in approach are those relating to the following.

- The ratio between practice and theory, often reflected in the ratio between contact hours (between students and between students and teachers) and study hours, and in the academic or practical content of the final extended essay.
- The ideology or philosophy of coaching, with the main distinction being that between a single preferred approach and a broader, 'integrative' philosophy.
- Following on from the chosen ideology: the specialist areas that play a leading role in the programme, such as organisational science, leadership, communication and behaviour, clinical psychology, psychoanalysis, etc.
- The ratio between individual, paired ('coaching') and group learning, and between different learning activities, such as active experimentation, reading and listening, and writing and self-development.

Emphases may be very differently assigned, in terms of both the areas of competence in the previous section and the methods of learning and working together. It is important to take account explicitly of the fact that participants in educational programmes will do more experimentation with their clients as well during the period of training, for example when:

- they enter into a new coaching relationship and draw up a contract;
- they 'try out' new techniques with existing clients;
- they 'use' their client relationships to carry out measurements, such as a tape recording, or more informally in self-reflection and research.

Change, experimentation and research within client relationships can give rise to a range of tensions, of which the programme facilitators should be aware. The following contains examples of recurring questions, and my own thoughts on those questions.

- 'I am asking among friends and acquaintances for a coachee to help me gain experience. Can I charge a fee?' Yes, charging a fee, even a nominal or symbolic amount, makes the coaching relationship more significant and more genuine, and there is a better chance that the coachee will turn up on time!
- 'How do I ask permission to make a tape recording?' You will be surprised how understanding most coachees are when it comes to making a tape recording that may help to further your professional development. They are there to further their own development, after all. Make it clear in advance who exactly will be listening to the tape, and when you will destroy it. Give them the option to come back later to the recording and what you learned from it, if they wish. Be aware that sharing your recording and notes with them may have a strong impact on the relationship and the coaching.
- 'Is it ethical to try something out on my client without asking permission?' In a sense, we as coaches are trying something out with every intervention. Don't forget that you are also trying out something 'on yourself' within relational coaching because, through the relationship, you yourself are also part of what you are doing. Try to make as much as possible explicit in advance and to agree with your client what you are going to do. This will also provide you with more relevant feedback.

I myself have experience of coach education in different institutions, and for internal coaches, ranging from a two-day course in coaching skills for partners in a consultancy firm, a five-day coaching module for an educational institution for management consultants, to the two-year part-time MSc programme *Ashridge Masters of Executive Coaching* (AMEC) that we developed in 2006. To give an idea of the potential make-up of an in-depth coaching programme, here follows a brief overview of the AMEC.

9.2.1 First year of a masters programme
Year 1 is designed around five two-day workshops ('Module 1') taking place over an extended period of about nine months, i.e. approximately the same length as many coaching contracts. In addition to their own coaching relationships, participants are encouraged to enter into a 'co-coaching' contract in pairs, in which they put the material from the workshops into practice by coaching each other. They also

write a personal reflective learning journal ('Module 2') in which they relate the more content-related parts of Module 1 to their own coaching practice.

Module 1 – 'Relational Coaching in Practice'

The five two-day workshops in Module 1 cover the following aspects of executive coaching:

Workshop 1 – Developing coaching strategies
- The nature and purpose of coaching
- Choosing coaching interventions
- Choosing a focus for coaching
- Building the 'working alliance'.

Workshop 2 – Psychological theories of personality
- Models and approaches in psychology and psychotherapy
- Where do my preferences lie?
- How free am I to 'choose' an approach?
- Coaching as a relational process.

Workshop 3 – Repetition and change: working with patterns
- The emergence of patterns
- Addressing patterns and 'stuckness'
- Patterns in groups – 'team coaching'
- Patterns in organisations – 'organisation coaching'.

Workshop 4 – Creative change interventions
- Perspectives on organisational change
- Supervision and perspectives on coaching
- Seven perspectives on the coaching relationship
- Creative change interventions.

Workshop 5 – Professional identity in the coaching relationship
- Articulating your coaching proposition
- Cultural identity – differences and diversity in coaching
- Ethics and professional identity: dilemmas and considerations
- Ending the coaching relationship.

Each workshop contains a number of hours of group supervision for participating coaches, in groups of 5 to 7. At the end of the module participants are asked to write a short account of their own development as a result of those five supervision meetings. The supervisor responds to that account with written feedback for the participant.

Module 2 – 'Reflective Learning Journey'

At the start of the AMEC, every participant receives a copy of the *Personal Reflection Log*, which helps them to prepare for and reflect upon each of the workshops in Module 1. The Personal Reflection Log comprises:

- A list of 12 recommended articles or book chapters, also recommended in Module 1, and a longer list of background literature.
- 10 study tasks (an average of two per workshop) for the participant, consisting of questions about the above recommended reading list. The intention is to help the participant integrate the theoretical subject-matter into the participant's own coaching practice.
- 10 reflective tasks, most of which are related to the specific coaching qualities and ambitions of the individual participants. These tasks encourage participants to reflect on their own current and future coaching practice.

The Personal Reflection Log is an exercise in reflecting on practice and integrating the relevant theory. Participants produce a written response to the various questions in the log, subject to a minimum length of 10,000 words.

Module 3 – 'Coach Accreditation'

The coach accreditation module, which is discussed in more detail in section 9.3 below, is offered frequently (on average, around ten times a year) and is separate from the other modules so that participants can also obtain accreditation in the second year of the Masters programme.

9.2.2 Second year of a Masters programme

Year 2 of the Ashridge Masters in Executive Coaching (AMEC) consists of a joint and an individual study programme within the discipline of coaching. The joint study element takes place within four three-day workshops (in Module 4) and consists of further exploration and consideration of the four building blocks of every coaching relationship: the coach, the coachee, the relationship and the organisation. The individual study element (Module 5) consists of an individual reflective inquiry in which one or more of the participant's own coaching relationships are subjected to closer scrutiny.

Module 4 – 'Inquiry into the coaching profession'

The aim of this module is to enable participants to reflect on the relevance to their professional practice of four key areas in coaching: the coach, the coachee, the coaching relationship and the organisational context. Participants embark on a joint exploration, and guest speakers with an internationally acquired reputation within the coaching profession supervise them in that process.

The four three-day workshops in Module 4 cover the following aspects of executive coaching:

Workshop 1: the coach and his/her perceptual system

- Human perception, including thresholds, distortions, illusions and selective attention
- Common factors as effective factors (see also Chapter 3)
- Common factors over which the coach has influence
- Coaching and perception: how am I seen by my clients?

Workshop 2: the coachee and limits of coaching

- Human self-regulation, including regulation of thought and emotion
- Emotions and their impact on change, and on barriers to change
- Domains of coaching, life stages and process stages in development
- The importance of boundaries: with therapy, of our own professional competence and between different coaching domains (such as mediation, counselling, mentoring, career development)

Workshop 3: the coaching relationship and the 'in between'

- The co-created relationship; co-creativity
- Unconscious processes in relationships
- Critical moments in coaching relationships and 'moments of meeting' (see Chapters 7–9 of this book)
- Power and influence in coaching relationships.

Workshop 4: working with the organisation through coaching
- The organisation of the coach: my unique product/market combination
- The organisation of the coachee and the organisation in the mind of the coachee
- The 'business' of the coach: internal/external, marketing, sustainability
- Coaching as an organisational intervention.

Module 5 – 'Inquiry into coaching in action'
This module consists of a reflective exploration in which the participant, as a professional coach, is at the centre, in relation to at least one coachee. Participants receive an introduction to the field of qualitative and social-constructionist research in the first workshop of Module 4 and then are free to choose their own research method. The coach's own relationship with one or more specific clients is chosen as a subject for study and gives rise to questions about
- the participant's personal biography and history as a coach;
- the (partly unconscious) choices at the root of their work as a coach and their work with this particular client or these particular clients; and
- the coach's own impact and added value.

All participants receive support in the form of coaching by another participant and in the form of case-work supervision within a small study group. Participants develop and design their own inquiry and report on it in the course of Year 2. The inquiry encompasses the following elements:
1 (Beginning of Year 2, ideally before the start of Module 4): Analysis of current practice, including an outline of the nature of the contracts and client issues. Participants describe critical aspects of their own coaching practice such as tensions, conflicts, unresolved doubts and counter-transference.
2 (During Year 2, ideally after the first workshop of Module 4): On the basis of the above analysis, each participant drafts a reflective inquiry proposal, which serves to plan and prepare for the reflective inquiry. In this proposal, the participant specifies:
   a) Aims and expected results of the inquiry;
   b) A description of the coaching assignment(s) or coaching relationship(s) central to the inquiry.

   c) Explorative questions and hypotheses expressing what
      participants are most curious about in relation to the dynamic
      between 'self' and 'client' – and their own responses to that
      dynamic specifying a possible relation to client themes or
      dynamics.
   With this proposal, the participant seeks support from one of the
   AMEC supervisors, who will then act as a tutor of the reflective
   inquiry.
3 (Over the next 3–6 months): Execution of the Reflective Inquiry,
   in which participants explore their own coaching practice in detail,
   bearing in mind the inquiry proposal.
4 (Conclusion of the Inquiry): Reflection on the completion of the
   Inquiry and articulation of the results of the inquiry. Special attention is devoted to:
   a) Reflections on the self as a coach-in-context, including a reflec-
      tion on the question why this particular context and these par-
      ticular clients;
   b) Reflections on one's personal strengths and limitations as a
      coach, including an answer to the question of which obstacles
      or limitations were overcome during the inquiry process;
   c) Reflections on one's possible future development as a coach,
      including a possibly changing context and client base, with a
      time horizon of at least 5 years.

Participants produce a 'reflective inquiry report' of 10,000 to 12,000
words that describes the complete learning process outlined above. In
that essay they demonstrate that they are capable of:
- successfully completing a full reflective inquiry process in relation
  to their own practice, making use of qualitative analytical
  methodology;
- integrating the theoretical models underpinning their coaching
  practice and relating them to their own personal development;
  and
- identifying and analysing their own behavioural patterns as a coach,
  and relating them to their own practice, and drawing relevant
  conclusions based on observations and the application of theory.

9.2.3 How coach education addresses the various areas of competence
The main challenge with coach education is, in my experience, to
reconcile the outcomes of education with the required qualifications

of a coach. Traditionally, when designing training programmes, we specify learning outcomes that should be as measurable as possible. It often turns out that the aspects that are easiest to measure (such as increase in knowledge or experience of specific activities) are not always the most important qualifications. If you ask coaches themselves what they benefited from most within their education, they mention mainly practice and personal feedback. However, the results of this type of training practice are not easy to measure. The best way to measure the skills and insight that coaches obtain from practice and feedback is, in my view, through the application of a good *accreditation process*, which is discussed in the following section.

If we look at the areas of competence in section 9.1, we notice that education primarily addresses the 'outer layers' of the onion: knowledge, strategic skills and specific interventions.
- Knowledge and strategic skills grow by reading and talking about them, and a test in these areas is easy to design.
- Behavioural skills and interventions can be practised, and improve on the basis of feedback and suggestions.
- Values, however, and the attitude of the coach to some extent, are much less easy to 'train in', because they are based at a deeper level. With the aid of discussion groups and self-exploration, however, it is possible to generate demonstrable differences in values, as expressed in attitude, choices and behaviour. Meta-analysis shows that the effects of moral education are significant, albeit small ($d \approx 0.25$; see Schlaefli, Rest & Thoma, 1985 and Lipsey & Wilson, 1993).

In designing the AMEC, we attempted to make a difference at the deeper levels as well, by devoting close attention to reflection on the coach's own standards and values (by means of reflective tasks), and development of the coach's own reflective capacity (by means of reading material and practice in meta-reflections and displaying acquired skills).

9.3 Coach accreditation

The coaching profession has not yet reached a point where it can describe objective criteria that demonstrably lead to better coaching. There is, however, a general consensus on the need for a code of ethics and on the so-called 'common factors' (see Chapter 3) as objectively established effective ingredients of coaching. Otherwise, we will have to rely on review by fellow coaches, and preferably review by several different colleagues, because each new coach will have a slightly different opinion. It helps to have prior agreement on the ethical principles, including the code of conduct, and on the assessment criteria to be applied.

This peer review for and by fellow coaches is usually referred to as *accreditation*. Coach accreditation can lead to stringent quality standards if the assessment is rigorous and the accreditors grant approval only if they are all persuaded that the candidate in question meets all of the applicable accreditation criteria[2].

9.3.1 Accreditation criteria

In connection with the coach competences outlined above, we at Ashridge use the following seven *accreditation criteria*.

1 *Theory*: knowledge and understanding of theoretical concepts underpinning coaching.
2 *Relationship*: establishment and maintenance of an effective working alliance within the coaching relationship.
3 *Behaviour*: the application of specific coaching skills, identifying creative options and supporting by means of coaching strategies.
4 *Assessment, contracts and boundaries*: clarity of analysis of client and organisation context. Clarity of contract and understanding of boundary issues.
5 *(Organisation) Change*: understanding of organisational change. Takes into account social, economic and political realities, systems and cultures of the organisation.
6 *Effectiveness*: demonstrating effectiveness in coaching interventions, and monitoring the effect of coaching on the client.
7 *Self-awareness and professionalism*: demonstrating the capacity for:
   a) self-reflection and awareness of the coach's own coaching processes and styles;

---

[2] At Ashridge we have accredited 45 executive coaches in the past four years using this new process. Around a quarter of them were told to come back later on submitting their material and a further quarter were not accredited on the day itself but were asked to come back with one or more new pieces of work.

b) registering subject-matter concerning power and identity;

c) acting in accordance with ethical principles.

The accreditation criteria are always measured on a scale of 1 (demonstration of poor or limited competence) to 5 (demonstration of broad and far-reaching competence).

Besides submitting three detailed pieces of work (case study with log book, tape recording with verbatim and live coaching – see below) which meet the above accreditation criteria, an Ashridge Accredited Coach must meet the following *entry criteria*.

1 The coach must display good listening behaviour and be able to maintain concentration while listening over extended periods.

2 The coach must have demonstrable skills in working with people from different levels of seniority within organisations.

3 The coach must enable clients to achieve their own desired outcome themselves, without accepting personal responsibility for the outcome of coaching.

4 The coach must be able to justify when being able or unable to work with a client, depending on the previous relationship with the client. The coach must also be able to assess when an issue lies outside their area of expertise, for example when a referral to a specific type of counselling is necessary, e.g. for addiction or relationship therapy.

5 In a broader sense, the coach must be able to decide when to continue independently and autonomously and when to seek support. Compared with some other consultancy activities, coaching can sometimes be a solitary profession, if only because the work is done at a distance from colleagues, sources of assistance, or the coachee's organisation. Moreover, the client's expectations are often high but incompletely revealed, so are largely unknown at the outset.

6 An accredited coach should commit him/herself to a clear code of conduct with the aim of monitoring ethical standards for coaching and to inform and protect coachees, customers and other interested parties. An example of a suitable code of conduct is the Ashridge code for coaches in Appendix E of this book.

7 Experience of individual coaching, demonstrated by at least 30 sessions of intensive one-to-one (including coaching) conversations over the past two years. This does not include psychometric

feedback conversations and conversations within the context of a managerial relationship. At least 20 of the 30 sessions must consist of coaching conversations within an ongoing contract for a minimum of three sessions. Candidates are requested to produce a summary of coaching hours (including dates and client details) over the past two years, or over a shorter period if that yields sufficient hours.

8   An accredited and practising coach should, in my view, make use of individual or group supervision at least once a quarter, or more frequently if more coaching is undertaken. A ratio of 1 hour of supervision to every five hours of coaching or two hours a month in a busy practice is what we expect of accredited coaches. Candidates are requested to produce a summary of supervision hours (including dates and details concerning the nature of the supervision) over the past two years, or over a shorter period if that yields sufficient hours.

9   If psychometric instruments are used, a level B qualification from the British Psychological Society (or the equivalent in other countries) and experience and specific qualifications for the use of each psychometric instrument. The same applies to 360° feedback processes: the specific instrument must be used only if the coach is appropriately qualified.

10 Coaches are asked to keep full client case notes relating to every coaching conversation. This is helpful if questions or misunderstandings arise in subsequent sessions, but it is primarily an instrument of continuing professional reflection and preparation for forthcoming sessions. Some obvious areas for making notes are:
a) information about the client;
b) information about other interested parties and the organisational context;
c) a summary of the questions and issues raised during the session;
d) critical moments during the coaching;
e) the working alliance and other processes within the coaching relationship;
f) results, aims and learning outcomes achieved in the coaching relationship;
g) different coaching approaches used and how they fit in with underlying theory or other presuppositions;
h) learning and evaluation of outcomes.

Session notes need not be produced on the accreditation day, although we assume that other materials submitted, especially the case study and the verbatim transcript, are based on those notes.

Once a month we hold a three-hour workshop to prepare for accreditation, at which:
1 peer review takes place on the basis of the materials available to date; and
2 participants practise live coaching with each other and obtain feedback from one of our 11 accreditors.

9.3.2 Accreditation process
Part 1 – prior to accreditation
Prior to accreditation, the coach makes sure that he meets the initial criteria outlined above and prepares the following materials:
1 The accreditation process starts with a *self-assessment* by the coach. This is an appraisal of his own competence on the seven general assessment criteria (accreditation criteria) above. The candidate coach rates himself on a scale from 1 to 5 and gives a single-paragraph justification of the rating awarded. Together with the other material, the self-assessment should be submitted two weeks before the accreditation practicum.
2 The *case study*[3] should relate to a recent coachee whose coaching journey has been completed or who is in the course of a substantial number of sessions. The case study should be 4,000 to 6,000 words in length and based on the notes made by the coach during sessions with the client in question.
3 A *tape recording* of a recent coaching conversation, comprising twenty minutes of consecutive coaching as far as possible. This may be with the same client as in the case study. The recording should be accompanied by a written reflection, so the following materials are required:
    a) A tape, mp3 or video recording of 20 minutes of live coaching;
    b) A *verbatim transcript*[4] of the recording ('verbatim' means literally word for word, i.e. including repetitions, 'ums and ers', and preferably indications of listening signals, laughter and interruptions);

---

[3] For an example of a case study, see Appendix C.
[4] For a shorter example (ten minutes) of a verbatim transcript of part of a real coaching conversation, see Appendix D.

c) A brief introduction giving background information about the context, the client, and the session in question;

d) A written commentary on the recorded coaching highlighting what the session demonstrates.

e) Written feedback from the client (optional).

4 A concise coaching curriculum vitae or the coach's own coaching profile.

5 A log of at least 30 sessions of coaching over the past two years (see entry criterion 7 above).

6 A log of at least eight supervision sessions over the past two years (see entry criterion 8 above).

All materials should be submitted two weeks before the accreditation practicum and are assessed by two or three members of the accreditors' panel, who will also be present during the practicum itself.

Part 2 – the accreditation practicum

The actual accreditation process starts with a live coaching conversation lasting 20 minutes. An assessment group consisting of two or three accreditors and one to three fellow coaches also taking the practicum will observe the coaching conversation from another room via video screens. All assessments are made against the coaching accreditation criteria and the candidate receives full feedback at the end of the session. Candidates are therefore expected to act as peer assessors of other coaches as well as undergoing the assessment themselves.

A typical individual timetable during the practicum is as follows:

9.00 Welcome the candidate; check that the materials submitted are complete and explain the process and procedure.

9.15 Welcome the coachee (often a candidate for a later practicum who wishes to experience the process in this role first). The coachee is welcomed in another room and settles in there prior to the live coaching.

9.25 Start of the live coaching, which is videorecorded and observed from an adjoining CCTV room. The candidate is given the tape to take away afterwards.

9.45 Assessment discussion of the live coaching, with scoring on the accreditation criteria.

10.15 Assessment discussion of the case study and verbatim transcript, ending with scoring on the accreditation criteria.

Candidates often receive the accreditors' detailed comments in the margins of their work when their documents are returned.

11.00   End.

There are usually several candidates, so the time taken is correspondingly longer, with the live coaching and feedback sessions taking place as a group, and feedback on the case study and verbatim transcript individually.

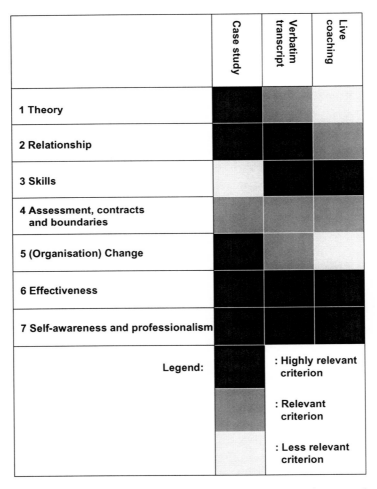

Figure 9.3 *A summary of the 7 accreditation criteria and how relevant they are to the three main pieces of work submitted by the coachee during the accreditation process.*

The table above (Figure 9.3) shows how the three main pieces of work in accreditation measure up differently against different assessment criteria. Clearly, live coaching places most emphasis on coaching behaviour, while the verbatim transcript provides an opportunity to look at the building of the relationship, and the case study provides additional information concerning theory and organisational change. The table also shows that the most important assessment criteria are probably:

- (6) *Effectiveness*, which involves reaching the outcomes of the coaching contract and helping with change and movement for the coachee; and
- (7) *Self-awareness and professionalism*, which involves being able to reflect on the coach's own coaching relationships and coaching interventions, including such things as ethics and cultural diversity.

In this form of coach accreditation we are very aware that we are using extremely subjective measures, the scores and opinions of the randomly assigned accreditors, all of whom are very experienced coaches themselves. As a test of the accreditation process itself, we had ten different Ashridge accreditors read through a case study chosen completely at random. All gave their scores on the 7 accreditation criteria (see Figure 9.4).

Clearly, the mean scores and range of scores given by our ten accreditors vary considerably. Some are gentle or positive in their assessment (e.g. A2 and A10), others much more critical (e.g. A1 and A9, who would have had the case study re-done). It is also noticeable that some give very uniform scores on the different dimensions (A8 always scores between 3 and 4), while others show a much wider spread of scores (A9 scores between 1 and 4.5). It will really make a difference, therefore, which accreditor you get as a coach. However, these differences become smaller through comparison with the other parts of the accreditation process, and the conversations held between accreditors.

In addition, it emerged that the scores in the table correspond more than might appear at first sight: if I calculate the correlation coefficients of each pair of scores and then take the average, the scores

	A1	A2	A3	A4	A5	A6	A7	A8	A9	A10	M	SD
1. Theory	3	5	4	4	4.5	5	4.5	4	4.5	4	4.25	0.59
2. Relationship	2	3.5	3	3	4	3	3	3.5	2	3.5	3.05	0.64
3. Skills	3	4	3	3	2.5	4	3.5	4	3	4	3.40	0.57
4. Assessment, contracts, boundaries	3	5	4	4	4	4	4	4	2.5	5	3.95	0.76
5. (Organisation) Change	2	3.5	3	2	3	2.5	4	3	4	4	3.10	0.77
6. Effectiveness	2	3.5	3	3	3	4	3	3.5	2	4.5	3.15	0.78
7. Self-awarenessand professionalism	2	3	2	2	2.5	2	3	4	1	3	2.55	0.83
M	2.43	3.93	3.29	3.00	3.36	3.50	3.57	3.71	2.71	4.00		
SD	0.53	0.79	0.49	0.82	0.80	1.04	0.61	0.39	1.22	0.65		

Figure 9.4 *Scores of ten different Ashridge accreditors (A1–A10) on all seven accreditation criteria, for the same case study, with mean values and standard deviations.*

appear to correlate on average to the extent of $r = 0.56$, so there is indeed a substantial degree of correspondence in the interpretation of the seven criteria by these ten accreditors.

Part 3 – maintaining accreditation

After obtaining accreditation, coaches are entered in a recognised coaching register such as, in our case, the Ashridge Accredited Coaches Register (AACR). Maintenance of accreditation is guaranteed on condition that the coach continues his or her own coaching practice and undergoes regular supervision.

One way to implement this is via an annual re-registration process which requires a summary of coaching and supervision activities undertaken, with certain minimum requirements, such as:

1 a minimum of 20 hours' activity as an executive coach;
2 a minimum of 5 supervision conversations, individually or in groups;
3 a minimum of 5 hours of other continuing professional development activities related to coaching.

In addition, it is usual to organise some form of 're-accreditation' activity once every five years. This is more a conversation with fellow coaches with the aim of professional development, than an accreditation practicum as described above. It is sometimes organised on the basis of a tape recording of a recent coaching conversation.

9.3.3 How coach accreditation addresses the various areas of competence
Coach accreditation is an ideal way to assess the full range of competencies of a coach. The accreditation criteria have been chosen in such a way as to cover the whole spectrum of coach competencies.

- The criteria of Behaviour, Relationship, (Organisational) Change and Theory cover different specific areas of competence of the coach (see section 9.1). Coaches are therefore assessed on all of these dimensions.
- The criteria of Assessment/contracts/boundaries, Effectiveness and Self-awareness/professionalism measure more reflective competencies. They assess the quality of an (internal) 'conversation' about the coach's own competencies. They therefore focus mainly on the coach's own attitudes, values and convictions (see section 9.1).

With a range of coach competencies as broad as the human personality itself, running from values and convictions to specific behaviours, it is not surprising that three of the criteria for testing these competencies are in fact 'meta-criteria', which look at how coaches themselves relate to their own competencies.

- The criterion of *Assessment/contracts/boundaries* (4) looks at the way in which coaches reflect on the boundaries of their own professional activities, and the embedding of their own work in an organisational context.
- The criterion of *Effectiveness* (6) looks at the way in which coaches reflect on the outcome of their own professional activities.
- The criterion of *Self-awareness/professionalism* (7) looks at the way in which coaches reflect on their own reflection (i.e. an appraisal

of 'meta-reflection') and deeper-lying values related to power, diversity, identity and ethics.

Accreditation is most effective when it is used for assessing behaviour and attitude and for developing ethical competencies: the accreditors observe each coach *in vivo*, and invite them to explore and assess their own approach. In fact, accreditation is a unique opportunity for a coach to receive feedback on their own way of working with genuine, paying coachees. I am therefore an advocate of regular re-accreditation, however expensive and time-intensive the process may be.

Summary: education and accreditation of the executive coach

The **areas of competence** of a coach are exceptionally wide, covering the entire personality spectrum.

1   **Beliefs** may differ widely, but confidence in the coachee's potential and openness to convictions other than those of the coach frequently recur.
2   The **attitude** is one of respect for the coachee and involvement in the coachee's learning process.
3   The **areas of knowledge** are very wide-ranging, from organisational change and change management, psychotherapy and communication, through personal development, coaching models and interventions, to self-knowledge.
4   The **skills** are also wide-ranging: building a relationship, coordinating expectations, recognising interactional patterns and mental models, and dealing with emotions.
5   In the description of **coach behaviour** I adopt Heron's model, which distinguishes six styles: directing, informing, challenging, discovering, supporting and releasing.

Coach education focuses on developing (a substantial) part of the spectrum described above. Types of coach education range in practice from training courses lasting a few days to academic masters programmes. The latter can be expected to address the full spectrum of areas of competence.

The design of an existing masters (MSc) programme is outlined in this chapter.

A process of **coach accreditation** can be a good way to test the quality of a coach, i.e. to certify or validate coaches. A coach accreditation process normally specifies the materials that the coach must submit, the assessment criteria, the accreditation process itself, and how to maintain accreditation once it has been achieved.

The design of a successful accreditation process is outlined in this chapter.

Chapter 10
Continuing Professional Development of the Executive Coach

'You're not working, you're just sitting there listening!', a client told me recently. Such assessments of the coach's work are found not only among clients, but also among coaches themselves. They feel honoured to be doing the work; sometimes, indeed, they find it too much of an honour for their 'low' levels of competence or qualification (see some of the doubts of less experienced coaches in Appendix A). Client and coach are both easily tempted to underestimate the work and then may lose sight of the fact that individual support by means of coaching conversations is a solitary and vulnerable activity[1]. The coach is alone in the room with the client, and feels internal and external pressure to achieve something with that client, without knowing exactly how, or if he or she can do that, or 'what on earth' is going to happen. This is very stressful, and a first step in professional development is often to face up to that stress and seek help. Before we look at potential sources of help for the coach, I will start by outlining the various forces to which the coach is exposed.

We can use Porter's well-known 'Model of 5 forces' to map the pressures on coaches to some extent (Porter, 1979; see also the four-force model used by Fineman, 1985). We can differentiate five different forces that exert pressure on the practice of coaching, and hence on actual coaching conversations:

1 the 'new entrants' or the arrival of competitors, in this case the other, competing aspects of the coach's life and work;

---

[1] Although the opposite is also possible of course, and is not uncommon: boundless over-estimation of their own abilities or a sense of omnipotence in coaches. But the cause is probably exactly the same as the cause of underestimating one's abilities: the *stress* that comes with coaching.

2 the 'negotiating position of suppliers' or professional requirements needed in order to act as a coach – in a nutshell, professional accountability and accreditation;

3 the 'tensions between existing players', in this case the coaching conversations and everything that takes place in them;

4 the 'negotiating position of buyers' or clients of coaching, i.e. the coachees and their expectations of the coach; and

5 the 'threat of substitutes' or other colleagues and coaches.

Summing this up in a single figure (Figure 10.1), I arrive at five different areas of potential anxiety and stress. The main aim of continuing professional development is to enable coaches to handle, and continue to handle, these forces and to maintain and enhance the quality of their own performance. Factors that appear to be important in continuing professional development are:

1 new knowledge and skills, or maintaining knowledge and skills;

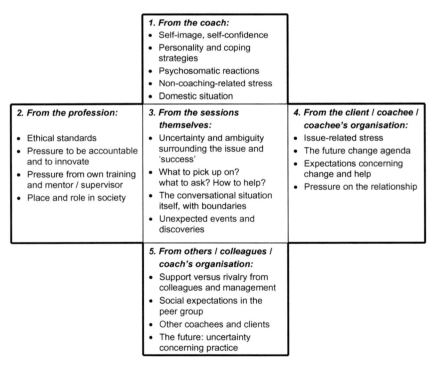

1. From the coach:
• Self-image, self-confidence
• Personality and coping strategies
• Psychosomatic reactions
• Non-coaching-related stress
• Domestic situation

2. From the profession:
• Ethical standards
• Pressure to be accountable and to innovate
• Pressure from own training and mentor / supervisor
• Place and role in society

3. From the sessions themselves:
• Uncertainty and ambiguity surrounding the issue and 'success'
• What to pick up on? what to ask? How to help?
• The conversational situation itself, with boundaries
• Unexpected events and discoveries

4. From the client / coachee / coachee's organisation:
• Issue-related stress
• The future change agenda
• Expectations concerning change and help
• Pressure on the relationship

5. From others / colleagues / coach's organisation:
• Support versus rivalry from colleagues and management
• Social expectations in the peer group
• Other coachees and clients
• The future: uncertainty concerning practice

Figure 10.1 *Five sources of possible stressors for the coach.*

2 space to process and reflect on events and situations that occur in practice; and

3 gaining a third, more objective position with a new perspective on the coach's own work (precisely in the way that coaching helps to relieve a coachee's stress, but now for the coach).

There are three forms of continuing professional development, all three of which can be immensely valuable for coaches: individual, with fellow coaches, and with a supervisor or supervisors. In the following sections I give an introduction to each of these three forms.

10.1 Individual professional development: reflective practice

Individual professional development is in a sense the safest but also the most solitary. The coach embarks alone on a quest for new knowledge and skills, possibly in consultation with a guru or mentor. The coach decides how far to go, and in which direction, on his or her path of development. Individual professional development may involve literature study, a reflection on the coach's own coaching sessions by means of tape recordings and evaluation forms, or participation in workshops and lectures. But only if the coach practises with real coaching conversations or role-play will those activities go further than just self-development.

Individual development for coaches can begin before and after every coaching conversation, when they read through their notes one more time and add some more observations. Many professional coaches write up a log after each session, an account of the session that takes the issues raised and their own actions in the session one reflective step further. The *coaching logbook* is often a good starting point for supervision relating to the session in question.

In chapter 11 I provide a starting point for individual professional development by means of literature study. I have selected 12 inspiring books which I believe hold useful lessons for coaches, and state how they influenced or changed me as a coach.

10.2 Co-coaching and peer consultation

Professional development with fellow coaches is of a very different nature compared to individual development. The coach is exposed to the observations and interpretations of professional colleagues and is, in a sense, 'coached' by them to become a better coach. The development activity is two-sided, and geared towards learning both in the role of coachee and in the role of coach. It is still relatively safe, because 'co-coaches' generally go easy on each other: they know that the roles will soon be reversed and that they will be under scrutiny themselves.

An advantage of co-coaching is the mutuality of the contract, which makes it easier to find time for it (it benefits both colleagues!) and usually ensures that no money need change hands. That mutuality is also a disadvantage, because it may restrict the other person in their freedom to use coaching interventions and may even make certain disruptive non-coaching interventions more likely, such as suddenly starting to talk about one's self while listening to your coachee. I believe therefore that in co-coaching it is a good idea to agree on firm boundaries within which the coaching will take place; for example, by working in one coach/coachee combination for the first 45 minutes, then having a 15-minute discussion, and then spending the next hour in the same way but with the roles reversed.

The main advantage of peer support from fellow coaches is also its main disadvantage, therefore: the mutuality in the relationship during the consultation contrasts with the relationship that the consultation deals with, the coaching relationship. In coaching, the roles of coach and coachee are sharply divided and different. That division of roles probably contributes greatly to the value of coaching. It ensures that you work with someone whom you trust and respect, who is placed fully at your disposal, about whom you know little and with whom (at least in theory) you are not in competition. The fact that you do sometimes feel competitive with your coach can also be a part of coaching, while forms of rivalry among co-coaches are more difficult to discuss. In general, trust, safety and freedom are less strong in co-coaching because no professional boundaries are imposed on that relationship.

A good way to handle this in peer coaching groups is by freeing up one of the coaches present to take on a supervisory role (De Haan, 2005). This coach can concentrate fully on the other coaches' learning without personally contributing issues to that meeting. This role calls for great discipline in a peer-only setting and is better taken on by an external, often paid, supervisor. In this case it is called group supervision – see section 10.3.2 below.

10.3 Coaching supervision

Note: like terms such as mentoring and coaching, different practitioners use the word 'supervision' to refer to different activities. In Germany and the Netherlands, the word is widely used as a synonym for coaching. In this book I use supervision always in the specific sense of supporting helping professionals, i.e. coaches, consultants or therapists, in the practice of their profession, with regards to specific assignments and client relationships (as in Hawkins & Shohet, 1989). Supervision is a learning activity in which coaches learn with regards to existing work with clients, by systematic reflection and by practice. Participating in supervision relates to attending a coach training programme more or less in the same way as consultancy relates to training in other professions. The supervisor is more of a consultant than a tutor or trainer. Little research has been carried out into supervision as yet. Lambert & Arnold (1987) summarise the early research and Chapter 8 of this book refers to more recent articles.

Professional development with a supervisor is often a kind of 'mentoring' (see Chapter 1) for coaches. The coach is exposed to the scrutiny of a more experienced colleague with the (mutually agreed) expectation that this coach will be honest and open in feedback. This may be a cause of anxiety – just as coaching may very well make the coachee anxious – whether supervision takes place individually or in groups.

Proctor (1988) describes three functions of professional supervision and of continuing professional development more generally. The above forms of professional development (individual development and co-coaching) cover mainly the first and last of these three, while in my experience only supervision can provide a sufficiently safe environment for all three.

1 *Formative* – Further developing skills, learning from others and from feedback, and broadening one's own potential roles and professional practice.
2 *Normative* – Laying down and reinforcing professional standards and best practice. This is a 'quality control' or peer review of professional coaches, by a qualified and recognised authority.

3 *Restorative* – Supporting coaches in order to enable them to face
   and remain working with difficult issues or emotionally charged
   situations; a safe place where coaches can distance themselves
   from the anxieties in their practice, start to process doubts and
   anxieties and reflect on their own personal patterns and
   projections.

For my part, it was mainly in supervision that I learned how powerful
and omnipresent the phenomenon of 'transference' is in coaching –
and in other relationships. It is often extraordinary to see how a
coachee's transference may pervade the supervision session, without
the coachee being present, i.e. only mediated by the coach. Transference phenomena enable coach and supervisor to 'open more doors' to
the coachee, i.e. to generate genuinely new and unanticipated perspectives on the coach's clients and the material that they contribute.

A useful and widely adopted model of coach supervision was provided
by Hawkins & Shohet (1989). It has become known as the *seven-eyed
supervision model*, because it gives seven different perspectives on a
single account contributed by a 'supervisee'.
1 The subject matter or coaching situation contributed: what the
   coachee brought to the coach and how he or she did that.
2 The coach in that situation, including coaching strategies,
   approaches and interventions.
3 The relationship and the process in that situation, i.e. what happened between coach and coachee.
4 The counter-transference of the coach in that situation, i.e. the
   coach's reaction to the situation.
5 The transference here and now: relationships between the situation
   contributed and the situation now.
6 The counter-transference of the supervisor now, in this situation,
   as a result of the contributions and the process now.
7 The broader context such as the organisational context of coachee,
   coach and supervisor, with associated roles and organisational or
   political repercussions.

Simply running through these seven perspectives during a supervision
session provides a wealth of new insights for the coach contributing
the situation. It is an elegant model. However, in my view, it does not
bring out the full symmetry of the situation or all of the levels at which

transference can 'reverberate'. In truth, the reverberations of transference between conversational platforms do remind one of the infectious spreading of hubris within certain Greek families that provide protagonists for the tragedies. For this reason I believe a good description of the phenomenon of transference should allow for the contagious linking of a multitude of arenas and perspectives.

Following on from these considerations and because I myself often organise supervision of coaches in groups, i.e. with four to eight participating coaches, and with more roles than simply coach and supervisor, I have developed my own version of the Hawkins & Shohet model (1989), which is easy to remember and to apply in groups and, like the other model, yields a wealth of new insights. This version mainly emphasises the different relationships at issue in supervision, whether or not they are in the room at the time, and the many forms of transference that can reverberate within and between those relationships, during the 'here-and-now' of the supervision itself. I call this my *seven-ring model*, by analogy with Hawkins & Shohet's seven eyes. Each ring stands for a *working relationship*[2] that can be viewed from three perspectives:
1 what the 'client' contributes to the relationship (including transference);
2 what the other person, i.e. the coach, supervisor, colleague, facilitator, etc., contributes to the relationship (including countertransference); and
3 what happens between them at every moment (in other words, the 'process' or the co-created relationship).

Since there are seven rings in total, there are three times seven, i.e. a total of twenty-one perspectives on each account that the 'supervisee' brings to supervision. It is true that this is an explosion of perspectives compared with the Hawkins & Shohet model (1989), but it is still easy to understand because the rings are interlinked, forming part of the same *chain* of working relationships. The first ring is entirely within the coachee's organisation and the last ring connects all of those involved with their own organisation and with other working relationships, and so forms a natural end point for supervision. These are the seven rings that can be considered during (group) supervision.

---

[2] The ring has been a symbol of a relationship since time immemorial, as in a wedding ring.

1 Relevant relationships within the coachee's organisation, such as those between the coachee's immediate team members.
2 The relationships that link the coachee with colleagues, or with the coachee's own organisation.
3 The relationship that links the coachee and the coach, i.e. the essential ring that is the main focus of the coaching, as well as the supervision.
4 The relationship that links the coach and their own supervisor, or one of the fellow coaches in a supervision group, by means of a coaching conversation here and now in the supervision.
5 The relationships that link this supervisor or these supervisors with their own supervisor, or with fellow coaches in the supervision group.
6 The relationships between those supervisors and their own supervisor (and so on), or the relationship that individual members of the supervision group have with the facilitator of the supervision group.
7 The 'matrix' of relationships that each of these people have outside this specific chain of relationships, both individually (such as other work and personal relationships of each of the people concerned) and in common (such as those with the social contexts around them). Parental figures and other important early relationships will play a key role in this ring, as they are known to be vital sources of deeply ingrained transference patterns.

This chain of coaching relationships is depicted in Figure 10.2.

The strength of this approach comes to the fore in situations where emotions are passed on from one ring to the next, often because the emotions cannot be dealt with adequately in a given ring/relationship and are therefore 'carried forward' to the next relationship/ring. Something I have often seen myself in supervision is an 'upwards' movement of certain strong emotions and anxieties; for example, certain tensions within the coachee's organisation. The latter may lead to strongly felt but poorly understood tensions between the coach and coachee. The coach may emerge from such a situation with a coachee with an uncomfortable feeling that prompts a referral of this very coaching conversation to the coach's own supervisor. During the supervision, the supervisor or one of the observers notices a certain tension in the room. If the supervisor or observer is able to put a name to that tension, and to relate it in some way to the coaching situation and thereby indirectly to the coachee's organisation, we often observe a sigh of relief and evident relaxation in the coach/contributor. Finally, a lingering feeling of unease has been pinned down, and finally the coach understands something of his or her own emotions and motives in bringing this particular situation, this conversation and this client, to supervision.

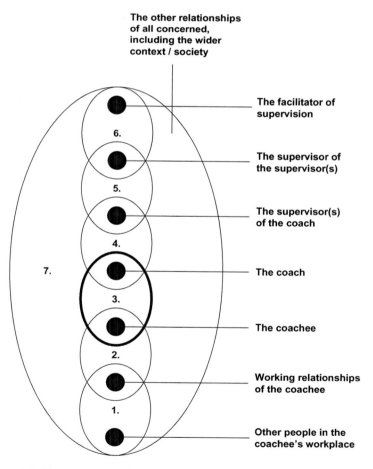

Figure 10.2 *The seven-ring model: a supervision model that devotes attention to (transference) phenomena which 'reverberate' from one coaching situation to another.*

Sometimes it doesn't work that way. Certain tensions are not recognised or named during supervision either, and only later, when the supervisor is in conversation with others, perhaps their own supervisor or coach, is it possible to make sense of what was an uncomfortable meeting. The original client and the original organisation can still benefit from that observation; for example, if it is 'reflected back' by the supervisor during a subsequent supervision session, so that the coach can clarify things for the coachee in turn.

The specialist fields of coaching and supervision, viewed from this perspective, resemble a kind of hydraulic system which pumps unpalatable and poorly understood emotions upwards, always with a slight delay (because they are 'off-line'), and then pumps hypotheses and new dawning insight back down towards the coachee's organisation.

Harold Searles (1955), who wrote at length about the phenomena of supervision, also discovered that there are in fact two ways in which emotions can be pumped upwards (i.e. from ring 1, to ring 2, to ring 3, or starting at, say, ring 3, and going up to ring 4, to ring 5, etc.).

1 *Unconscious identification* – in which the coachee starts to behave in the same way as others in the organisation; the coach starts to behave like the coachee, the supervisor like the coach, and so on. I myself like to call this form an *inverse projection* (see De Haan, 2005, Chapter 12), because it is in fact a change of role between two relationships: the linking person behaves in one situation as the recipient of certain behaviour and certain emotions, and in the second situation starts to act as the source of that same behaviour and those same emotions. The classical example of unconscious identification is that of the father who scolds his older son, who then goes on – often using exactly the same posture, tone of voice and gestures – to scold his younger brother or, if he doesn't have one at hand, a pet or even an inanimate object.

2 *Complementary unconscious identification* – in which the coachee displays certain behaviours or susceptibilities from the organisational context in the coaching conversation, triggering a particular response in the coach, who then goes on to display the very same response in the treatment of the coachee and this conversation in supervision. I like to term this a *parallel projection* (see De Haan, 2005, Chapter 12), because the protagonists here continue to

display the same behaviour, and continue to act in the same way, from conversation to conversation. A classical manifestation is the coachee who talks despondently about his or her own work situation, where many people are despondent, whereupon the coach starts to feel despondent and can't see the point any more, not even in talking about this organisation and this client at supervision – if the coach does so nevertheless, the feeling of despondency returns just as before, and that emotion becomes contagious for everyone in the supervision group. Only when someone explicitly points out that the atmosphere has become despondent or 'flat' or 'heavy', can they reflect on that fact and identify a link with the coachee and the coachee's issues.

10.3.1 Process of individual supervision

Individual supervision is a form of individual *mentoring*, because it involves coaches bringing their practical issues to someone who is both their coach and their colleague. The supervisor is therefore a sort of mentor who can both use coaching interventions and reflect in a more advisory fashion on the coach's practice and the issues raised. Contracts and forms of discussion in individual supervision are therefore very similar to what is usual in coaching and mentoring. In a conversation lasting an hour and a half to two hours, a variety of practical issues and situations can be discussed. The supervisor is often looking for parallels between this supervision situation here and now and the situations contributed to supervision, and also for parallels amongst those various contributed coaching situations, because those parallels and resonances often say more about the person of this coach and about what he or she unconsciously brings to their own coaching conversations.

Individual supervision is ideal as a place for coaches to bring their case notes, coaching logbook or marketing materials, because they can count on more one-on-one time than during group supervision. It is also a good idea for individual supervision to work on the basis of audio video recordings or literal transcripts of conversations, if only because recordings and accounts of this type provide more information to the supervisor, including information that coaches would not bring to supervision on their own account. There is evidence in the literature (Lawton, 2000; see also Chapter 8) that coaches do not bring all of their most pertinent issues to supervision, and that it is sometimes too painful for them or they have too much awe for the supervisor to discuss more vulnerable issues. Signs of these more vulnerable areas may sometimes be picked up by the supervisor, and recordings of actual coaching sessions sometimes provide useful material to that end. It is often sufficient to listen to just a few minutes of recording, which may provide enough material for many minutes of supervision.

Individual supervision is a very specific conversational relationship with its own objectives and techniques. Due to the nature of the relationship and what is discussed in it, there is certainly a risk of overstepping certain boundaries, which would make the supervision less effective.

- Supervision is more than giving advice. The intention is not that supervisors merely explain how they would handle the problem outlined, or constantly provide advice on how to tackle things differently or better. What it is, is a *coaching relationship* in which supervisors mainly help clients (coaches) to make sense of their own issues and their own professional practices. It is important that supervisors continue to facilitate the coaches' thinking and do not dominate the conversations with their own thinking.
- Supervision is more than coaching because, due to the nature of the relationship and the issues raised, the supervisor can be expected to voice their opinions more than a coach would do. Individual supervision is therefore a combination of coaching and advising, as in professional mentoring relationships.
- Supervision is not therapy. Because a coachee, a coach and a supervisor are always present during supervision (although not all physically in the room!), three people who also have 'coaching-type' links with others in turn, there are, as has already been mentioned, many opportunities for 'resonance' or the joint discovery of insights into other relationships, via the fascinating phenomenon of transference. This is in fact the territory of therapy, so supervisors should be aware that even small interventions may lead them into very personal areas, which bear limited relation to the task at hand. A therapeutic conversation can even be an unconscious 'defence against supervision' by the coach. Take for instance coaches who finds therapy less anxiety-provoking than talking about their own coachees with a more experienced colleague. Hawkins & Shohet (1989) provide helpful ideas for ways to monitor the boundary with therapy.

It is not strictly necessary for the supervisor to be a more experienced colleague who has notched up more 'flying hours' than the coach. The most important thing here is the division of roles between mentor and mentee, in which the supervisor explicitly assumes the role during sessions of someone who can 'think along' with the coach on the basis of their own experience and whose own issues are not under discussion here.

A major drawback of a process of *individual* supervision is that the participating coach does not take a coaching role during the supervision itself, at least not to any great extent. The process mainly involves looking jointly at the actions of the coach, as undertaken at other places and times, with other people. It is good for the supervisor to be aware of the exclusive 'coach role' that is all too easily adopted during individual supervision. It is difficult to lay that role down temporarily and to invite the coachee to self-coach, for example by asking the coachee how *they* would coach with that issue, or by embarking on a role play in which the supervisor plays the role of the client's coachee. Both methods are much less effective in practice than a genuine live coaching session, for which you need another participant, and which therefore takes you into the territory of group supervision.

10.3.2 Process of group supervision

In group supervision it is much easier to map out and explore a longer chain of coaching relationships. In my view, this makes it a better instrument than all of those outlined previously in this chapter as a way of exploring the coaching relationship, including transference phenomena and relational patterns. A method of group supervision, which focuses primarily on exploring the coaching relationship, is as follows. The facilitator/supervisor asks the group of coaches present[3] to start by giving a brief account of what it is they want to contribute,

---

[3] In group supervision, the ideal configuration is a group of three to eight coaches and one supervisor. It is still possible to work well in a larger group, for example with an inner and outer circle, where the coaches in the inner circle act as supervisors and those in the outer circle merely as observers. Even as an observing coach, you can still learn a lot from supervision; indeed, it may be easier to 'co-resonate' and to pick up transference phenomena in the situation. In that case, therefore, it is important to bring observations from the outer circle into the inner circle at set times.

and whether they would prefer to work as coach or coachee, bearing the following in mind.

- The role of coachee is best suited to those who have specific issues arising in particular (and preferably recent) coaching conversations. This role gives the participant ample opportunity to contribute the issue and to discuss it in detail.
- The role of coach, on the other hand, is ideal for those who have requests related to one's own style of coaching and for those who would like to practise certain interventions or techniques.

In this first, stock-taking round, we generally find that approximately as many issues arise that lend themselves to the coachee role as issues that lend themselves to the coach role. On the basis of the issues raised, the supervisor can divide the group into pairs who will examine certain issues from those two roles. Other characteristics of the issues raised such as similar subject-matter or recognisable aspects of the context often suggest certain pair combinations (man/woman, organisation-specific features, etc.). It is also possible to put together a trio of two collaborating coaches and one coachee.

The coach of the pair can then act as supervisor in a conversation lasting approximately 15 minutes, which is discussed afterwards in the whole group. This means that the live coach/supervisor in the session also has access to supervision, by the other group members and just after the coaching session. For every 15 minutes of live supervision, a minimum of 15 minutes are needed to give the supervisors a chance to discuss the live coaching afterwards. The supervisor of the whole group can concentrate on facilitating the meeting and shifting the coaches' attention during the meeting towards the coachee during this meeting, towards the coachee outside this meeting, and vice versa. All seven rings of my supervision model as described above can be used:

1 the relationships within the client's organisation;
2 the relationships of the client and his or her own organisational context;
3 the coach and his or her relationship with the client;
4 the coach and his or her relationship with their immediate supervisor (this is the first relationship in the here-and-now of this session – the central relationship of the first 15 minutes of conversation);

5   the coach and supervisor and their relationship with the other
    supervisors in the group (this is the second relationship in the here-
    and-now of this session – the central relationship of the second 15
    minutes of conversation);
6   the relationship between those supervisors (participants) and the
    supervisor/facilitator of the supervision group (this is the third and
    final relationship in the here-and-now of this session, usually coming
    into more prominence towards the end of the second 15 minutes
    of conversation);
7   all other relationships between the group members and between
    them and others outside the group.

Fascinating resonances often develop between all seven rings
of relationships, from which coaches can learn a lot. Over the history of a well-progressing supervision group, they may find crucial
new insight for their coaching practice at all of these different
levels.

Group supervision sessions are generally longer than individual supervision sessions. Around three hours is common, with a short break in
the middle. Three hours is plenty of time for three conversations along
the lines of the above approach, so six participants can easily receive
personal supervision in the role of coach or coachee during one session.
Besides the wealth of insights and the chance to practise in different
roles (coachee, coach, supervisor), this approach has the additional
benefit that coaches experience the supervision as safer and so find it
easier to contribute more vulnerable issues, because:
1   other group members are also exposing themselves to scrutiny in
    the same session;
2   a group like this has a self-correcting tendency, so sharper expres-
    sions of feedback are balanced by other points of view;
3   the supervisor who gives feedback from an 'external', 'authoritative'
    position, does not dominate the session, because the participating
    coaches contribute most of what needs to be said, which makes the
    supervisor less threatening as an 'authority' in the field.

The only aspect that perhaps makes individual supervision safer than
group supervision is precisely the fact that a participating coach shares
their issues and questions with just one other person. On the other
hand, I have often seen participants of a supervision group develop as

'comrades in adversity' relating to the fact that everyone has to 'lay themselves bare'.

Two further advantages of group supervision.
1 In a group supervision model like the one introduced above, there is less risk of providing unnecessary advice: facilitating and supervising are separate contributions at separate times.
2 There is also less risk of participants turning the supervision meeting into a therapy session, again thanks to the self-correcting ability of the group and the supervisor's ability to monitor this type of boundary in the group facilitator role. In addition, supervision groups generally meet much less frequently than therapy groups.

Summary: professional development of the executive coach

Continuing professional development for executive coaches helps them to build an independent **third position** with new perspectives into their relatively isolated practice consisting purely of one-to-one conversations. A third position similar to the one executive coaching often provides for leaders and managers.

Continuing professional development can take place in three different ways:
1 **Individual professional development**, often in regular consultation with a mentor. The safest and most autonomous method, but also the least likely to yield a true 'third position'.
2 Peer development: **co-coaching** or **peer consultation**. Still relatively safe, with more opportunity for an independent perspective from a 'third position'.
3 **Supervision**, both individually and in groups of coaches, under the direction of an experienced fellow coach. This is generally the most vulnerable way of working on one's own development, but also yields most independent perspectives and feedback.

Where coaches develop with the aid of professional support from a fellow coach, i.e. in the form of supervision, there is ample opportunity to observe transference phenomena. Supervisors can make use of the **seven-ring model**, where each ring symbolises a relationship. These linked relationships are:

1 relationships within the client's organisation;
2 relationships between the client (the coachee) and the coachee's colleagues within that organisation;
3 the relationship between the client and the client's coach (the 'supervisee');
4 the relationship between this coach and this coach's supervisor;
5 the relationship between this supervisor and this supervisor's supervisor(s);
6 the relationship between this supervisor (or these supervisors) and his or her (or their) supervisor, or the facilitator of their group;
7 the relationships between all of these parties and others outside the chain.

A **method** for individual supervision:
1 Stock-taking of the issues of the coach and the supporting material contributed to this session (logbook, tapes, reflection accounts).
2 Mentoring in relation to the issues raised.
3 Future: plans, new issues and things to try out.

A **method** for group supervision:
1 Stock-taking of issues from participating coaches, with particular attention to coach and coachee roles during this session.
2 Dividing up into coaching pairs.
3 Coaching/supervision conversation lasting 15–20 minutes.
4 Reflection/feedback/supervision conversation lasting 15–30 minutes.
5 [same procedure for the other pairs].
6 Brief review of the entire meeting.

Chapter 11
Library of the Executive Coach

11.1 Introduction: coaching and reading

Over many years of working with a wide range of coaches as their client, colleague and supervisor, I have noticed that many of us love to read. We find solace and inspiration for our work in books, even if it is often difficult for us to explain exactly how reading informs our practice. We value insights from psychology, philosophy, spirituality and even 'self-help' manuals, as well as the sublimation of those insights in poetry, prose and drama.

Why we want to read such a variety of books is not entirely clear. Perhaps the tenth book in the series in this chapter, Alice Miller's *Das Drama des Begabten Kindes* [The Drama of the Gifted Child], may shed some light on this. The origins of our pleasure in reading may lie in our childhoods. Books, like the mother's breast for the infant, represent a source of comfort and instant sustenance which is there whenever we need it.

Of course the act of coaching is very different from the act of reading. While books on the subject may inspire and educate, coaching tends to be acquired mainly through practice and supervision. There is, however, one similarity between coaching and reading which I find interesting. I refer to the practice of visiting and revisiting a topic contributed by a friendly companion – each time trying to bring an open mind and a fresh outlook to such a 'meeting of minds'. Reading, as well as coaching, I feel, is best done 'without memory and desire', as Wilfred Bion once (1970) famously said.

This short 'reference library' of twelve books, one for each month of the year, is classified as follows. I start with three very different works of fiction: an epic by Homer, a dialogue by Plato and a novel by Yalom, all of which say something about the rich history of this profession. These are followed by three books that, taken together, define the coaching profession very well; one on helping conversations by Stroeken, one on executive coaching by O'Neill and one on psychological approaches within executive coaching by Peltier. Next come three classics from the counselling and psychotherapy literature: Heron's book on counselling interventions, Rogers' book on making contact, listening and 'becoming whole', and Malan's book on therapeutic techniques and their area of application. Finally, I wanted this reference library to reflect a caring for solitary coaches with their many slights and injuries, so I added a book on coaches' cradles and early nurture by Miller, a book about looking after yourself by Foucault and another about looking after coaches by Hawkins and Shohet.

The following sketches of those twelve books do not claim to be introductions to or summaries of the works in question. Many of the books chosen are too complex to be summed up in the space of three pages. Equally, these descriptions are neither eulogies nor reviews. Anyone whose main interest is in what the books have to say will find no better source than the books themselves.

What I hope to share here is my enthusiasm for the books in question, and the feeling that they may contain inspirations that actually make a difference in everyday coaching conversations. I therefore try to relate the books to my own practice as much as possible. To that end, I start by describing the place the work in question has in my own library, followed by a brief characterisation of the book, a personal reading, and finally a number of insights or innovations inspired by the book. I hope the reader will approach these sketches and the books themselves in the spirit of Bion: without memory and desire, and will take some pleasure from their reading.

11.2 A historical overview in fiction

11.2.1 Homer's Odyssey: the triumph of mentor-coach Athena
One of my greatest inspirations as a coach is the literature of classical antiquity. The lasting words of ancient writers often help me to step back from everyday worries and anxieties, from the uncertainties in

my coaching conversations, and encourage me to focus more on the underlying patterns and potential for learning.

It is the chorus in Greek tragedy – from any one of the thirty-one surviving plays – that I find the most inspiring and intriguing coach in antiquity, which is why I devoted the last chapter of my book *Fearless consulting* (2006) to the unique roles and coaching skills of choruses in Greek tragedy. For the purposes of this library, however, I would like to focus on another, much older Greek classic which defines coaching – or at least mentoring – for me: Homer's *Odyssey* (8th century BC).

The *Odyssey* is an epic tale transcribed around 800 BC chronicling events thought to have taken place in the aftermath of the Trojan War, four hundred years earlier.

It is the story of Odysseus, King of Ithaca, who when the story begins has been away from his home for twenty years – ten years fighting in the great war against Troy and another ten years searching for his ships, which have been scattered across the seven seas by the god Poseidon. Poseidon has done this as an act of revenge on Odysseus' supporter, the goddess Pallas Athena, who outwitted him in the war with her Trojan Horse. Now, in the opening pages of the *Odyssey*, Athena manages, with some difficulty and only thanks to the fact that Poseidon is away travelling, to persuade the other gods to lift the barriers on Odysseus' home-coming. At about the same time, Odysseus' son Telemachus, who is then twenty years old and has no memory of his father, sets out on a voyage to find him.

Much of the *Odyssey* recounts the journeys of Telemachus and Odysseus in an ingenious manner involving flashbacks and parallel cuts. However, for me it is Athena who is the real protagonist of the *Odyssey*. Odysseus, as Poseidon's victim, is primarily occupied with a succession of perilous, sometimes crazy but usually heroic adventures that gradually bring him closer to his home and faithful spouse. His son Telemachus only makes a risk-free journey to the peaceful Peloponnese. It is Athena who undertakes the most challenging task: an ambitious and compelling reconciliation with her father Zeus and a fight to the bitter end with her angry uncle Poseidon. Athena is the real heroine of the *Odyssey*, precisely because she brings about her heroic reconciliation, not in the role of lead character but in the role of helper and coach to the house of Odysseus.

To achieve this, Athena assumes the form of Mentor, whom we encounter three times in the narrative:
1 as himself, a distinguished adviser and old friend of Odysseus, standing up to the carousing Suitors in the public assembly (Book 2);
2 as an incarnation of Athena, accompanying and 'mentoring' Telemachus on his long journey (Books 5, 6 and 7);
3 again as an incarnation of Athena, telling Odysseus how and when to fight and, most notably, how and when to stop fighting and let peace return to his island (Books 22 and 24).

Mentor's mentoring style is sincere and specific, and is still widely observed in mentoring today. It is typified in Book 22: 'Come hither, friend, and stand by me, and I will show thee a thing'.

For humans the *Odyssey* tells the story of Odysseus' return but, for the gods, the *Odyssey* recounts the victory of Pallas Athena, the goddess of female intelligence and the arts, and a personal coach, over destructive male forces of nature personified by Poseidon.

The *Odyssey* should be read by modern coaches for the 'classical mentoring' it contains. After all, our own coaching processes can be a real odyssey for our clients. They are usually full of unexpected encounters with (internal) demons, similar to the prototypes in the *Odyssey*, such as the primitive cannibal Polyphemus, the devouring monster Scylla, the monstrous whirlpool Charybdis, the tempting Sirens and the enchantresses Circe and Calypso. Moreover, in the figure of Athena/Mentor the *Odyssey* shows us how coachees may take their coach with them outside the sessions, where the demons stay with them.

The many Greek gods and demons in the *Odyssey* help us to consider and study our clients' inner demons and ambivalences. Athena personifies very well the concept of a 'guardian angel', which in coaching can initially be personified by the coach and later hopefully fully internalised by the coachee.

11.2.2 Plato's Meno: the encounter with the numbfish

Plato lived at a time when Greek society, having reached its full civic bloom in the previous century, was beginning to develop consultancy and coaching as a way to support and reflect on the great virtues and accomplishments that it had created. Obviously, words like consultancy and coaching were not yet in vogue, but sophists and philosophers had started to apply themselves to exactly the same trade as consultants and coaches do today: the betterment of leaders and the education of future leaders and professionals.

Plato was not only one of the leading coaches of his day, but also had the ability to reflect on his profession and pose questions which are still as open, profound and fresh now as they were then. He did this by creating a new literary form, the dialogue, which is in both form and content 'coaching'. One of the earliest of Plato's great dialogues, the Meno (6th century BC), provides challenges that can help modern coaches to reflect on their profession. Indeed, the main question of the Meno is still relevant for executive coaches today: *can one learn excellence?* In this dialogue, this question is discussed between Socrates and Meno in an aristocratic household in ancient Athens.

The Meno is structured as follows. Meno introduces his question and Socrates, acting as his coach, asks him first to share his own ideas about it, and what he understands by the word 'excellence'. Meno then has three attempts to define the Greek word *arethè* which spans our own concepts of (leadership) excellence, virtue, and robustness.

Meno's three definitions are then examined closely by Socrates. Together they find fault with each one of them, leaving both Socrates and Meno in a bewildering state of not-knowing, of not having the faintest idea what this 'excellence' really is. They do not give up, but return to the original question, rephrasing it as: 'What conditions need to apply for one to be able to learn or teach excellence, whatever this "excellence" may be?' Finally, Socrates sketches his ideal of the person who is both able to lead with excellence and understand what it is, and who is therefore able to teach it. But such a man wouldn't be easy to find because, according to Socrates, he would be 'like Tiresias among the dead in Hades, of whom it is said that he is the only one living consciously, while all others live as flitting shades!'

Next to this form of a truly explorative coaching conversation, the *Meno* also has a lot to offer in its content. In my view, the content of the *Meno* hinges on a pessimistic point that Meno raises and that Aristotle later calls 'Meno's dilemma': how can we learn what we do not know? For even if this would cross our path incidentally, we would not even be able to recognise it. This almost sounds like a play on words, but in my coaching practice it is a very real problem: how can my coachee learn what he has failed to learn so far in his life as a leader? How is real learning possible in areas where it has not happened up to now, where the coachee does not even know what to search for?

Socrates also finds the dilemma worrying because it undermines learning itself. He invokes a radical definition of learning to counter it: 'learning is remembering'. And he proves his point, by interviewing an uneducated slave in the company about an advanced mathematical subject (at least in the 5th century BC!): what is the length of the side of a square with a surface area of 8?

Just like Meno in the longer dialogue, the slave attempts the solution, becomes baffled by not knowing, attempts again in response to probing questions from Socrates and ultimately finds the right answer $(2\sqrt{2})$. Because the slave does it all by himself, Socrates can show that the slave now *remembers* knowledge previously buried within!

The most painful, but I believe at the same time most inspirational moment in the *Meno*, is when Meno has exhausted his wits, applied all of his knowledge, produced three definitions and had to retract them, and then bursts out saying to Socrates: 'they warned me about you, even before I met you, that you always go around embarrassing yourself and embarrassing everyone else . . . now I feel hypnotised, enchanted, even bewitched . . . with your big flat nose you don't only show the traits of a numbfish, but just like that fish you paralyse everyone who comes close to you! I am completely lost' (Plato, 4th century BC).

I believe it is the best thing for coachees, and even for coaches themselves, to regularly meet a numbfish that completely embarrasses and baffles them, paralyses them and perplexes them, so that again and again they think afresh about their issues without the dangerously tempting, self-gratifying voice within that tries to convince them that either they have already resolved them, or, just as stifling, that they will never be able to learn anything about them.

More generally, I believe it is a good thing to read Plato regularly, as he makes us realise that in spite of all the good work we may do as leadership tutors, sophists or coaches, we do *not* ourselves know what leadership is, and we do *not* know what excellence is. We do *not* know what we are purporting to teach, however much gurus 'in' leadership and excellence make us believe that leadership and excellence are known attributes. In fact they are not: they change with the particular person exercising leadership or excellence, and are notoriously hard to teach even by those who have mastered them, as is clearly demonstrated by the fact that even superb leaders usually lack the capacity to make others more excellent or better leaders. Only by reminding ourselves regularly of this can we retain a questioning, searching approach in the face of wishful thinking.

11.2.3 Yalom's When Nietzsche wept: *the mid-life crisis*
Coaches are often 'called in' in times of crisis. Sometimes they are asked to suggest ways forward in a leadership development crisis when previous routines no longer seem to work or when a recent promotion has opened up a very different and challenging new leadership context. Sometimes they are asked to miraculously 'improve' the style of a leader who has come under criticism and may even have been given a 'last chance' with the coach.

It is for this reason that it is good for coaches to be familiar with the so-called mid-life crisis, through personal experience or through reading. The novel *When Nietzsche wept* by the well-known psychiatrist Irvin Yalom (1992) describes an intensive mid-life crisis and its resolution by coaching.

When Nietzsche wept is one of those cleverly conceived historical novels which depict what *could* have happened but did not. Lou Salomé, Friedrich Nietzsche and Sigmund Freud *could* have spent the last months of 1882 meeting the famous Viennese doctor Joseph Breuer, as in the novel, but most probably none of them did. What did take place in 1882, however, was the very first 'talking cure', as it was described by Dr Breuer's patient, Bertha Pappenheim, who passed into history under her pseudonym of Anna O.

When Nietzsche wept evokes the fascinating Viennese *fin-de-siècle* world into which psychoanalysis was born and which saw the invention of psychotherapy. The novel relates the unfortunate outcome of that very first 'chimney sweeping cure' – another very apt epithet by Pappenheim, one of whose symptoms was that she was unable to communicate in any other languages than English at certain times – that eventually gave birth to psychoanalysis.

As well as being an engaging read, this book serves as a comprehensive and profound introduction to the thinking of three great scholars, Joseph Breuer, Friedrich Nietzsche and Sigmund Freud. To me it is particularly endearing to witness the young Freud here in the role of pupil – of Breuer – and not yet as the expert he would later become.

The story of the novel is written from Breuer's perspective, so we read his thoughts almost as a 'voice over' on events. Yet, despite the fact that Breuer is the central character, I feel drawn to Nietzsche. To paraphrase one of Nietzsche's book titles, he is depicted as very human but not all too human, and he practises his coaching with detachment, sensitivity, fearlessness and selflessness.

The main tenets of Nietzsche's philosophy are cleverly summarised in the novel and Yalom even manages to emulate Nietzsche's poetic and axiomatic writing style in his diction. Irvin Yalom shows us how groundbreaking ideas such as the will to power, eternal recurrence and choosing and loving your fate (*amor fati*), can be used by coaches, especially when dealing with a mid-life crisis.

Yalom reflects a great deal on coaching in the novel, especially the initial stages of the journey which are explored in fascinating detail. The first fifty pages are devoted to the active anticipation of the client, the second fifty explore the client's issues and the third fifty pages address the contracting process. As a consequence, the actual coaching journey between Nietsche and Breuer does not begin until page 155!

The novel form allows us to learn what happens *around* the consulting room, and to appreciate how a coach can be affected before and after coaching conversations. Breuer's and Nietzsche's equally fictional case notes support this learning.

When Nietzsche wept presents psychotherapy as something entirely experimental and existential, which befits the setting in a time when coaching or therapy had not yet been invented. However, Yalom's own approach to his therapeutic work is also existential and can be characterised as similarly experimental, which makes this book fascinating reading on several levels.

When the actual coaching in the book begins there is a lot of experimentation around the question 'Who is the client?'. Also, the two protagonists experiment continuously with their coaching style: Breuer begins with a directive style and then tries to lure and tempt Nietzsche into the coaching in an almost manipulative way. When Nietzsche takes over, he too begins as directive and even authoritative, but later settles down in a style which is almost psychoanalytical. The final pages show how a deep friendship, uniquely mutual and open in both men's lives, has developed during these sessions, which have helped at least one of these men to overcome his mid-life crisis.

11.3 Milestones in the coaching literature

11.3.1 Stroeken's Kleine psychologie van het gesprek: *a vade mecum for helping conversations*
Kleine psychologie van het gesprek ('Brief psychology of the conversation') provides, in brief, a sound foundation for every coach. From his extensive practice as a psychoanalyst, the author takes his readers on an exploration into the forms helping conversations may take, the kinds of conflicts, ambiguities and transference clients may bring with them to those conversations and the type of baggage the coach himself brings with him. What I like about this book is its simplicity and its informal invitation to accompany the author on a journey through striking examples and powerful insights into the world of conversations.

Harry Stroeken starts with the basis of every conversation, and certainly of any helping conversation: listening. He compares listening to picking up a vibration, a subtle tone of a specified frequency. I continue his musical metaphor in my reflection on the book. The two biggest mistakes with listening in helping conversations, according to Stroeken, are as follows. On the one hand, there is the risk of not picking up the vibration, i.e. of not sensing the actual idea or intention. On the other hand, there is the risk of reverberating with the vibration, as a result of which the vibration takes us over and we are no longer able to observe it impartially.

Stroeken goes on to explain what can happen for others, in a sense, 'by itself' if we only listen well. The other person feels automatically encouraged to say more. This virtually always puts a 'counter-vibration' or counterpoint on the table, an ambivalence or a conflict, with questions or dilemmas surrounding it, something the other person is unsure of, is conflicted over, and so on. Stroeken shows what can happen if you listen to both vibration and counterpoint, without giving more consent or assent to either.

The ambivalences start to develop further. For example, they become deeper and display their connection with other ambivalences, in other keys, with a longer history. A whole series of 'harmonics' now becomes apparent to the listener. We also see how the vibration here and now gains a special significance, how what the other person says also has direct repercussions and resonances, here and now in this conversation. Sometimes this makes it even more difficult to keep really listening, and to confine yourself to just listening. The harmonics associated with yourself, or with this conversation, have more grip on you and exert more pressure on you to limit yourself to vibration or counterpoint, i.e. to send the ambivalence packing or cancel it out. If you look at what these harmonics suggest in you, you become just as involved as when you listened to only part of the ambivalence, to the vibrations or the counterpoints, in the earlier introduction.

Stroeken also looks at the longer term of helping conversations, at what happens when you manage to sustain this form of proper listening through many conversations. He describes first of all how the vibrations that the coach perceives appear to belong to the 'classical repertoire', or to a 're-issue of an old composition' (due to transference), or indeed to a 'première', after remaining implicit for many years (due to repression, e.g. banned to the coachee's dreams). Stroeken describes how the coach starts to feel more like a musical instrument himself, one on which very unfamiliar melodies are sometimes played, or on which a chord is touched which cuts through you like a knife.

The phenomenon of transference is dealt with at length: Stroeken describes it as 'feeling like a mannequin that is dressed and undressed at your conversational partner's pleasure, according to his or her fantasy. Sometimes you are the recipient of unfair criticism, sometimes of love that is not meant for you. Sometimes you are tempted to cry out: "no, no, that's not me. That's only what you think."' Stroeken describes how helping relationships ultimately appear to fade away in sorrow and grief: over the fact that the original vibrations that gave rise to the piece of music being (re)performed here and now, can no longer be changed, so we are all condemned in a sense to keep playing the same old tune.

Stroeken is inimitable in his treatment of sorrow during the series of conversations. A first performance of a piece that has existed only in dreams to date is accompanied, for example, by loss, loss of options, wishful thinking or sweet fantasies about how the piece of music might turn out. By listening closely and picking out harmonics, the coach always takes something away from the score. Similarly, sorrow also turns out in a different way to be a theme towards the end of helping conversations. The loss here is the loss of the helping relationship itself. This too is accompanied by feelings of grief, which are often imperceptible in the first instance (because they are unconscious). It is again up to the coach to pick up subtle vibrations and counterpoints, and to be aware that things said earlier about loss now relate to this relationship.

Stroeken's journey therefore begins with picking up a single vibration, and ends with sorrow over an entire piece of music. One constant, which continues to move us in that journey from page to page is Stroeken's immense trust in his conversational partners. He has complete confidence that every client, every conversational partner, will contribute a tone, and then counterpoints and harmonics, and ultimately the performance of a genuine and personal symphony. He shows that the coach need do little to bring all of this about: simply be available and listen with attention, empathy and respect. This huge confidence in the completion of helping conversations also extends to us as readers of the book, in our role as silent 'conversational partners'.

Stroeken explicitly addresses himself to lay people in conversations, to 'those people who give some thought to their conversations, in their occupation or otherwise', to everyone in fact. And he entrusts all of his psychotherapeutic insights to that wide readership, unreservedly. He shows that conducting helping conversations is a great art, which requires a lot of study and experience and conceals many pitfalls. But at the same time he believes that his readers are able to do something useful with his examples and insights, even with esoteric matters such as transference and counter-transference, resistance and the helper's syndrome. He entrusts that knowledge to them without being oversensitive about the need for the study of medicine or dream analysis, or for accreditation or ethical codes, as you find in many other texts.

11.3.2 O'Neill's Executive coaching with backbone and heart: *the coach as partner*

The library of the executive coach should contain one preferred introductory text about coaching, if only because with some regularity colleagues and clients will ask: 'If I were to read only *one* book about coaching, which book would you recommend?' For the past couple of years my answer to that question has been Mary Beth O'Neill's book *Executive coaching with backbone and heart* (2000).

This book introduces the concept of executive coach as a *partner* to the executive. Indeed, the author applies this perspective of partnership throughout *Executive coaching with backbone and heart*, ensuring that all ideas about 'good coaching' in the book are just as much ideas for 'good leadership'. O'Neill believes that executive coaches should offer a full and mutual partnership to the point that the coach almost becomes a 'co-manager' or manager for the executive. We suggested something similar in the title of our book, *Coaching with colleagues* (Erik de Haan & Yvonne Burger, 2005), but never have I come across a book that is more consistent and congruent in this respect.

Many tips and ideas suggested for coaches could just as easily have been written for the client. The paragraph headings of Chapter 2 provide an excellent example:
- Identify and sustain a goal for yourself in every session
- Manage yourself in the midst of ambiguity
- Increase your tolerance for reactivity within you and in others around you
- Bring immediacy to the moment.

O'Neill also writes extensively about the fact that the presence of a coach converts a dual relationship with the executive and his issue into a *triangular relationship* consisting of (1) the executive, (2) his issues and (3) his coach. Separate from the sessions themselves, the start of coaching will inevitably alter the relationship of the executive to his issues. This is one 'common factor' that is often overlooked in the literature on coaching (see Chapter 3).

Having identified the coaching relationship as a triangular one, the book then devotes attention to other triangles that leaders may create in response to challenges and stress, and how important it is for leaders and for their coaches to become aware of these triangles. Unconscious triangulation is shown to be an insidious process that spreads anxiety throughout the organisational system.

As its subtitle indicates, this book expounds a 'systems approach' to the coaching of executives, building on Salvador Minuchin's 'structural' approach to family therapy. This systems or structural approach, with its emphasis on boundaries, roles, homeostasis and equilibrium, is an appropriate model for bringing the organisation into the central focus of coaching. Therefore this approach helps coaches to shift perspective from the executive to the executive's organisation, and back.

Of particular value in this book is the variety of perceptive metaphors to help coaches reflect on their profession. Metaphors appear even in the title, where the contradictory pulls of being straightforward, frank and authentic ('backbone') and at the same time being sensitive, compassionate, and siding with the coachee ('heart') are beautifully expressed. Again, the author intentionally suggests a double benchmark with the terms backbone and heart: for coaches *and* for leaders.

Other metaphors I liked include:
1 the image of the coach as a small gyroscope constantly moving and rolling under the influence of powerful external forces, while its inner mechanism stays perfectly level and balanced;
2 that of the spider's web as the flexible, resilient, anchored but ultimately vulnerable pattern of connections linking the coachee and others inside the organisation;
3 recurring dancing metaphors, up to the point of 'a dance through rough water while trying to get beyond knee-jerk reactions . . . '.

Clearly, this book is just as much about leadership as it is about coaching. Indeed, it made me realise that there is as great a potential in the model of a 'leadership style of coaching' as there is in the model of a 'coaching style of leadership' that so many write and talk about.

It also makes one wonder about how different the coaching profession really is from leadership. I always thought it was very different indeed, but since reading this book, which compares the two very closely, I am not so sure anymore.

I think *Executive coaching with backbone and heart* displays the very best of the so-called directive style of coaching, or business coaching. Of course this is only one approach to executive coaching, as we will see in the following book description, but O'Neill introduces it exceptionally well.

11.3.3 *Peltier's* The psychology of executive coaching: *systematic inspiration*

Had I been aware of Bruce Peltier's book *The psychology of executive coaching* (2001), I would probably not have written *Coaching with colleagues* (2005) or might have produced something else entirely. Peltier starts from exactly the same premise as my colleague Yvonne Burger and I did in our book: that an executive coach can learn from the theory and practice of psychotherapy.

When Peltier's book was brought to my attention, I was preparing the English edition of *Coaching with colleagues*, and I was most happy to refer to it. It is a sophisticated translation of many different therapeutic approaches into executive coaching practice and indeed covers the field of sports coaching as well, another field which appears to hold many lessons for executive coaches.

Peltier starts with the premise that coaching skills are similar to those used for counselling and therapy. He believes that some theoretical knowledge about these other fields will make coaching practice more effective and gives practical guidelines for setting about the task, with systematic checklists and illuminating case studies.

His definition of executive coaching is 'the use of psychological skills to help a person develop into a more effective leader'. These skills are applied to specific work problems given as examples. Peltier suggests that the executive coach should select from the various approaches those which best fit with their own view of life and which employ their personal core competencies to best effect. His views are therefore in line with the latest insights into the effectiveness of psychotherapy (see Chapter 3 of this book).

The psychology of executive coaching gives an introduction to some of the main influential strands of counselling and psychotherapy: psychodynamic, behavioural, person-centred, cognitive, systems, hypnotic, socio-psychological and existential approaches take up the bulk of the book. Uniquely, Peltier includes in his overview the sports coaching literature which he also summarises into valuable themes and 'nuggets' for the executive coach. There are also useful chapters on intake, ethics, the coaching of female executives and (especially for psychotherapists) how to start your own coaching practice.

For me the strength of this well-researched book lies in the qualities of its summaries. It also asserts very boldly that psychotherapy should form the basis of all coaching in business, where many coaches would think that general management and organisation consulting also have something to contribute in that respect, or would even argue that coaching is specifically *not* therapy.

The relatedness of executive coaching and psychotherapy will always be a moot issue. Whichever position one may wish to adopt, I think most readers will agree that it is worthwhile for the executive coaching profession to work towards a situation where most coaches are as well trained, well supervised and well accredited as are most psychotherapists. Peltier's book certainly helps us to move towards more careful and considered training and continuing professional development of coaches.

For executive coaches there are two reasons to return to this book on a regular basis. The first is the presence of carefully edited checklists that give overviews of phenomena that we all encounter in our coaching conversations. The checklists that I found most helpful are the ones listing psychological defence mechanisms, styles of distorted thinking, and family roles or valencies that our coachees may take up in the work place (such as the scapegoat, cheerleader, placater, jester, etc.)

The other reason to revisit this book is that it provides a rare insight into how therapists see and experience the field of executive coaching. In this way it gives us a useful 'outside perspective' on our profession. The last chapter, which is devoted to helping therapists move into the coaching world and set up a coaching practice, reminds us of some of the underlying foundations of our work and competencies that we often tend to take for granted.

The exhaustive overview of approaches, the literature reviews, the many checklists and the translations from one profession into another make this a book of 'systematic inspiration' for coaches that is a useful supplement to our own *Coaching with colleagues* which discusses some of the schools of therapy in greater depth.

11.4 Milestones in psychotherapy

11.4.1 Heron's Helping the client: *specific helping interventions*
John Heron's 1975 book *Helping the client* has become a classic in 'helping the coach'. Originally written for counsellors, no other work is more frequently used to provide focused training for coaches. Moreover, entire generations of managers have been trained in coaching styles of leadership on the basis of this book.

Helping the client presents six forms of helping behaviour that can be adopted by coaches, facilitators and counsellors[1]. Three of the six: directing, informing and challenging, are defined as authoritative and coach-centred, and the other three forms: discovering, supporting and releasing, as facilitative and coachee-centred. The book provides ample opportunity to study these six categories of coaching and to bring them to concerns and emotional states of the coachee.

I like to present Heron's six categories in a specific way that links them with my own model of different coaching approaches in Chapter 1 of

---

[1] I have renamed Heron's 'six categories of counselling intervention', as in De Haan & Burger (2005), as follows: prescriptive-directing, catalytic-releasing, confronting-challenging, supportive-supporting, informative-informing, cathartic-discovering.

this book. For this purpose, I'd like to add to Heron's dimension of 'who is central' to the interaction another dimension relating to attention to strengths or weaknesses; in other words, to draw a distinction between supporting and confronting.

Figure 11.1 shows the window onto the behaviours of the coach, which was given earlier (in Chapter 1), where Heron's categories are included in the ovals.

This interpretation of Heron's model allows one to explore and improve coaching behaviours in the widest sense:
(A) The four quadrants in Figure 11.1 contain the four different 'basic approaches' of a coach that were also distinguished in Chapter 1.
- *Problem-focused coaching*, which is related to many cognitive-behavioural approaches such as GROW, rational-emotive coaching and, more generally, any form of coaching that uses step-by-step models.
- *Solution-focused coaching*, an approach which has seen increasing interest in recent years and is related to appreciative inquiry.
- *Person-focused coaching*, which is humanistic in nature and places the person of the coachee at the centre as far as possible.
- *Insight-focused coaching*, which is related to forms of coaching born of psychoanalysis.

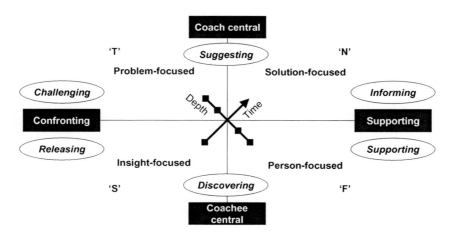

Figure 11.1 *The Window onto the coach: six specific behavioural styles of coaches*

(B) Those same quadrants turn out to be good indicators of the personality of the coach. This emerges from clear personality differences between the founders of the different approaches (Corsini & Wedding, 1989) and can also be illustrated with the aid of a well-known personality typology, that of Jung and Myers-Briggs (Briggs Myers, McCaulley, Quenk, Hammer, 1998). Jung (1921) distinguishes four *functions* within the personality: 'F' (Feeling), 'N' (use of intuition), 'T' (Thinking) and 'S' (Sensing). The model assigns one dominant function to each personality. In the Myers-Briggs procedure, most people ultimately choose a profile in which they recognise themselves, with a single dominant function. Statistical research (Briggs Myers *et al.*, 1998) shows that people with a dominant 'F' or 'N' choose counselling and coaching professions more frequently on average.

What I notice in working with coaches who know their Myer – Briggs preferences is that:
- coaches with a dominant 'T' function often have a preference for problem-focused coaching;
- coaches with a dominant 'N' function often have a preference for solution-focused coaching;
- coaches with a dominant 'F' function often have a preference for person-focused coaching; and
- coaches with a dominant 'S' function often have a preference for insight-focused coaching.

Summarising, I have seen some confirmation of the hunch that the personality of the coach plays a role in the choice of his or her own coaching approach, and this merits further investigation.

(C) The diagonals in Figure 11.1 are also relevant to the coaching profession (see Chapter 2 of De Haan & Burger, 2005). The diagonal pointing from insight- to solution-focused coaching is the *Time* dimension, where insight-focused coaches devote more attention to the here-and-now of this session, or even to the past as far as the issue is concerned. The other diagonal can be seen as an indicator of so-called *Depth of Intervention* (see Chapter 1), where person-focused coaches tend to focus on deeper, more personal levels of intervention than problem-focused coaches.

Back to *Helping the client*, which has given us such a straightforward yet far-reaching model. Its first few chapters are worthwhile for the way in which Heron shows much empathy and understanding for what it means to be a 'helper'. The rest of the book is useful mainly for its detail. The book lists a variety of specific supporting behaviours for each of the six categories of intervention, while it also lists manifold ways in which each of the categories may degenerate into something that is no longer helping. In this way John Heron offers both support (in the many examples of behaviours) and challenge (by reminding us of possible degeneration) to coaches, helping us to improve our interventions with clients in every moment of our coaching session.

11.4.2 Rogers' On becoming a person: *sharing something of me*
When it came to selecting a book from the founding fathers of the main currents of psychotherapy for this series, there were many options that seemed relevant to coaches, from Freud's *Psychopathology of everyday life* (1904), to Watzlawick, Beavin & Jackson's *Pragmatics of human communication* (1967). After some thought I finally decided on this seminal book by Carl Rogers because I believe his 'person-centred' ideas translate most easily into coaching practice. *On becoming a person* (1961), and its sequel *A way of being* (1980), were written 'to share something of me, Carl Rogers' – a statement which is exemplary of Rogers' very personal stance as a therapist.

Rogers believed that if we share who we are in our most private and intimate world, we will discover many more similarities than differences. We will also find that sharing such extremely personal information has a healing effect. He describes counselling as an effort to relate to the most intimate thoughts and feelings of the client: if the counsellor can welcome the client fully into counselling, allowing him or her to express their most personal internal processes, the client will become more fully 'themselves' and thus a more fully functioning person.

It is moving to see how warmly Rogers himself welcomed and listened to his patients, how he was able to reflect back the emotional essence of a longer statement with amazing parsimony and simplicity of expression, and how freely he shared his own feelings in the moment. See the videos we still have of Rogers at work, such as *Carl Rogers counselling an individual on hurt and anger*, or *Three approaches to psychotherapy: Gloria*.

The philosophy of counselling that Rogers advocates is no more, and no less, than fully accepting and welcoming the client – allowing the client to express himself or herself as fully as possible. In Rogers' view many counsellors and coaches can do a lot *less* than they are doing now. They don't have to add to the conversation or offer feedback, nor do they have to interpret, assess or evaluate what the client brings.

Rogers devoted a life-time of quantitative research and writing to this central hypothesis, inquiring into which attitudes and behaviours of counsellors are most welcoming to clients or what exactly happens with clients when they feel welcome.

In *On becoming a person* Rogers concludes that fully welcoming the client into the relationship is more about attitude than behaviour. He identified three 'core conditions' that he believed to be necessary and even sufficient for a successful counselling relationship.
- *Empathy and Warmth*: An understanding of the client from within and a positive regard for the client, or caring for the client.
- *Acceptance*: Unconditional acceptance no matter what the client brings to the conversation.
- *Congruence* or genuineness, in other words, what you see is what you get.

Rogers also assumes a large degree of symmetry within the counselling relationship, as these core conditions imply that the counsellor welcomes himself or herself into the relationship first, in order to welcome the client, or as Rogers put it: 'Can I let myself fully enter, so that I lose all desire to evaluate or judge?'

Modern research (see Chapter 3) shows that Roger's core conditions describe a large proportion of the measurable improvement in therapy. Rogers also had a view on what very specifically does *not* lead to a measurable improvement: an *evaluative attitude*. He stressed that counselling should bring about an internal 'locus' of evaluation but not add any external evaluation from the counsellor. This would only make the client more dependent, more uncertain and weaker.

I will try to do what Rogers does so well throughout *On becoming a person*: speak personally. My greatest revelation on reading his work focused on the difference between judging my actions myself or through the lens of other people's judgements. I think I became stronger and more autonomous by becoming aware of Rogers' concept of the 'locus' of evaluation, the place from which judgements are made.

I have attempted to apply these insights in my coaching work, encouraging my coachees to think for themselves and follow their own judgements. And I have gradually become more interested in my coachees' judgements on what they were experiencing. Rogers has also helped me, as a slightly introverted and reserved coach, to share more of myself during coaching, and to become more relaxed about showing how I feel and what is going on within me from moment to moment.

11.4.3 Malan's Individual psychotherapy: the science of coaching
There are many books about psychotherapy, but very few are so hard to put down as Individual psychotherapy (1979) by David Malan, a book I read and re-read with renewed benefit for my coaching conversations each time.

Individual psychotherapy is a bold and courageous book that, despite its firm grounding in the psychoanalytical tradition, takes a critical look at Freud's legacy. It investigates which of Freud's ideas are worth keeping, because they are supported by evidence; and which should be discarded, because they consist of 'oversimplifications based on a narrow and unsatisfactory view of human instinct'. Apart from this new, critical look at Freud's work, Malan was courageous in suggesting different ways of approaching psychotherapy itself, by opting for short-term psychoanalytical therapy with particular clients, a combination which was revolutionary and ground-breaking at the time when Malan was writing.

The book is constructed around a series of case studies, which Malan uses to explore the inner workings of the human mind. He begins with frictions and small conflicts in everyday life, and ends with pathologies that take many years of daily analysis to heal, if in fact they can be healed.

After addressing unconscious communication and the role of the therapist, this book moves on to descriptions of various disturbances and syndromes, including complicated and life-threatening ones that coaches fortunately will not have to deal with. But in my view the executive coach can still benefit from reading Malan's descriptions of deeper-rooted disturbances that affect and imprison clients.

Individual psychotherapy views individual psychotherapy as a science, in which practitioners explore case histories, gather evidence and test hypotheses. In his book, Malan shares with us the fruits of his own scientific exploration.

I am very impressed by how this book handles and builds on case studies. I feel that case studies often become a distraction in books on psychotherapy and coaching, hindering rather than supporting the author's main argument. Case studies can either become unnecessarily long-winded or rather remain too short and vague. Here, the case studies are treated as pieces of 'raw data', presented with precision and a wealth of follow-up data, leading to new knowledge and the testing of older (Freudian) suppositions.

This neat and thorough scientific work made me wonder what a science of coaching would look like, and how executive coaches in future could start to do more than just have their cases evaluated by their clients, or try to measure the return on investment of their own coaching.

In Chapter 10, Malan introduces two triangles that I remind myself of in almost every one of my coaching conversations. The first has to do with transference and links the parental figure, the 'other' in a situation described by the coachee, and the coach as three 'attractors' for any coachee to experience the same emotions with.

The second triangle[2] has to do with the main aim of any therapy, as Malan sees it: 'to enable the patient to understand his true feelings and experience them: as much of his true feelings as he can bear at any moment.' He shows us that the expression of any of these true feelings or impulses brings with it some form of anxiety, which is then often defended against. His 'conflict triangle' summarises this observation

---

[2] Both of these triangles were used in De Haan (2006). The second, 'conflict' triangle also motivated me to study critical moments of coaches in more depth. For that research, see Chapters 6 and 7 of this book.

and can therefore be used in our exchanges with our clients. These are the three angles of the conflict triangle:
- a defence, often the only visible part of this triangle;
- an anxiety that is defended against;
- some underlying hidden feeling, need or impulse.

A promising way to coach on the basis of the conflict triangle is first to name the defence that we perceive at this moment, then try to discuss the anxiety that underpins it, in order to arrive finally at the true feeling which remained hidden. As Malan shows in numerous examples, this is a powerful way to deepen the coaching experience while retaining the quality of the rapport.

The other chapter that I believe is a 'must' for every coach, is number 17, about breaks and termination. This chapter makes clear the degree to which termination is itself an issue of coaching that should not be approached lightly, especially in brief assignments where there is often not the time or the contractual scope to discuss the associated emotions in any depth. Malan sums up a number of fascinating phenomena that I also experience regularly in the later stages of coaching assignments, and shows how we can relate those phenomena to the agenda of the coaching itself in many cases. Everyone has residual grief and frustration stored up about earlier terminations in their lives, and the end of a coaching relationship often stirs that residue so that it starts to form a noticeable defence to the coaching. Then Malan's conflict triangle comes into play. The end of coaching is often an emotional journey comparable to the start of coaching, if we just open our eyes to it.

11.5 Books about care for the coach

11.5.1 Miller's Das Drama des begabten Kindes: *how did we actually become coaches?*
Here is a book that goes to the roots of why anyone becomes a coach in the first place. My only criticism is of its title which, in referring to a 'begabtes' or *gifted* child, plays into the hands of coaches' grandiosity and hubris. The title doesn't make it sufficiently clear that the author regards every child as exceptionally gifted, if only because it finds its own answers to the forces at work in its original family situation. This book is about all children, not just the

more talented among them. It shows how all of us grow up and deal
with some measure of frustration and trauma and how we find solutions
to the problems that those frustrations and traumas place in our path.
More specifically, this book is about the particular solutions discovered
by children who grow up to become helpers, coaches, consultants and
therapists.

Alice Miller (1979) writes about a moving drama, which is essentially
the same for every one of us. It is the story of the fragile and vulnerable
child arriving in a confusing world in need of parents or carers if it is
to survive physically and emotionally. As with every child, some of his
or her vital needs and wishes will not be fulfilled, which creates a sense
of disillusionment at a time when the child hasn't yet learned how to
deal with disappointment and frustration. This trauma can take many
forms and reach different degrees of intensity. Miller shows that every
child receives a certain quota of trauma, the weight of which may
depend on the early traumas experienced by its own parents, and the
nature of the solutions the parents were obliged to find.

Miller traces the child's solutions back to the source: unmet needs,
admonishments, expectations and demands during its early years. More
than enough experiences to teach the child gradually to repress its own
emotions and desires if they conflict with those of the environment.
This burying of emotions is always accompanied by deep pain, frustration and resentment. And those frustrations and resentments lead in
turn to new painful experiences, which have to be processed in turn.
Some of that anger and frustration may be taken out on parents or
custodians, but some of it is turned inwards, where it may lead in time,
in Miller's analysis, to outcomes as diverse as depression and
grandiosity.

The end result is that as adults we spend most of our lives trying to
ward off something that really cannot happen anymore, because it has
already happened, right at the beginning of our lives, when we were
entirely dependent on our carers. In other words, as adults we strive to
right the wrongs of our earliest experiences. Miller uses the image of a
prisoner obsessively polishing off a good meal in prison, while failing
to realise that the door of his cell is standing wide open.

Miller offers lots of examples to help us understand and appreciate
these patterns better. As we read, we become aware that no-one can

come through their childhood unharmed and without deep frustration and trauma. Maybe this is why we all remember so little from our early childhoods: we have all been repressing that painful information.

When reviewing the early childhood of people who later become therapists, Miller often sees children whose innate ability as carers puts them in a particular position of 'helpfulness' within the family. The coach therefore practised the role of coach at an impossibly early stage. Coaches often have a dual motivation, therefore: to help others, and so to help themselves. According to Miller, this motivation is often influenced by the desire to 'put right' something that previously went wrong. This can lead to extremely capable coaches. They started to practise at such a young age that they may be capable of amazing sensitivity and genuine empathy. They may also display a great deal of perseverance in difficult coaching assignments or if they get stuck, and they will probably be prepared to go to great lengths for their client and their coaching relationship. On the other hand, if coaches are unable to let go of their own 'need to atone' they can become dependent on the whims and improvements of their clients.

For these coaches, the original warding-off of one's own emotions and needs continues on a daily basis in adult life and indeed becomes a not inconsiderable part of their way of living and relating to others. That defence has to be actively maintained and requires regular and active maintenance, which can be expressed in two ways.

1 If a coach represses his emotions and needs so that they become fully unconscious, the coach will *still* find some other outlet for these emotions, such as:
   - A hunger for soothing or intoxicating substances.
   - A hunger for clients' positive feedback and praise. This is when admiration and love become equated in the coach's mind. The coach becomes susceptible to flattery, and a great flatterer himself.
2 If a coach splits off their emotions, attributing them to something or someone else, the coach becomes a bystander in relation to her own emotions; for example, she may split her emotions:
   - Either into parts of the self which become depreciated or which the coach becomes ashamed about. This may lead to a withdrawal into the role of coach even if there is no client or contract. The coach then tries to be everybody's coach, i.e., to

colleagues, friends and family, whether they want to be coached or not.

- Or into the coach's clients, which may lead to superior thinking and feelings of omnipotence, e.g. 'aren't clients hopeless', 'this person is well and truly in a rut', or 'I'll show him the meaning of leadership'.

It is particularly important for good coaching that coaches do not allow their personal needs and neediness to come between and impede them from really being with their clients. I believe there is one crucial lesson we can take from this book: that it is important to know why we became coaches in the first place, what it is that drives us – consciously and unconsciously – to practise this profession.

This is sometimes a challenging and revealing book, because it shows how ambivalent, self-serving and unconscious our own choice to become a coach really is. How much this choice may expose our own neediness, and how important it is therefore to take the opportunity to explore that neediness, e.g. with a coach or supervisor of our own. In my view, a coach must have at least a rudimentary understanding of what it means to be a coach, and why he has become a coach. A good coach has, at least once, seen the small and lonely child that is behind his achievements, behind his antennae and empathy for others. A good coach has, at least once, mourned what this small and lonely child has missed out upon in life, and a better coach has learned to embrace that loss and their own fate, as Nietzsche so eloquently put it in his *amor fati*. Only then will many of us truly be able to help our clients genuinely and teach them to embrace their own fate in turn. In my view, there is no better way to begin acquiring those insights than by reading *The drama of the gifted child*.

11.5.2 *Foucault's* Fearless speech: *the care of the self*
The last works of the great French philosopher Michel Foucault before his tragically early death in 1984 as one of the first generation lost to AIDS were devoted to the 'care of the self'. He asked himself how 'care of the self' became an issue for individuals and in Western culture more generally, and then explored what types were originally proposed.

Foucault suggests that this concern first emerged in 5th century BC Athens. As an introduction to his ideas I have chosen his 1983 University of California lecture cycle, now edited and published as *Fearless speech*.

Fearless speech is all about the ancient Greek concept of *parrhesia* – 'saying everything', 'speaking fearlessly', or 'free speech'. The lecture cycle charts its history over more than six centuries, from the first use of the term by the tragic poet Euripides to the Cynics and later the Stoics in ancient Rome.

The Greeks were interested in the ways in which kings handled their 'coaches' or advisers. Was a king able to join in the game of *parrhesia*? How did he react when the adviser spoke fearlessly? Did he show his tyrannical side by punishing his advisers for speaking fearlessly, or did he play the 'good king' and tolerate everything a coach said to him?

Foucault talks about a sort of *parrhesiastic contract*, which still embodies the essence of executive coaching today: the sovereign, the one who has power but lacks insight, addresses him or herself to the person who has insight but lacks power, saying to this 'coach': 'If you tell me the truth, no matter what this truth turns out to be, you will be rewarded rather than punished.' *Parrhesia* was linked to the care of the self: by speaking fearlessly, the philosopher alerted others, especially ambitious young men and leaders, to the importance of care for the self.

Fearless speech is not without its anxieties in modern coaching practice either: a coach speaking 'fearlessly' to the coachee makes the situation more anxious for the coachee. Coachees already struggle to lay bare parts of themselves and expose their situations and issues to the scrutiny of the coach. If the coach responds with critical feedback, that struggle is made all the more difficult. Equally, *parrhesia* is about the anxiety of being a coach: digging deeper and uncovering more, the coach knows, is not how to court popularity. On the other hand, the coach may do just that, because what is uncovered may lead to a breakthrough for the coachee.

A good coach does not take the client (only) at face value, which can be cosy and convenient but provides too little learning. A good coach looks at issues, stories and situations from multiple perspectives and with an eye for new and meaningful interpretations.

As Foucault demonstrates, fearless speech engages the client in a new, undiscovered relationship – thereby bringing the coach not only into a new relationship with the client, but also into a new relationship with himself, or herself. Fearlessness takes precedence over propriety and etiquette, so fearlessness is perhaps not for all coaches, and needs to be handled with care. It is an important and significant moment when the coach decides for the first time to speak fearlessly *about* the coachee, *to* the coachee.

The premise of *parrhesia* is an asymmetrical relationship (see also De Haan, 2006): it comes from 'below' and is directed 'upwards', to someone in a much more powerful role, to someone who has the absolute say regarding the continued existence of this relationship. *Parrhesia* therefore requires not only fearlessness but also humility. The fearless coach is aware not only that they are being placed in a dependent position, but also that the client has complete autonomy, and controls the future and the outcomes of the coaching. Client dependency is meaningless in this context.

One of the most common obstacles for an executive or consultant who wants to get the most out of coaching is self-love. Self-love makes leaders self-confident and ambitious, but it can also make them their own greatest flatterers and stand in the way of them really knowing themselves 'warts and all'. In fact, self-love can make it difficult for leaders to accept a coach in the first place. Unfortunately, there are still many executives who could benefit greatly from coaching, leaders whose self-love does not permit them to expose themselves to the scrutiny and attention of a coach. I often have to do a lot of work in order to build a sound relational basis in which fearless speech can feature.

More specifically, Foucault shows how the concept of *parrhesia* is at the very root of one of the most interesting and radical forms of coaching, sometimes called paradoxical or provocative coaching (see Farrelly & Brandsma, 1974). This is particularly helpful in certain situations when the coach feels manipulated by the coachee or when the coachee mounts a powerful defence to learning opportunities (see Chapter 1). Provocative coaching tackles these defences head on; for example, by hurting the coachee's pride and mobilising irritation and resistance. There are many similarities between provocative coaching and *par-*

rhesia as practised by the ancient Cynics. Foucault supplies many examples which give the reader an idea of what this form of *parrhesia* involved.

11.5.3 Hawkins' & Shohet's Supervision in the helping professions: and who takes care of the coach?

Supervision in the helping professions by Peter Hawkins and Robin Shohet is rightly considered to be the 'bible of supervision'. Hawkins and Shohet cover all aspects of supervision meticulously and, with their clear descriptions of a range of aspects of supervision, have generated a band of devoted followers of which I count myself one.

The book is introduced with a quote from Juvenal, '*sed quis custodiet ipsos custodies?*' ['but who will take care of the carers?'], which I feel says it all: this is a book about taking custody of the custodian, caring for the carer, developing the developer, and coaching the coach. The authors express the importance of this mission beautifully when they write about the fight of British miners in the 1920s for 'pit-head time'. Pit-head time was the right to wash off the grime of the work in the boss's time rather than take it home with them. Supervision, the authors believe, is pit-head time for those working at the coalface of personal distress, disease and fragmentation.

Hawkins and Shohet begin by reminding coaches of a few radical and perhaps disheartening truths concerning the helping professions.
- What brings us to this work is often an insufficiently processed need to be in control, or to help ourselves by projecting our own neediness onto others (see also Miller's book in section 11.5.1).
- In order to be supervised coaches have to temporarily move out of the luxury of 'helping' into the uneasiness of 'being helped'.
- The process of becoming a coachee ourselves exposes our vulnerabilities and anxieties around becoming dependent, which makes supervision so keenly difficult for helpers.
- The supervisory role itself will be felt unconsciously as an 'escape route' out of being supervised: in that role one can rise to the status of 'super-helper' or 'helper-of-helpers'.

After establishing these 'home truths', the authors move on to their descriptions of professional supervision for which the book is so well known and appreciated. They present a process model of supervision (summarised in Chapter 10 of this book) which is particularly good at increasing the number and depth of perspectives during supervision. This 'seven-eyed' model helps the supervisor to expand his or her perspective: from simple case-driven supervision to the dynamics of the session itself, and to aspects such as ethics, diversity and the influences of organisational culture, aspects that they then deal with in specific chapters.

The most fascinating of these aspects of supervision is transference, and Hawkins and Shohet show how transference can spread from conversation to conversation. This refers to the unconscious signals that find their way from the client organisation to the coaching relationship and from there to supervision – these signals are translated as behaviours, but remain poorly understood until someone draws explicit attention to them and is able, say, to make a suggestion as to the origin of the behaviour. What makes transference so fascinating is the way in which it spreads mysteriously from context to context, but also the fact that it can become more and more sublimated in helping conversations.

Transference is a two-way street: coaches can bring their own behaviour from the coaching with them, and behave in supervision in the same way they behaved earlier with their coachees (parallel transference); and a coach can 'take on' the client's behaviour during supervision, i.e. start to behave in the same way the coachee did earlier (inverse transference). The following is an example of inverse transference from one of my recent supervision groups.

The coach was an English management consultant who had been sent by his English client organisation to a subsidiary in Italy where he was to coach a senior manager. He described how he found the exuberance of expression and emotionality of his new coachee difficult to handle. During supervision he was given a coach with whom he discussed the challenges posed by this new client. At the end of that short coaching conversation one of the supervisors drew attention to the fact that he seemed to have changed; he had never seen him so animated and extravert. We realised that he had copied his coachee's behaviour, especially his gestures, and he agreed when we asked him if this had been the case. It is surprising that he first felt almost intimidated by his client, and then was able to do the same with someone else. Now that I have observed this several times, during supervision but also during coaching, I believe this is an unconscious way of learning, that helps us to handle strange behaviour by first adopting that behaviour ourselves.

In this way, supervision helps us to look at coaching from a different perspective – according to Hawkins and Shohet, from as many as seven different perspectives! During supervision we are more aware of the presence of several parallel relationships (the coachee/organisation relationship, the coach/coachee relationship, the coach/supervisor relationship, to name the most important), which develop further at every moment and feed each other with the discoveries and insights of the helping conversation. Considering one relationship gives us an insight into what might be happening in the other relationships linked to it.

What I like about *Supervision in the helping professions* is that the authors provide clear and straightforward figures and tables that actually help us to discover more in the various developing relationships. Another piece of wisdom from this book which will benefit the less experienced supervisor concerns the four beliefs that may get in a supervisor's way, making it difficult to do a good job and learn from it together with other coaches:
1   I must be competent;
2   I must be in control;
3   I must be consistent;
4   I must be comfortable.

Something to bring up in a supervision group, often with the immediate result that many of those present admit to having trouble with at least one of these beliefs, and sometimes all four of them – which then allows them to work in a more relaxed manner!

Summary: library of the executive coach

An example of a reference library for the executive coach, with one inspiring book for every month of the year:

1   A historical overview in fiction:
    • Homer's epic in which Athena appears as Mentor, one of the first coaches in world literature.
    • Plato's dialogue in which Socrates demonstrates how coaching can generate knowledge within the coachee.
    • Yalom's novel which explores in fiction the origins of therapy, and thus of helping conversations in modern times.
2   Milestones in coaching literature:
    • A brief vade mecum from Stroeken about conversational technique from the perspective of psychoanalysis.
    • O'Neill's guide to executive coaching and how coaches can learn something from executives in organisations.
    • An overview of the influences on coaching from the perspectives of psychotherapy and sport, by Peltier.
3   Milestones in psychotherapy:
    • Heron's classic summary of coaching interventions.
    • Rogers' classic text on counseling relationships, and how we can become more ourselves through those relationships.
    • Malan's classic text on short-term psychoanalysis, with a wealth of carefully analysed case histories.
4   Books about concern for the coach:
    • A worrying yet solicitous book about the early life of the helping professional, by Miller.
    • A book about how the helping professional shaped concern for the self in early times, by Foucault.
    • A book about how the helping professional shapes concern for the self in present times, by Hawkins and Shohet.

There are of course many other wonderful books, not to mention films, plays and operas, from which the coach can draw inspiration.

Chapter 12
Future of the Executive Coach

All the signs are that the current interest in coaching is not a fleeting trend or fashionable hype, but indicative of a fundamental shift in our society and culture, including corporate culture. It would seem safe to assume that, at least over the next few decades, this shift will continue and become consolidated. Coaching will increasingly become a genuine partnership between professionals, an aid to help them keep their own performance up to standard, and will become a permanent feature of every professional working environment like, say, the telephone or photocopier at present. This development reminds me of a painting by Palma il Giovane in the Jesuit Church in Venice, in which every mortal in the composition is accompanied by his own personalised (guardian) angel to guide them on their journey heavenwards (see Figure 12.1). In that case, coaching contracts will probably become more long-term: 'five sessions a year over a period of four years', and broader in scope, and more often contain an element of career guidance.

My expectation is that the consolidation of coaching may bring about a further professionalisation of the consultancy profession. There is already much talk of team coaching and organisation coaching, but in my view this is primarily from a marketing perspective. Because the term 'coaching' sounds attractive, it is linked to other consultancy activities. Later on, I hope professionals will be able to state more precisely what they mean by team coaching or organisation coaching, what the differences and similarities are with other forms of team facilitation and organisation development, and why they themselves are qualified to work in that area. And that in turn might herald the advent of more professional training programmes for facilitators and management consultants. It is not inconceivable that the sound research that has been carried out into the effectiveness of psychotherapy may give

Figure 12.1 *The painting* Three episodes of the archangel Raphael *by Jacopo Palma il Giovane (1619) shows how the archangel helps John the Baptist, Tobiah and Hagar to find the way to development, freedom and a well, respectively. It is no coincidence the Raphael (literally, 'God cures') is often called 'guide of souls'.*

a definitive answer on what works and what doesn't work, more widely within the consultancy profession. There is a great need for such clarity, especially for clients.

Professional coaching organisations will continue to flourish and the profusion of conferences, committees, symposia, etc. will increase still further. These organisations will seek to play a role in the further consolidation of this field. But it is difficult truly to get to grips with something that is as rich as human experience itself, and as varied as people are different. The most important area for attention in this professionalisation process in my view, therefore, is monitoring a proper balance between standardisation and regulation on the one hand, and the essential uniqueness and vulnerability of coaching on the other (see Chapter 2).

12.1 The role of research in coaching

Executive coaching is a remarkably rich and effective instrument for learning and development in the workplace. We need have no doubts about the effectiveness of professional coaching, because we can have confidence that the convincing results of meta-analyses in psychotherapy (Chapter 3) are also valid within the coaching profession. We can also properly assume that a high degree of effectiveness can be demonstrated for very diverse approaches to coaching, and for very different organisational contexts and individuals. The factors in the coaching intervention that actually make a difference are in all probability 'common factors', such as the motivation and self-regulating ability of the coachee, the coaching relationship, and personal attributes of the coach.

The time is now right for a new research paradigm to replace the 'effectiveness'/ROI paradigm in coaching (as summarised in Chapter 5). It is now time to find out what these common factors do in practice, i.e. *how* they encourage or bring about change in the coachee. What is a 'coaching relationship' exactly, for example, and how can we improve that relationship under different conditions?

Future avenues for research within coaching that may yield considerable benefits are the following.
1 The setting up of a *coaching database* or 'coaching science' as David Malan (1979) has started to develop within psychotherapy, where case histories are monitored over extended periods and it becomes possible to chart the long-term effects of the coaching intervention.
2 More research into the relevant *language* of the coachee, or into *our* own language as a coachee (bearing in mind that coachees are not fundamentally different from coaches). What terms can we use to describe the coaching from the perspective of the coachee? What are the most important distinctions we should apply when comparing different coaching experiences as coachees? This question was also posed in Chapter 5 and in De Haan, Bertie, Day & Sills (2008), and a number of initial responses were given, but it is still much too early to reach any conclusions in this respect.
3 More research into the *coaching relationship* and different possible coaching relationships. As a starting point for that research, it is

worthwhile looking at different personalities and whether specific combinations of personalities produce greater or different effects.

4 More research into the effects of individual coaching on the coachee's *organisation*. This will be difficult to study because it means involving others outside the close confinement of the coaching relationship. However, only part of the 'client system' of coaching has been investigated to date, namely the coachee and the effects of coaching interventions on coachees.

5 More research into *moments* of coaching. There is still much to learn from the moment itself, and what happens in it that makes a difference within the session and via the coachee, for the coachee's organisation as well.

6 More research into the *basic building blocks* of coaching. Although much has been written about phenomena such as listening and service relationships, many questions remain unanswered in this area.

To put it briefly, even if no further classical outcome research is necessary, there is still a lot to do. I have no idea how future research will develop. But, with the expanding practice of coaching, I am convinced that our knowledge of helping conversations will increase further and, with it, our appreciation of such conversations. For me personally, as for many practising coaches, the question of the future *within a single coaching conversation* will always remain the most interesting one. How can you keep that future open, and continue to ask questions about it . . . ?

12.2 The role of coaching in organisations

What can the role of coaching be within our rapidly changing society, a few characteristics of which I outlined in Chapter 2? If you consider this question pessimistically, executive coaching can already be viewed as a sort of outlet or safety valve, or perhaps a sticking plaster over the wounds left by increasingly solitary workplaces, failing support and increasing fragmentation and oppression. According to that view, coaching actually serves to uphold a process that is extremely harmful not only for organisations but for our society as a whole: a process of fragmentation, growing inequality, declining sustainability, a lost sense of place within our ecosystem, and the isolation or suppression of large parts of human emotionality in the workplace. Coaching helps to maintain processes like these because:

1   Emotions during coaching are indeed welcome, so that fragmenta-
    tion can be healed or kept in check to some extent by coaching,
    and a lack of permanency, equality or protection can be processed
    to some extent during the coaching – which may allow them to
    continue to fester in other arenas.
2   Market forces and scarcity make that access to (professional) coach-
    ing will remain exclusive to an elite, so that the luxury of individual
    support by an executive coach itself is a discriminating and frag-
    menting force within organisations.

I admit that this is a somewhat cynical perspective. However, it is a
perspective that regularly occurs to me of its own accord just after
coaching conversations, when I notice once again that I am left with
a huge amount of tension from an unsafe or fragmented organisation
when my coachee leaves the room.

I am certainly not the only person to observe the increasing fragmentation and conflict in modern society. Sociologists and philosophers
have been writing for over a century about secularisation, the loss of
a guiding, commonly accepted morality, and the consequences of
increasing bureaucratisation and capitalism, using metaphors such as
'iron cages' and 'polar nights of icy darkness', to quote just one of them,
the sociologist Max Weber. Philosophers are in agreement about the
phenomenon, but less so when it comes to its interpretation, i.e.
whether we should describe the modernisation process as a lapse of
morality, or as a liberation and a route towards a new morality. This
perhaps depends more on their own personal preferences. What everyone agrees on is the fact that the 'prevailing morality' has declined
in influence as a moral compass. Modern man now has to set out alone,
with or without the help of an authority or a coach, to find his own
moral compass in these anchorless times.

Baritz (1960) shows very convincingly how consultants and coaches,
and also more generally all sorts of applied social scientists, essentially
fail to offer a new 'compass' or even to help in finding one, when old
value systems decline. He wrote: 'From the pioneers in industrial psychology to the sophisticated human-relations experts of the 1950s,
almost all industrial social scientists have either backed away from the
political and ethical implications of their work or have faced these
considerations from the point of view of management.' According to

Baritz coaches will moreover be constrained by the fact that strictly speaking they will be able to co-determine and influence the means towards a goal, but the choice of the goal itself to a much lesser extent.

There is a real risk that coaching will only play a role in reinforcing *individuals* in modern working relationships, and in providing a counterbalance to oppressive or fragmenting influences in modern organisations. If that is the case, coaching will do little more than maintain and teach us to live with the *status quo* in organisations. However, the hope and promise of *relational coaching* is that coaching offers more than that, i.e. that as the result of experiencing a more healing and liberating relationship in the coaching, coachees will be better able to enter into or create that sort of relationship within their own organisations as well. Only if we can tackle fragmenting and oppressive practices directly do we stand a real chance of bringing about a sustainable long-term improvement.

I believe, however, that something can be learned from the history and practice of helping conversations on another level as well, taking our cue from the way in which therapists and coaches have been able to handle and largely resolve their own conflicts and misunderstandings. I refer to the battle between the schools of thought that have dominated a large part of the modern history of helping conversations. This tribal warfare was not settled, as so often happens in conflicts, by one or more approaches conquering all of the others and not even by an uneasy compromise between all of the parties, but in a radically different manner. The different schools and approaches gradually came to realise, with the help of vast quantities of research data, that a more obvious and much more attainable victory was one in which everyone was a winner. A victory in which they were all proven equally right. In my view, such a victory is the only permanent victory as well when it comes to fragmentation and oppression, and to conflicts between different systems of values or beliefs as we see so widely nowadays.

The judgment of the famous Dodo (see Chapter 3) has resulted in an additional important insight which can have a positive influence in organisations and society. And that is despite the observation that all convictions are 'equally good', neither eclecticism ('piling everything in a heap') nor nihilism ('disparaging everything') proved to be the right conclusion. The meta-analyses in psychotherapy have demonstrated clearly that, while the theoretical approach taken by the therapist does not matter, *commitment* to one approach (or a coherent theoretical system) does matter a great deal in terms of effectiveness. This too is a useful idea to apply to fragmentation and oppression, conflicts and exclusion, in a broader social sense. Which fragment you belong to, which system of values you adhere to, need not matter, but the fact that you are committed to it, and derive meaning from it, may be vitally important for the effectiveness of your contribution.

How can we use this idea to provide an answer to fragmentation and oppression? We can develop the understanding that what divides the fragments is their views and mental models, while what unites them is their commitment and conviction. This answer may be the beginning of a more interconnected organisation or society, in which partners are aware that they have much more in common than they thought, including the fact that none of them can lay exclusive claim to the 'right' conviction or the 'right' morality.

The role of coaching in present and future organisations and, in a wider sense, in society, is a relevant question for a *relational* coach and an important *open* question with which to conclude this book. Everyone's social and organisational role defines a *relationship*, a relationship between individual and system, or between individual and other individuals. It is moreover a relationship that is relevant for the coaching itself. Hawkins & Shohet (1989) refer to this relationship and role as the seventh 'eye' on coaching and, in my own model for supervision in Chapter 10, section 10.3, I also assign this wider context to a seventh 'ring' of relationships. What is important for coaching, therefore, is how it is imbedded in society, and what is important for society is how it wishes to make use of helping conversations.

Summary: future of the executive coach

Coaches may be able to expect the following in the **future** (see also Chapter 2).
- Continuing growth and consolidation of the profession.
- Increasing awareness of the (instructive!) friction between general knowledge about coaching and the uniqueness of a coaching relationship.
- A more external and independent form of regulation than self-regulation.
- Increasing awareness of the vulnerability of coaching.

In my view, new and relevant areas for research are the following.
- Systematic exploration of (long-term) **case histories**.
- Formulating a **language** of the coachee that expresses how they experience the coaching.
- Research into forms of **coaching relationships** and their effects on the coaching itself.
- Research into effects of individual coaching on **organisations** in a wider sense.
- More research into **moments of coaching** (see Chapters 6, 7 and 8).
- Research into the **building blocks** of coaching.

A possible future role of coaching within organisations and society:
- (first order) **reinforcing** individuals and helping to **process** fragmentation and oppression;
- (second order) **raising awareness** of a different type of relationship, which can spread to other relationships via (conscious and unconscious) transference;
- (third order) **serving as a model** for a method of handling conflict:
  - recognising that every viewpoint is of equal 'value' and that no view or position is 'better' than any other;
  - valuing the common factors, such as commitment to your chosen viewpoint;
  - teaching that common factors such as commitment and allegiance could be explored and exploited further.

The community of therapists and coaches by and large appears to be capable of undergoing such a positive change, so why should this not also be possible for their clients, the individuals and organisations for whom they work?

Appendix A
80 Critical Moments of
New Coaches

1 All moments are critical

(i) 'I can't describe one critical moment; all of my coaching sessions to date have been very critical. Especially the uncertainty about the course the proceedings will take, even though feedback shows time and again that the coachees view the sessions positively. They say they find tools they can use to make progress in their work.'

(ii) 'At the moment I am still finding nearly everything critical because it is the first time I have worked formally in the role of coach. I am still exploring my own role and the role of the coachee. From time to time I find it difficult to find instruments to use: talking is all very well but the coachee also needs tools or exercises.'

2 The very beginning – acquisition

(iii) 'Taking on a coaching assignment: discussion with the main client in the organisation, which may or may not be in the presence of the coachee.'

(iv) 'I found it difficult to propose coaching to someone in the first place, to ask whether individual coaching by me might be a solution. How do I know, or sense, whether a potential coachee would appreciate a coach? I find entering into a coaching relationship difficult, so I don't quite know how to approach it.'

(v) 'I find getting to know new coachees the most critical part, time after time, because you don't know how people will react. Perhaps they're not willing, or not open to coaching and it often turns out that those are the very people who need coaching.'

(vi) 'It was a significant moment for me when she eagerly accepted my offer of coaching. I wasn't sure if I should go ahead with my offer because it would have consequences for the relationship. Nevertheless, I am almost certain that it will turn out well for both of us.'

3 The very beginning – the first conversation

(vii) 'The first conversation with my client was my most critical moment. How do you prepare for it? How will he react to your approach? Will it all be over inside of half an hour? And so on.'

(viii) 'I had the first contact with my coachee this week. A first "rendez-vous" like that is always critical: what will she look like, how will she come across, what will she think of me?'

(ix) 'A woman I know fairly well is referred to me for coaching. She comes straight to the point. Her current manager has told her she needs to figure out why she keeps getting into conflict with people. That is what she wants to figure out with me. Almost right away, she starts explaining why she acted in such and such a way and how it is mainly down to the other people. I ask some questions, and she answers them in the same way. After a while, when I steer the conversation towards the coaching, objectives, arrangements, etc., she loses interest. She thanks me for a "useful conversation", but doesn't believe that talking any more will resolve much, surely I don't know either why people are against her. What I found most critical about this was directing the conversation and putting myself forward as a coach (with someone I knew, in this case). My intention was to let her get a few things off her chest, experience my attention, etc. But then it made sense to discuss the coaching options with her and give her joint responsibility for the arrangements. I let this run its course. In retrospect, it was exciting for me to ask the question of whether this was indeed the right match and to bring the subject of her own responsibility up for discussion.'

(x) 'Our first session went well, until we started to discuss the coaching plan. He suddenly came out with some very unpleasant remarks. I was tempted to go on the defensive, but managed to avoid it. I asked him a question about his behaviour towards me. That got him thinking. At the end of the session he told me that had been his biggest learning moment during the conversation.'

4 The very beginning – building a relationship

(xi) 'Gaining the coachee's confidence so that essential problems can be discussed. She knew me as a member of the management team with a reputation for being demanding and straight-to-the-point. Now I was to be her coach. In the beginning she said her main problem was lack of time. That was true, but it was hiding something more important: the fact that she was facing burn-out and had come to a deadlock in her project and was unable to break through the impasse. So we had to develop a common idiom at the start and I had to discover where she was experiencing problems. The moment when she stated that she had a problem and that she trusted me was indeed a breakthrough in a sense. Now she is very happy with the coaching and gives me too much credit for it.'

(xii) 'I experienced a coaching situation with a colleague in which I found it difficult to tune in to his way of thinking. This colleague was a self-made man in his profession and quite a few years older than me. He was struggling with assignments that he had to carry out and wondering how he was going to handle them. He seriously doubted himself. To the outside world, this coachee radiated strength and forcefulness, but inside he had serious doubts about himself. His outward appearance made everyone assume that he knew how to cope with all sorts of problems so, like a magnet, he attracted all kinds of issues and problems. Sometimes he got hopelessly bogged down in them. My problem in this coaching journey was that my own world view and that of my colleague were so different that it was very difficult for me to gain an idea of his thinking and his standards. This made it difficult to mirror, challenge or explore. Most of the summaries that I gave during our sessions revealed that I had slightly misunderstood him, and as a result the session became a cascade of misunderstandings and incomprehension. It was therefore very frustrating to have to bring this journey to an end after two sessions.'

(xiii) 'I had an initial session, intake and initial exploration at the same time. The critical moment came when I asked about her private situation. Would she trust me to such an extent in this first session? Luckily, she did, but I heard myself expanding upon and defending why I had to ask that question.'

5 Am I good enough?

(xiv) 'The fact that the coachee chose me gave me a lot of confidence and room to work. I do experience some pressure because she has a lot of experience of therapy and because she took a personal effectiveness training course recently.'

(xv) 'I find it difficult to coach senior people, who have so much more work experience than I do.'

6 Am I doing it well enough?

(xvi)   'What I find difficult as a coach is the fact that I sometimes attach
         too much importance to knowledge. Whereas, if I know about
         something, I also want to come up with solutions. Something else
         I find myself wrestling with as a coach is the question of whether
         you mainly go along with the coachee's needs, or whether you
         can also give feedback off your own bat, even if the coachee isn't
         expecting such feedback or is not yet "ready for it".'

(xvii)   'My most critical moment was when I followed my coachee
         entirely in what she was saying in a coaching conversation, and
         kept "playing back her words". In the end, this left little scope for
         a solution to her problem. I always had the feeling, up to and
         including the next conversation, that I had forced something.
         And so I was afraid that my approach had disrupted the coaching
         process towards her longer-term goal. My "not quite knowing
         what to do" left me at a crossroads: giving back what she said or
         bringing the conversation back to her original question. The
         latter didn't seem like something a coach should do – I was afraid
         the conversation would get bogged down. This example shows
         that, even if I don't know what to do, I often decide just to do
         something. But perhaps I can still change that during the conver-
         sation and then ask for feedback about my approach.'

(xviii) 'When I don't understand what the question is or how to tackle
         it. People frequently confide their their issues in collaborating
         with each other to me in confidence and as yet I am not always
         effective enough in coming up with tools to achieve a solution.
         The awareness of the problem and the potential contribution of
         the manager himself in that respect and the overriding impor-
         tance of bringing about further change and development within
         the division in partnership. To put it briefly, the welding together
         of individual experience and objectives to create a common inter-
         est of greater value. A critical example was a direct request to
         contribute towards the team coaching of a management team in
         the form of a workshop where, besides the naming of individual
         and collective objectives, questions such as personal relationships
         and how to optimise such relationships also came into play. I felt
         rather powerless in the face of such dilemmas.'

(xix)   'Not knowing what to do: having the manager foist an under-
         performing colleague on you with the announcement that his
         performance must improve spectacularly within a given period or
         he will be dismissed. It was clear that the manager didn't expect
         anything of the coaching and had in fact already drawn his own

conclusions. I just barged right in, not knowing what I was actually supposed to do. I hadn't discussed the conditions for the coaching with the manager, or its scope. The employee was dismissed after six months. I was left with a feeling of failure.'

(xx) 'An IT specialist has been working on a project for a year. He is wondering if his results will actually be used and says that he doesn't understand how things work in his organisation. It annoys him that everything works so irrationally in his organisation. I attempt to expand his understanding of the context. And I explain, using examples, that "irrational behaviour" may have a sound logic behind it. He himself has a tendency to explain a lot of technical things to me. After a while I try to draw him back to his original request for help. I strongly get the impression that I am not helping him any more, but he neither confirms nor denies this. After a few weeks he reports in sick due to "relationship problems". I don't know what this refers to and ask for an explanation, but he isn't able to back it up. I wonder if he might be depressed. He doesn't rule it out; I now hear for the first time that he has had depressive symptoms in the past. The company doctor wants him to return to work by gradually working more hours. My advice is to consider psychological help. I failed to spot an important underlying problem in this case.'

(xxi) 'A critical moment was when my coachee had received blunt criticism from a colleague and sought my opinion about it. I agreed with the colleague's comments in essence, but was nervous about telling him this. I was tense because I was afraid he'd hold it against me.'

(xxii) 'Tackling my coachee about her style of speaking and the abstract language she used, which did not connect with others.'

(xxiii) 'Bringing up the subject of the unproductive coaching relationship, and getting out of it.'

(xxiv) 'Entering into conversation with a manager who was not happy about having me as his coach.'

7 There's something there . . .

(xxv) 'A critical moment is when I can tell there is something going on behind all of the information being communicated to me, but I can't yet put my finger on it. In that case I'm not quite sure what to do. In hindsight I think I should have reflected that fact back, but in the heat of the moment it didn't occur to me.'

(xxvi)	'Critical moments are moments when you have to be very open yourself in order to coax someone out of his shell. You point something out, such as an awkward response, and mention it directly which makes me feel like working on the edge.'
(xxvii)	'A very anxiety-provoking moment for me in the relationship with my coachee was the realisation that he has taken on a consultant who might potentially turn out to be a better manager for the office than he himself. I haven't said as much. Not yet. I'm not sure how to tackle this. I have, though, asked how he plans to handle the new, useful insights from this new employee who is his intended right-hand man. And what kind of effect these new ideas have on him?'
(xxviii)	'A coaching conversation with someone who, as far as I am concerned, is telegraphing the fact that she has lost all purpose in her current work but responds with denial to all attempts to bring this up for discussion, even when I confront her with the facts she has told me. Clearly, it doesn't help to keep pressing harder on the same button, but where is the button that does work?'

8 There's nothing there . . .

(xxix)	'I find it difficult when I have absolutely nothing to go on, or when the question is very open.'
(xxx)	'A critical moment is when my coachee doesn't give an example, or not until late in the conversation.'
(xxxi)	'When a lot is said but leads nowhere. In that case I find it difficult to act worthy as a coach. How do you bring structure to the conversation and how do you help the coachee to focus and gain insight?'
(xxxii)	'The people who see it as something compulsory are difficult.'

9 What do I unleash?

| (xxxiii) | 'The impetus was my coachee's current inability and desire to learn how to set better boundaries, and to be more assertive in certain work and other situations, so that the effectiveness of her efforts would lead to improved results. During the conversation we acted out a sort of role-play where I reflected the potential feared reaction of the "adversary", as soon as she expressed |

her opinion openly. Gradually I unearthed all sorts of irrational, obstructive convictions that were deeply rooted (in her youth) and were imposing many restrictions on her, both at work and in her private life. This was a critical moment because I could see she was becoming very aware for the first time of her way of thinking, preserved for so many years, and seemed to be determined and inspired to change it. That this would directly affect her position in family relationships was inevitable. In the end things only improved, but I wondered whether and how I could find a balance, as a coach, between objectivity and responsibility.'

(xxxiv) 'I am currently coaching a woman who works as a consultant to a non-profit organization. She was at home for a few months at the start of this year due to overwork. She has now returned to work and wants to get off to a good start. Objectives of the coaching are (1) to strengthen her understanding of her strong points, needs and stress factors; (2) to deepen her understanding of the sort of work that suits her best, and (3) to formulate an appropriate career strategy within the current organisation. A critical moment for me was when we reached a sort of personal core after two sessions. On the one hand, I felt we were really getting to the root of her problems and that was great, but on the other hand I found it scary that I was getting into something that I did not know how to handle. And what then? Where does the coach end and the therapist begin?'

10 The coachee's emotions

(xxxv) 'The coachee in question was sent by his manager for coaching and for referral to a programme in the area of assertiveness. After a conversation with the coachee I told him that, on the basis of his story, I had a feeling that something else was the matter. The coachee started to shake all over and burst into tears, then it all came out about how he had been feeling in recent months. At that moment I didn't know what to do as the coach, apart from showing concern, and I asked the coachee if he was happy for me to refer him to the company doctor. In hindsight, that was a good decision. At the time, however, I was pretty nervous about it.'

(xxxvi) 'With one of my coachees I conducted a reintegration programme. It was only partly voluntary. In one of our sessions the man became very emotional. It was the first time I had seen that side of him, he is generally a very rational man. He threatened to stand up, walk out the door and never come back. I could feel I was getting pretty warmed up and quickly asked myself what that would mean for him and for the organisation. I asked him very calmly what would be the point of that, apart from getting him out of a difficult situation at that moment in time. That surprised him and he took time to think it over and reply. We both saw that moment as a turning point in our sessions. It gave him the space to return to the organisation in a new position. The course of sessions was completed successfully.'

(xxxvii) 'A new project worker in an organisation where job losses were likely felt threatened by a number of workers who were jealous because she did have a job. She was very distressed by this, and I didn't know how to advise her.'

(xxxviii) 'What I always find critical, time and again, is when emotions get really high. For example, when my coachee is particularly angry or disconsolate over events in his work, such as the actions or behaviour of others. Because you are so close to the root of the other person's problem at times like these, I am always afraid that I'll say or do the wrong things, which may ultimately have a considerable effect on my coachee's development. I am keen to help and guide, but not in the wrong direction. So then I doubt if I'm doing the right thing.'

11 My own emotions

(xxxix) 'Moments when I experience a degree of resistance or irritation in myself. For example, I remember a conversation with an internal coachee that took place in response to her desire for further personal development. In accordance with her wishes, she was given the opportunity to expand her range of duties and thus the responsibility to shape and interpret those duties herself, with help from others. She made no initiatives to take ownership of those duties but waited until I asked how it was going and then reported that nothing had happened. She didn't feel responsible for her own development. That irritates me and I have to take care that my irritation doesn't form a barrier in subsequent conversations.'

(xl) 'A critical moment for me is when I get annoyed about the behaviour or attitude of the other person. For example, when the employee doesn't come to the realisation and thus the belief that he has to change or he won't get ahead. When do I as the coach call it a day? Perhaps a somewhat dramatic turn of phrase, but that feeling sometimes comes over me when I have a conversation like that.'

(xli) 'The coachee had only been employed for a week and had just come back from the introduction days at our organisation. During that time she had talked at length with a former colleague of mine about the inclusions and exclusions in our team. The coachee told me that she was very happy with these conversations and they had done her good. It was critical for me because I had exactly the same good feeling about the inclusion of the coachee in our team and it concerned me personally that I hadn't thought in advance that inclusion and exclusion might be a subject for discussion. It hadn't occurred to me.'

12 My own doubts

(xlii) 'Sometimes I'm afraid I have communicated too much of my own doubts, for example about a situation raised in a conversation.'

(xliii) 'My coachee didn't know how to handle a particular situation. I wasn't able to give him good advice at that time because I hadn't had any experience of such a situation myself and found it hard to put myself in his shoes. Which coaching style do I use in such a case?'

(xliv) 'Moments when I don't know what to do are when my coachee says he is faced with a delicate issue. I always ask him to describe the situation and then ask why it is a delicate issue for him. We then analyse the possible consequences of doing A or B and look at what he feels comfortable with. So far so good, but then he always asks what I would do. I never know to what extent I should share my own opinion, so as not to influence him. The factors I consider in reaching a decision might be completely different from his own and not necessarily any better or worse.'

(xlv) 'This coachee also says that I act as his "conscience". That is very flattering, but it also puts me on a pedestal, by which I mean that he expects his 'conscience' to be infallible, and I am certainly not that. Plus you can only fall off a pedestal! So I don't know how to handle this situation.'

(xlvi) 'When the manager I am coaching makes me feel that I have to supply the solution: "Should I do A or B?"'

'The situation involves a new manager. She has a lot of potential but knows she needs a challenge from her environment in order to really raise the bar higher. Her manager is not so demanding. In her words: "He doesn't ask how it's going, as long as nothing goes wrong everything's fine, I don't receive any criticism, he is always positive. So what actual use am I in this organisation?" My own idea: she does not experience her own challenges as compelling enough to give her the stimulus she needs. Nor does it come from her manager. A short account of the moment when we reached a stalemate:

My question: Why do you need a critical environment?

Coachee: That's what I'm doing it for, for my manager and colleagues.

My question: What do you want to achieve yourself?

Coachee: If I perform better the people around me like it, but they do anyway,

so what is the point of putting in the extra effort.

My question: Do you take your manager seriously?

Coachee: No, not really.

And there you have it . . . stalemate!!! I could only think it was time to surround herself with different people, but that's easily said.'

13 Deferring my judgment

(xlvii)   'I can't cite one critical moment right away, but I do frequently experience tension between consulting and coaching. It is difficult not to offer an opinion but to allow the coachee to arrive at his own conclusion on how to handle the situation raised in the conversation. I also have trouble with objectifying situations presented by my coachees who are part of the same organisation. I notice that I have my own "opinion" on the situation. This is because, in many cases, I know the people and the organisational culture in question. Plus, my coachee often knows in advance what I think about it all. As a result of my consulting and judging, I am often afraid of coaching too much in one specific direction.'

(xlviii) 'A difficult point that frequently recurs is when I am discussing with someone how he could tackle something. Because I work in the same field, I often already have a clear idea of how things should be done or what the end result should be. However, the fact that someone else is working on a job means of course that the result is not always the same as if I were to do it myself (leaving aside the issue of whether they do it better or worse). I find it difficult to let go.'

(xlix) 'The direct question from a coachee: do you think I am suitable as a manager? That was difficult because I had my doubts but didn't want to offend, discourage or demotivate him.'

(l) 'At a particular moment the coachee opted for a strategy that I personally did not support. I found it very difficult to remain objective and not to air my own opinion, for example by asking leading questions. I saw the solution in front of me but the coachee clearly couldn't see it, or not yet.'

(li) 'I have always known what to do. What I find difficult is to draw a distinction between myself as a manager who has solutions and wants to offer them, and as a coach whose primary duty is to foster trouble-spotting and problem-solving capabilities in the other person. Sometimes you feel you have to be content with a second-best solution on the part of the other person. Sometimes I am asked outright what I would do. In those cases, I just outline my method of working.'

(lii) 'When my coachee let off steam over a situation we both found very annoying. I was at risk of falling into the trap of joining in and having a good grumble.'

(liii) 'My coachee is trained as a psychologist and psychotherapist. She works here as a policy adviser. She came to me in a period of burn-out, saying that she had already tried several approaches and was seeing a psychologist but so far nothing had come of it. She knew why she was feeling so bad, but lacked the energy to break out of the vicious circle. While I was telling her how I would set about working with her and that we would try to find her strengths together, she was regarding me very suspiciously. I heard myself talking enthusiastically and could well imagine that the sessions would not hold out much hope of salvation to her either. Nevertheless, she started the coaching course. She was so low that she really needed some help. After several sessions in which she had showed an upward trend in my view, we had studied things in depth and were making plans to find a different position for her, she started coming up with completely unreal

> career choices. Professions that required a minimum of four years'
> study. Nothing that *was* within her grasp appealed to her. At
> that point she took it into her head that all of our conversations
> up to then had been pointless. I found myself getting rather irri-
> tated by this. Later, I realised it was escape behaviour and dis-
> cussed that with her.'

14 Breakthroughs

(liv)	'Critical moments are when someone's awareness is raised as the "penny drops".'
(lv)	'Seeing, hearing and feeling that the other person has suddenly arrived at an understanding, so that everything is different from that moment on.'
(lvi)	'There are many critical moments, especially in a positive sense. I mean the feeling of satisfaction when things are going well, and you have helped someone achieve what they wanted to achieve.'

15 Directing the conversation

(lvii)	'The moment when you feel you have to start to create structure in the conversation still gives me cause for doubt. What is a good comment or question? And questions arise such as: what will come out of this conversation? What should I offer, or should I offer nothing at all?'
(lviii)	'What I find critical are the moments when I have to decide whether to go along with the coachee on a certain path or whether to branch off as a result of an intervention on my part.'
(lix)	'Individual coaching: striking a balance between business context and personal growth.'
(lx)	'When I confronted her with her behaviour for the first time. In our conversations we had been going round in circles. A recurring argument was the pressure of work she had to perform under. I wasn't able to break out of the circle, until the moment when I confronted her with her behaviour: by constantly bringing up the pressure of work argument, she didn't have to change her behav-iour. As a result of the confrontation, we were able to reach a deeper level and break out of the circle. It was a critical moment because I didn't know how she would take it and had the feeling I was entering someone else's territory.'

(lxi) 'Coaching conversation with a colleague who has come to me for career advice. His dilemma is whether to continue with all of his current activities including a national presence, or to take a step backwards but to add sparkle. Full of enthusiasm, he explains how he invests his time in the national network. I think that this is precisely the dilemma and wonder how to confront him with it. Since he is a very analytical and highly educated man, I try a roundabout route. I throw at him: "So you're leaving your employer and customers in the lurch." Coachee: "???" Coach: "Your employer and customers are entitled to a properly rested worker but you're clearly not taking it seriously, you're just tiring yourself out in your free time."'

(lxii) 'My most critical and frustrating moment was one when I didn't know what to do any more. I was coaching someone whose issue was how best to handle her immediate colleague, who was causing her a lot of stress. She had a number of learning issues, because she *appeared* to realise that she couldn't change her colleague. Our sessions were about "what I can do to handle this better". However, she seemed to keep coming back to the fact that her manager needed to deal with her colleague, and similar frustrations, instead of looking at her own behaviour. I frequently brought her back to our objectives and confronted her with these, but this helped only temporarily. In the end we worked out a number of options for her to change the current situation, but it took a lot of pushing and pulling on my part (I was often pushed into the role of expert, which I usually managed to avoid by throwing the issues back at her, but this didn't always work). In the end I cut to the chase and said: "the choice is yours, if you want to change this you will have to take action yourself. If you don't, what more do you want to get out of these sessions?" Then she said that she agreed with this, but never took any action and the sessions were terminated. I realise that I wasn't clear about her learning objectives in the end, that I was mainly supposed to be a listener and give her advice from time to time. I (not she) found it necessary to make her realise that her own behaviour also played a role in the situation. She saw that to some extent, but not enough.'

(lxiii) 'My coachee is a director of a support service. Our sessions are often about his management team, which is not functioning as a team. A critical situation that has occurred more than once is the moment when he says that he has given up on his MT. They work well as individuals, but not as a team. He sees no point in investing any more energy in them. When he comes to this conclusion he is no longer open to reflection about his own behaviour and doesn't want to explore it any further. I am not able to pursue it because he is pulling the strings and changes the subject.'

16 Matching coach to coachee

(lxiv)	'I am fairly extrovert myself. My coachee, on the other hand, is fairly introverted. Time and again, I find it exciting to be able to see during conversations whether or not my comments are hitting home, or whether or not he agrees with them. Usually I don't find out until later, when he comes back to it. I ask about it directly on a regular basis, but I still have the feeling that I don't know exactly what is going on in him and whether or not I am helping him.'
(lxv)	'A critical moment was a coaching conversation dealing with introversion. The person in question was so shy that making contact with other people was too much for her. Even with me, she found it difficult to make contact and at the end of an hour's coaching I was exhausted because *I* had been hard at work, not *her*. She was mainly physically present and I was always speaking because she said nothing, not even when I allowed long silences to descend. In the end I decided to mirror her behaviour very forcefully (doodling while she was giving an answer, not making eye contact, saying nothing in return), which forced her to adopt another role. This turned out well, but it could have backfired.'
(lxvi)	'When and how to make the transition from more substantive matters to personal matters. I find that particularly difficult with introverted coachees who have little, or very subtle, expression.'
(lxvii)	'Someone who didn't want to change or develop himself, or denied suggestions for development. Or someone who wanted something that I seriously doubted he could do. Or someone who wanted something I was sure was impossible.'
(lxviii)	'I am coaching one director who, in my experience, can be a bit blunt and sometimes rather clumsy. His own interests can be heard in many of his comments and he often reacts against his environment. If you examine this one on one, he does make progress: he does understand things, but in fundamental terms nothing really changes. I haven't been working with him for very long. I am trying to find a balance between timing, i.e. when and how to say something, and the structure of the relationship, i.e. when to let something go. And I wonder in fact if he does want to change. He must be getting something out of it, or he wouldn't continue to display this behaviour. He is also dead set against "psychobabble" from the outset. "Pragmatic" is his watchword. There's nothing wrong with that in itself, of course, but it does close the door to tackling things from a more fundamental angle.'

17 Limits of coaching

(lxix)	'Coaching often goes unnoticed, and is not connected with a coaching contract or explicit coaching conversations. The disadvantage of this is that I sometimes don't realise until later that I'd have done better to have tackled it differently.'
(lxx)	'My coachee, who is also a colleague because I am an internal coach, was clearly in a jam in terms of workload. I wasn't sure whether to tip off his manager in order to support my coachee.'
(lxxi)	'I find it a challenge to learn how a coach can best handle the "professional distance" between coach and coachee. My most critical moment was when the coachee confessed that he had feelings for me. I didn't quite know how to handle that situation.'
(lxxii)	'I heard via my manager that my coachee is getting a "bad" reputation in the organisation. He wouldn't say who had made the comments, but it seems my coachee isn't coming up to expectations. I can't quite place these comments. I've only heard good things about my coachee, in fact. Even from immediate colleagues and other people within the organisation, I've only heard reasonably positive things about him. How do I bring this up? His promotion is now up for discussion as well and in my view that is undeserved.'
(lxxiii)	'Specifically, I find it difficult that I am hearing criticism about my coachee in the corridors and I'm not sure how to get that over to her. I don't know if it makes sense to raise the fact that people are criticising her behind her back. I *would* like to do something with the content of the criticism, but how do you broach that? Is that something she should find out for herself? And how do you make the first move towards that?'
(lxxiv)	'At a specific point in an evaluation conversation, my internal coachee described her experiences with a manager. She had observed the manager in various situations and, using a number of examples and scenarios, was able to set out the pluses and minuses clearly. At the same time, on the basis of my role as her senior, the series of coaching sessions concerned the secondment of the same manager: whether to extend or terminate it? After a quick internal assessment, but without proper consultation with my coachee, I made use of her information. Quite rightly, she tackled me about this. Of course, I made my excuses straight away. I found it particularly annoying myself, and a clear error on my part. I should have known better. Straightaway we had a

useful conversation about mutual responsibility and trust, how to handle information, when to disclose information and what to disclose. But it was still difficult for me, to round off that conversation nicely. On both sides, different roles were inter-mingling: coach, coachee, manager, employee, colleague. In a nutshell, I found I had lost my grip.'

(lxxv) 'My coachee, a manager within the same organisation, is discuss-ing his problems with a female employee and wants to talk to her about them. He has committed the details to paper, such as his experiences and his feelings. We discuss them at length and I praise him for the way he put things down in writing and his planned approach. He short-circuits the results of the conversa-tion with his manager and decides to tackle it in his own way in the end. The critical part of this story is that, after the chosen approach escalated with the employee, I heard from my coachee's manager that he was hiding behind me. I found this disappoint-ing, because I felt used in the issue he had with his employee. At the time I didn't know what made more sense: to give him feedback about my feelings or to leave it at that, because he clearly didn't feel strong enough to speak for himself.'

(lxxvi) 'Because I have various roles in my position and have to deal with many different layers of management, I often end up in situations where I have advance knowledge or background infor-mation that my coachee doesn't or shouldn't have. In many cases, it is not my duty to share that knowledge with my coachee. Situations may also arise where I feel obliged to do something with the information I get from the coachee vis-à-vis senior management, such as give out a signal. At moments like that I really doubt what to do; until now I have been frank about such a dilemma with the coachee. But I think I always run the risk that the coachee will see it as a restriction that I sometimes represent several interests. In other words: I am often restricted by the fact that I am an internal adviser and coaching is only one of my roles.'

(lxxvii) 'The feeling that I can get rid of my coachee because there are "too many cooks", because there was already another counsellor present. I wondered if I should bring this up for discussion in the organisation, or let it go, and/or discuss it with the coachee.'

18 Impact of the organisation

(lxxviii) 'The most critical moment was when an employee, my internal coachee, broke off his training, stopped it after a year and then wondered where to go from there. It turned out that a traumatic experience within the organisation was his reason for stopping. As a result of the coaching conversation that helped him to handle that experience, he is now continuing his studies. I find it very difficult, when the organisation has laid down guidelines, to induce employees to set in train a development process themselves.'

(lxxix) 'Recently there was a "what next?" moment with a manager who is having problems with his department and the management of the company. While technically very capable, he frequently has angry outbursts that reduce his effectiveness. He is deeply affected by the fact that some people don't like him, and is keen to do something about it. During the sessions we look at how things could be different, with a bit of positive thinking, visualisation and NLP, but not long ago part of his department was transferred to another manager. So we're back to square one. I think that's a shame. A moment when I am not sure how to help him from here, and whether it makes sense generally.'

19 Team coaching

(lxxx) 'Team coaching: bringing different interests in team conflict on to the table and making them workable.'

Appendix B
78 Critical Moments of Experienced Coaches

1 Managing key conditions: context of the coaching conversation

(i) 'I have three meetings in a row with people from the same organisation. At my house, not at the company. I'm overrunning a bit, so the fifteen-minute break between appointments is always used up. So they see each other when they arrive and leave. They are very friendly and cheerful towards each other but I feel uncomfortable and think I'm not handling this right.'

(ii) 'I meet with a coachee at work. The room has thin walls and is much too warm. I don't get much out of the coachee. I want to leave, feel very out of sorts. After a while I decide to say so and suggest that we take a walk outside and hold a coaching conversation there. As we walk, we have a useful conversation about how he can start to make his work more interesting.'

(iii) 'At the start of a team coaching programme, very early on in the proceedings, you often get members putting demands on the table or quibbling over basic conditions. I find this annoying: you don't know the team yet, you barely know the team members, haven't yet formulated a common objective, either for the team or for the coaching, but you have to intervene immediately. You set the tone; you lay down your key conditions in a non-negotiable way: you can get off to a flying start or you can pack up and clear off. A tense moment.'

2 Managing key conditions: triangular contracts

(iv) 'It's exciting to see if the other person will let you connect with him, if trust will develop, particularly when someone feels coerced.'

(v)   'A manager asks me to coach one of his employees. I comply, but
       it remains unclear to me what the issue is. I ring the manager after
       the first session, with the employee's consent, to get a clearer idea
       of the manager's issue. In the course of the conversation I begin to
       suspect that he's doing a spot of file-padding: I think this employee
       is not to be given a second chance, his file must say that every
       option has been tried. The second appointment with the employee
       has already been made.'

(vi)   'Someone I coached very satisfactorily a long time ago and whom
       I meet regularly both as a friend and professionally comes to me
       urgently for help: will I coach his teenage son, because things can't
       go on this way, family crisis. I am keen to help him and suggest
       doing it privately, a personal meeting, nothing to do with the
       office, free of charge, as a favour to a friend. I do it, all goes well
       and the outcome is good but I don't feel very professional. Plus a
       fellow coach says it was stupid of me.'

(vii) 'A highly-trained specialist/project manager who had always had
       very good evaluations asks for coaching in order to improve in a
       number of respects following the arrival of a new boss, an interim
       manager. In a three-way conversation with the boss, the latter says
       he expects a more proactive attitude, more thinking ahead about
       what the directors in his account are busy with, and at the same
       time a sharper focus on results. We set to work. Half-way through
       the course I notice that my coachee is still displaying resistance to
       improving relationships with some key people in his network,
       because he has in fact given up. He also feels that his boss is asking
       the impossible of him and doesn't show enough appreciation for
       the steps he has already taken. I don't feel I can make much more
       headway with him like this, and am afraid I'll end up flogging a
       dead horse. I decide to introduce a progress meeting with his boss.
       In the second three-way meeting I ask my coachee's boss what
       progress he has noticed so far, what he is happy with and what, in
       his view, needs improvement. The boss is able to answer in very
       specific terms. However, in this meeting I notice something else is
       coming into play and ask the boss further questions about his own
       ambitions and how he sees the development of his team. He takes
       the subject very seriously. The conversation reveals why he consid-
       ers certain contacts important and what type of behaviour he would
       like to see from my coachee in specific situations. In a subsequent
       evaluation with my coachee, the latter says it is only now that he
       has a clearer idea, for the first time, of what his boss stands for. He
       also understands the urgency better, and the strategic direction of
       what is expected in his role. His motivation to work on this has
       greatly increased.'

(viii) 'One critical moment I remember is when I had been asked by the MD of a company to do some "remedial" coaching with his deputy. They did not share the same management style. The MD had briefed the deputy and he was happy to be involved in the coaching process. I had clear success criteria from the MD – which were to work with the deputy to explore the areas the MD was not happy with and determine a way forward. On my first meeting with the deputy, he told me that he was actively looking for a new job and his aim was to leave the company at the earliest opportunity. His mind was made up (we explored this). He did not want the MD to know this. This posed an ethical dilemma for me. In working with the deputy, some of the issues I would have explored with him were: how far he was willing to change his style; how this impacted his own values; what other options did he have, etc. In other coaching situations I have worked with clients to help them move on to new jobs. However in this case, I did not feel I could coach the deputy in leaving the organisation, though he would have liked me to. So we needed to terminate the coaching relationship before it had started – but with me unable to explain to the MD client why. We resolved this by my coaching the deputy to explore the best way to further his plan of leaving at the first opportunity, and him coming to the conclusion that it would be better if he were to tell his MD rather than hiding it from him. I suppose the critical bit was that for a while I really did not know how best to approach this – having loyalty to both clients.'

(ix) 'I once had a co-coaching relationship with the chairman of a medium/small company whom I had recommended to the MD of the company. I also informally coached the MD. At one juncture the MD said that he was planning to part with the services of the chairman, because (A) he had too much of a "large company" approach (he had been, but was no longer the deputy chairman of a FTSE 100 company) and (B) he was being needy and seeking to spend too much time in the company to the detriment of its ongoing work. I was torn as to how/whether to approach the chairman about this. I knew that this role mattered to him, that he was relatively short of work, and that we had a relationship where I could help him work through the issues that the MD had raised with me. I specifically asked the MD if I could speak with the chairman about this and he said he wanted me not to. My dilemma was whether to talk with the chairman and see if he had any inkling that would mean that we could work on the issue without betraying the trust of the MD and the privileged information I had from that coaching conversation. I also wondered whether I could drop a hint or make a suggestion. I didn't consider going back to

the MD as he had been emphatic and clear in his view. In the end
I had a general conversation with the chairman. He didn't raise
the issue and didn't want a discussion at that time. He was subsequently fired from his role. I still don't know whether I did the
right thing.'

(x)   'The client asks me to coach a colleague: high expectations, a
golden boy, a promising future. The colleague seems to want to
talk mainly about starting up his own business. I discuss that with
him and then start to think: I can't charge for this! And I can't
tell the client. I tell the coachee this and ask him to discuss it with
his boss or, if they want, to come together next time.'

3 Managing key conditions: 'reading' the coachee

(xi)   'A moment that is always difficult for me is at the start of the first
conversation, when asking questions following the coachee's initial
account. I can't yet tell how tense the other person is and find it
'a difficult situation' to judge what pace to set. I can't "read" the
other person very well yet. Later, when more has been said and
exchanged, when there has been some movement, I find it much
easier. "You can't see something that's standing still".'

(xii)   'In my early days as a coach, about ten years ago, I was supervising
a number of female professionals in a major accountancy firm. The
problem was usually to do with career development, sabbaticals,
etc. My client was young, around 25, blonde, wearing a suit and
gold jewellery: at first glance the kind you might describe as a dumb
blonde if you were to be sexist about it. She later turned out to be
far from dumb and very entrepreneurial but was often put in the
position of departmental ornament by her bosses because she was
attractive, sweet-natured and unassuming. I also misjudged her
initially, until our third meeting, when I found myself being a bit
too controlling and asked her: are we on the right track here? "Yes
of course", she said, "but we should also take a look at my previous
job. I talked about it a bit at the start but you didn't pick up on it
and then I decided to wait for my chance to bring it up again at
an appropriate time. And this is it". I felt strangely ashamed and
pleased at the same time: about being corrected on the one hand
and bearing joint responsibility on the other. I wished I had more
clients like her. I often look for ways to create joint responsibility
and am very satisfied when I manage to get someone other than
myself to take responsibility for the coaching process.'

(xiii) 'Feeling disillusioned after five years with her present employer my client has handed in her notice and has found a new job. It's our first meeting; we have been working together for an hour. She's charming to work with, we have covered a lot of ground – yet it is tiring – energy-sapping even. I suggest a break and a cup of tea in a different location. Suddenly she has lots of energy and is talking about what she really wants to do. This is totally different. We return to the coaching room and I am puzzled by something I can't put my finger on, so I observe how her energy has risen and fallen away again. Something shifts. We agree that we need to hold onto the positive state of mind for thinking about her new job, rather than falling into the trap of feeling overwhelmed that characterised her last job. I also sense there is a risk of me putting too much into this relationship, and I do not want to disempower her. Instead, I suggest we agree some ground rules for working together which include us explicitly taking joint responsibility for monitoring energy levels and intervening when we feel them slipping.'

(xiv) 'I have a first meeting with a coachee and he says nothing for the first few minutes, with a lot of facial expressions. I have never experienced this, I find it unusual, but I don't say anything, just smile. I believe he will say something in the end, and he does.'

4 Deepening by exploring

(xv) 'I was the change and HR consultant, working with staff of a global financial services company on the implications of a potential sale of a global subsidiary – I was involved in all the negotiations. The sale was aborted twice – slightly complex in that it also had a third party involved. I had positioned myself with the MD of the subsidiary as his informal coach – so there was no explicit contract but we had regular one to one sessions. On one such occasion, we were talking about the second "abort" and I managed to start helping him to explore how he was feeling towards the whole situation. He opened up to me, was very open about what he wanted but then talked about his relationship with his boss. It became clear that he didn't know what was going to happen to himself after the sale so he was inadvertently putting "spanners in the works" in the negotiations. As a result of this session, he went to his boss and asked him explicitly about his own future – another buyer came along and the MD was very upfront from the start that he was not part of the sale – the whole thing then went through smoothly.'

(xvi)   'This was a telephone coaching moment, working with a Belgian lady (in English) who takes her job and responsibilities very seriously but is not very communicative or assertive. We had spent two hours working face-to-face and had had one hour-long telephone coaching session during the preceding three months which had been dominated by a problem she had with a team member, X: "Who will do literally what he is asked to do but will not take ownership of the job, use any initiative or prioritise tasks. He has no professional objectives or goals." In our previous session she had decided that she would have a face-to-face session with X to explore the reasons for his behaviour and with her boss to discover the options for training or replacing X. We discussed her findings – she had gained some insights into X's motivation and his abilities and had clarified the situation with her boss about hiring and firing – but the crux of the matter was that deep down she believed that she had to solve X's problem, partly because her boss was not supporting her: "It's difficult to know what he's thinking and he doesn't do what he says". I was searching for something that would throw a different light on the situation to help my coachee to move forward. The moment happened as she talked more freely and openly about her own feelings about the individuals involved: X, her boss and the other members of the team. It became apparent that the situation was much more serious than she had described and that X's method of working was regressive, creating problems for colleagues and salesmen who fed into the department. By describing this, she was able to acknowledge that the situation had to be resolved and she needed the support of her boss to do so. To gain his support she needed to challenge him by offering two courses of action, both of which he had been avoiding. She appeared much encouraged by this and decided she would confront him the following week.'

(xvii) 'One of my clients, a finance director of a medium-sized company, had heard, just after his intake meeting with me, for a coaching programme, that the company was to be investigated. The operation of the management board was a central focus of the investigation. He was the last one in and knew that he had to change his communication style. Very soon, however, the supervisory board had reason to conduct an investigation into whether the composition of the board was correct. The coachee was well aware that his position was under discussion. Within a week, we went over his communication style, when it was appropriate and when not, and what he considered a suitable position in the investigation. It became clear during these sessions that he had to become much more conscious of the effect of his words. The combination of his strong drive in an environment where changes were viewed with a great deal of anxiety made his position very risky. In the end his interview with the consultancy firm took place the following week. It went very well. When it was over the firm rang him in the evening to say that, before the interview, they had been of the opinion that his position was no longer tenable. The good impression he made during the interview had caused them to change their minds. The meeting felt almost like an exam for the coachee. The fact that it went well meant he had "passed". This was the springboard for a successful coaching programme in which he was able to broaden his repertoire of behaviour permanently.'

5 Deepening by continuing to ask questions

(xviii) 'One critical moment occurred during conflict coaching of two people in an escalated conflict, where the failure of the coaching would result in one of them being dismissed. The conflict coaching of the pair was the springboard for team coaching of the entire team in order to create responsibility for results among the team as a whole. Distrust played a major role and at one point I heard myself asking the (awful) coach's question: "What do you need to restore trust?". "Not possible!", they both shouted. The thought crossed my mind: end of story, assignment failed, until I feverishly managed to dredge up the term "healthy distrust" from somewhere deep in my memory. I then asked them: with what level of distrust can you still work together? This was the turning point in the conflict and now, a year and a half later, the whole team is still working together.'

(xix) 'A female director of a welfare institution wonders why she can't deal appropriately with a fellow member of the management team who is not functioning properly due to a depressive illness. The coachee is experienced and competent enough but, in this case, she prefers to avoid confrontation even though her colleague is underperforming. At one point I asked her, have you ever had to deal with people with depression before? She went quiet and started to twist around in her chair. I held my breath, curious to find out what was coming. After a while (you could see her literally sinking with her mood) she said, "Yes, my younger brother was depressive and kept threatening suicide from the age of 11, and I tried to stop him". Ah, no wonder she felt uncomfortable having to deal with depressive people again. When this literally "came to the surface", it was a great relief to her, and to me. We didn't go into it too deeply, there was no need. After this conversation she took the time to process things herself. Then she was able to talk to her colleague, because the confusion was gone. This was a memorable moment for me, literally watching someone delving into her "subconscious". It did cost me the armrest of the chair, but that was a price I was willing to pay.'

6 Deepening by summarising and mirroring

(xx)   'During the early part of the coaching session, I asked Jane to "take some time to reflect with me on the leadership programme she is currently undertaking" and to "talk me through her main learning points". In doing so, I noticed that the story she was telling did not sound as healthy or rosy from my own detached position. I sensed potential elements of "groupthink" within her story, but did not display any reaction. Keeping my own perceptions within me, I stayed neutral and simply repeated some of her words about what had happened, then added "and how did you feel about that?" I was acutely aware not to impose any judgement about the story Jane was telling me. My aim was to find a way to get her to think more thoroughly about her experience. In reflecting back what I heard, I used many of her own words, but I spoke these in a more neutral tone (compared with her quite excited, positive tone) – as if I was indicating "did I hear you right, you said that . . .", and then I asked her how she felt about this. This stance seemed to work in that Jane did begin to think again and more deeply about her experience. Through this iterative process, she discovered some valuable insights for herself and about herself which seemed to have had been buried within her for some time.'

(xxi)   'My coaching client was a rather young man (early 30s) who had been recently promoted to a sales director role, for a small, but rapidly growing high tech company. He'd gone through a 360° feedback process and his agreed coaching agenda (with me) was to learn to develop a "more facilitative/coaching" and, ultimately, a "more empowering, leadership style". The critical moment for me, was when we'd reached the end of our coaching contract and were reviewing progress made against his original coaching objectives. I was expecting him to highlight changes he'd made, in the areas above – where he had, in fact, made some very positive progress. What he said surprised me, and reminded me, that it is often internal shifts of attitude or perception that bring about the most significant change for people, rather than specific behaviours to be learned or honed. His response to this "review" type question, "What did you appreciate most about the coaching?", prompted the following response: "It was actually an observation you shared with me. I remember saying that the people I know outside work (friends and family) wouldn't recognise me in this [360°] feedback ... that outside of work, I'm much more easy going ... enjoy having a laugh ... and people know me as being an outgoing, fun loving, and friendly kind of guy! So when you said that I seemed to leave the person that I am at the factory gate ... I thought, that's it! ... Why don't I bring more of who I am to work, rather than trying to be some sort of "caricature", of what I think a manager should be? When I started doing that I felt much more at ease – more myself – and the improved work relationships, just seemed to follow." So, the critical moment (and learning) for me, was: to review with my clients, more frequently, what's having an impact (sometimes not what I would anticipate), to allow that more expression, and to be more mindful of the fact, that the most significant shifts that happen, are internal ones.'

(xxii) 'The laid-off client who had held upper management roles with large *Fortune* 500s, travelled for them internationally, written speeches for senior VPs, who could only see herself as moving on to an editing or admin job until I held a verbal mirror for her, repeating back her own accomplishments to her in her own words.'

(xxiii) 'When I notice a pattern in the other person's responses that is preventing him from being effective, it is exciting to see if I can put it in such a way that the other person can hear it and, indeed, if I can point him or her towards the way out.'

(xxiv) 'During a coaching conversation I confronted the coachee three or four times with his own behaviour in a particular situation, where he put the "blame" on someone else. The coachee didn't like this and threatened to get up and leave. Despite this, I made another attempt. The coachee got up from his chair, then became very emotional and sat down again. Then came the acknowledgement and the "true" story.'

(xxv) 'An exploratory discussion with a new client, a financial consultant who has been referred to me. He said on the phone that he wants to learn how to convince his clients to follow his advice. I suspect he is someone who wants to develop the relational side of consulting for himself. While getting to know this client it strikes me that he is very evasive about his background. Usually I leave it to the client to decide what he wants to tell me about that, but it's taking much too long. I ask him whether all of that information is significant in terms of the aim that he wants to achieve. The client keeps on talking enthusiastically. I bring up the time aspect; in view of the time, could he be a bit more concise. That too has virtually no effect. I point out that he seems to be finding it difficult to rein himself in, and ask if that's also a factor in other situations. The client agrees, and the conversation takes a completely different turn: he recently visited a psychiatrist to investigate whether he might be manic. What do you do about this in coaching? Do you restrict the coaching programme to learning how to handle the relationship with consultancy clients better (my words), or do you aim for a more comprehensive course in which the consultant learns how to handle himself better (to contain himself) in his work (e.g. in the contact with his consultancy clients)? And who decides which choice is made? In consultation with the client, I decide to hold a three-way conversation with his boss to explore this further. I'm still struggling with the question of how, if the coaching becomes this comprehensive programme (which the client opts for), I can continue to confine my facilitation to coaching alone.'

7 Deepening by giving feedback

(xxvi)	'I am coaching a highly articulate person who acts very convinced of his own abilities. What he is saying sounds logical but I suspect it is not entirely true. I don't take to him much, although I do believe he has the best intentions in his approach to his work and is quite personable. The critical issue for me is how to confront him in such a way that I touch a chord in him that will make him open up rather than clam up. I don't experience such critical moments with people who are very senior in the organisation, but they do sometimes occur with people at lower levels.'
(xxvii)	'Sometimes in coaching you come across a situation where you don't know if you're broaching a topic that the coachee is willing or able to do something with. In career coaching I have confronted people with impediments that they can do relatively little about. One coachee had a pronounced droop to the corners

of his mouth. As a result his facial expression was always sad and offputting. A clear handicap in communication and an obstacle in his career. In my view it was absolutely a subject for conversation. However, I always find it tricky to touch on topics like these; to give some practical examples: "Sir, you stink, you have to do something about it"; "Madam, your facial expression almost always creates distance; I can't do anything about it, neither can you, but it's holding you back enormously"; "True, you want to become a director, but I don't think you'll ever be considered for it, any more than I am likely to make prima ballerina. In my view, you lack the basic skills".'

(xxviii) 'In an intake meeting a member of the board of a large organisation gives an account which leads me to conclude that he is on the verge of burn-out. At the same time, the newspapers have reported that his chairman is in the running for another job. He should really ease off the gas and make some structural changes to his situation, but at the same time the organisation will be making heavy demands on him to give his chairman more leeway. I decide to confront him head-on with the consequences of carrying on the way he is, point out that medication is not enough and experience shows that there are a lot of victims in his age group. My fear is that if I am too hard on him, I will lose him. Paradoxically, as he told me later, he had confidence in me because I didn't beat about the bush and he himself felt that he couldn't go on with things as they were. In the coaching sessions we continued to work on broadening his perspective on what was important in his life, making better use of sources of help, delegating more effectively in general and bringing about a major shift in his duties. A precondition was that he should make it very clear within his organisation what his needs and abilities were at that moment.'

(xxix) 'On Monday morning I met and started working with a senior guy. After 30 minutes or so I realised that what he was saying did not make sense to me – i.e. inconsistent and no logic. I gulped, thought to myself that I was putting my career on the line and decided to say what I was thinking. I said that I found that what he was saying did not seem to make much sense to me. After a while I said that it sounded like nonsense. He was taken aback, continued working with me and listened hard. On the Friday he told me that he had given a lot of thought to what I had said, and agreed that I was right. It had caused him to really think through what his vision should be. His colleagues applauded him and told him it was the best of the group.'

8 Deepening by contributing something oneself

> (xxx) 'If my coachee is not very forthcoming, I start talking about an experience of my own. It's exciting to see if my story will prompt the other person to step in and explore his own situation.'
>
> (xxxi) 'If I offer an insight, such as the suggestion: "Would it help to look at it this way?", and the other person doesn't pick it up, I sometimes have to suppress the inclination to offer it again instead of waiting or exploring where the other person is at. That is difficult because I am pretty convinced that it will help: if I just try it one more time.'

9 Deepening by means of transposition (homework, role-play, psychodrama, etc.)

> (xxxii) 'I can think of several where I have introduced a "right-brain" approach such as a guided fantasy to explore unwanted "baggage"; a flipchart drawing to capture feelings about an issue; walking a time-line to explore difficult options; using each hand to represent opposing drives and to explore potential integration – in all I experienced a moment of breathless waiting: asking a question, seeking their response to the activity and its impact, or just waiting for them to engage with the suggestion. Each time there is a sense of "Is this a step too far for now?"; 'Are they ready to engage with this issue in a deeper, more meaningful way and with this approach?"; 'Will it leave them worse off or able to move forward"? Always there is a sense of asking them to move into the unknown to a degree, and of moving into the unknown with them. Often there results a deeper insight, emotional awareness, clarity – which is what I am hoping. People can get upset at times in coaching but in the incidents described they (usually) engage and become intently curious to explore. My breathless anticipation includes a fear of what may be raised to awareness and a readiness to deal with whatever materialises. The worst seems to be that occasionally the activity fizzles out, the impact seems negligible and we pass on. I don't recall any dreadful consequence. Despite this when it proves very helpful I always experience it as walking on eggshells, on a tightrope, it feels precarious.'
>
> (xxxiii) 'This client was in a highly dysfunctional work situation. She was struggling to keep her sense of herself and her vision, when the men around her – both peers and bosses – were putting

political and psychological pressure (intentional or not) on her to conform to their conservative views. This client had a vibrant, eclectic, powerful vision for how her organisation could team with other local organisations from the local community to create a new and much-needed approach to long-standing issues around housing, land development, and growth – a vision that was being drowned by the resistance and lack of vision of these men. At one of our sessions she and I both were at a bit of a loss for how to get her head above water so she could breathe on her own again when I had an inspiration. I had her take a chair for each person with whom she was struggling, and set them in a semi-circle. I then had her conduct a meeting with them, saying exactly what she needed and wanted to say to each, without restraint. That simple (and I'm sure not unique) bit of role-play helped her take back her sense of herself and her goals. She referred back to it a number of times in our subsequent work together. She has since left the organisation for a much higher-level role with a significant pay increase (obtained in part through our working together).'

(xxxiv) 'I was working with a coachee who was asked to develop his emotional expressiveness by the board member he reports to. I worked through an exercise with him to remember a moment when he had not been expressive, and then to switch into a memory of a highly expressive moment, and then back into the non-expressive experience. The moment felt tense because here is this big man, we are well into our coaching session, where he defended a lot by rationalising why he needed the coaching (he needed 40 minutes only for that stage!). He turned to the exercise like "let's see what this can do for me", not cynical, but not believing either. We worked through it; we had a moment of silence during the switch to the non-expressive moment. I held the silence which was one of the hardest ones for me ever. And suddenly he burst out "oh my God, I can see it, I can see what I do wrong. It is so easy! I cannot believe that this realisation has only taken 3 minutes and yet it is critical for my future success and promotion to the board!"'

(xxxv) 'I'm reminded of some work I did last year with a client where she brought some poetry along to the coaching session. The session before she'd been exploring the way she presents herself in her organisation and how she holds a lot back. She had also spoken about her love of poetry and how important it had been to her during her life. I can't remember exactly how the idea emerged, but to cut a long story short, I suggested that next time she brought some poetry that in some way represented what mattered most to her, her essence etc. She took this piece of homework very seriously and came prepared with 3 books of poetry, with one poem from each. I must admit I wasn't sure how the session was going to go, but I needn't have worried. The poems were beautiful and moving in their own right, but more importantly they helped my client get in touch with her deeper values and passions that she had been neglecting for some time at work. This opened up a whole new area of work for us and marked something of a turning point for us both. Through this experience I learned about really trusting my client and being prepared to go with their flow – even if it felt quite risky at the time. I wouldn't necessarily replicate this approach with others, but it was the right thing to do with this particular person. I guess the critical moment was in making the suggestion and staying with it through the process.'

(xxxvi)   'A fellow coach who is very dear to me doesn't think much of my handing out homework: coaching works on a higher level: attitude, identity, changing people by means of a deeply-felt insight. I say a small change in behaviour can have a huge effect. We don't agree. I get the feeling he doesn't approve of me.'

(xxxvii)   'A brilliant professor had become hugely stressed during years of conflict in his faculty. He developed a sort of phobia: he couldn't drive any more, or fly, even though he was constantly required to at his level and in his position. It was getting him into a lot of hot water. We went together to visit people in other universities, taking my car. At one point I thought why not let him drive for a while. He was keen to do so. But oh dear, he drove so fast and recklessly that I had never been so afraid, my life flashed before me, my heart nearly stopped, although I felt I had to allow him as much room as possible. We survived, and he started driving himself again. Later on he bought a larger house, and after that he started flying again. He did make use of the room I allowed him, but it was a typical case of "phew, that was close!"'

(xxxviii)   'A professor is faced with a dilemma: do I stay at my current university where I was recently passed over for the position of head of department, do I go to another – less renowned – university, or do I take up an offer from abroad to set up something in my own specialty there? He set out the pros and cons of these three options during our first meeting. But that was as far as he got. In our second meeting he asks himself: how do I decide? I suggest that we start this meeting not with the options but with him; what drives him in his work, how he sees his future, and so on. And then explore the options on that basis. The client seems to like this idea, but keeps having doubts about whether one choice would suit him better than another. Each time he seems to be favouring one alternative, he stresses advantages of another, and vice-versa. I point this out, and the client acknowledges it. But this isn't helping him to decide. He has reached an impasse, and I can allow that impasse to continue in order to see how things unfold. I think it will be instructive. But the client is also under pressure of time: he has to decide next week. Can I also do something to support him? I decide to offer something completely different to what the client is used to. I invite him to participate in a focus exercise in which he explores from a physical awareness which option suits him best. He comes to a decision, but has he also learned how to handle a dilemma the next time round?'

(xxxix)   'First feeling swamped by a torrent of words from a client needing to unload a lengthy description of his story to date, why he was where he was, in great detail for about three hours. It was all I could do to get a question in here and there: "how had he coped?", get him to take a physical break, or to reflect back a summary. Questions designed to move him on were ignored until he had finished his account. I felt out of control and did not look forward to the next session – another verbal waterfall. When we met next, perhaps two weeks later and I took him out of his usual environment, to where I coach, and asked him a version of the "miracle question" with his answer to be drawn, not spoken. I was quite anxious that he would refuse, but felt I had to try something different. He went very quiet and spent 15 or 20 minutes drawing an intense image, impressionistic and holistic, unlike his detailed accounts as of very specific incidents. He was clearly moved and struggled to slowly convey his thoughts and feelings in words. I felt as if I'd plugged a leak but allowed something else to flow, which would take us somewhere of value. The image stayed in the background of many subsequent sessions. But in a relationship lasting about three years, covering much useful ground, I never quite captured the magic of that moment when a new language was found.'

10 Deepening by bringing up the transference here and now

(xl) 'The coachee uses long sentences and lots of words to describe the problem that he wants to work on in the coaching conversation. I summarise his issue: so, if I understand correctly, your issue for today is . . . "No", says the coachee, "that's not what I mean". I am surprised because I believe I have summarised his issue well, in his own words. He explains it again. Using identical sentences, and the same words. This time I interrupt with short questions intended to clarify and occasional mini-summaries. He is constantly confused by my questions, he "didn't mean" that, and the same with my summaries, "no, you misunderstand me". I suspect I *am* on the right track but his real issue is something else, even though the coachee keeps telling me I'm on the wrong track. We try again, with the help of keywords on a sheet of paper. I intervene: "I don't believe I can help you today, because I am obviously not able to understand what your issue is. I've spent the last fifteen minutes trying to clarify in various ways, but I'm getting nowhere. And I strongly suspect that you actually want to talk about a different issue today, but perhaps don't dare to put it into words." This is greeted with silence. The coachee goes pale and moist-eyed and, hesitatingly, comes out with a completely different story. This often happens in conversations, coachees have to gather the courage "to pop the real question" and first spend some time "beating about the bush". But I always find these moments very exciting.'

(xli) 'I am asked to coach a secretary whose boss I have known for 20 years, as a friend and client. The secretary was transferred to him from another colleague, something she sees as a personal rejection. During the sessions that follow I am worn out by the torrent of words, critical, perfectionist, that flows from her. I start to discuss alternatives with her, but she doesn't take me up on them, neither does RET work, nor conversational techniques, etc. I decide to confront her: spell out the effect of her constant blaming on me and so perhaps on her surroundings as well, offer alternatives, demonstrate, suggest she watch herself on video. I work and work and work, and nothing happens. Later, I ring her boss and tell him I want to stop the coaching if he doesn't tell her that he has a problem with her performance. The next time, it doesn't appear that he's done it.'

(xlii) 'I was coaching a controller. We had a contract for a year's work during which he wanted to become more participative, change the culture of his organisation through changing his leadership style which he recognised was quite directive and controlling. During one session he was musing about why his staff found him controlling and rather intimidating. He said, "I think I am a very good listener; I am skilled at handling appraisals and similar meetings and I don't understand how I create this effect". In that moment I said: "Yes, I think you listen with great skill, but even when you are listening to me I feel controlled by you". He replies, "What do you mean?" I go on, "It is as if you have two modes, one when you are persuading me of your view, and you are very persuasive and articulate, but even when you are in listening mode, reflecting back, paraphrasing and so on, I feel as if I cannot tell you anything you don't already know. It is as if you anticipate everything I am going to say. I can't take you by surprise, and therefore I feel I cannot influence you, so I think I understand how your staff experiences you. The trouble is that you are just so damned skilful that you do always seem to be in control". This felt a moment when I put myself at risk. I felt vulnerable and he was confused and needed to try and understand what I was saying to him, and it may have been a turning point.'

(xliii) 'It is my third meeting with a woman in a senior management position. She wants to work on a dilemma that she is finding very difficult: she is perceived as very authoritarian and controlling but she sees things differently, she sees herself as uncertain about her own behaviour and often seeking confirmation. In previous meetings we worked a bit on that uncertainty, with difficulty, on the basis of her biography. In this meeting she is quick to complain that we are not making much progress, she questions my expertise and does so in a very authoritarian and aggressive manner. I am shocked and feel initially under attack, and also guilty. Am I helping her enough? Are we in fact making any progress? Then I realise that she is doing the same thing here with me that she does in her work, and that I am responding in the same way. I bring up this pattern of interaction and tell her how I feel. This is very confrontational for her, at first she denies any parallel with her work and her issue. She wants to move on with "something useful". However, I feel I shouldn't give up so easily, and use this reaction to describe the pattern of our interaction again, including my own feelings of failure and inadequacy. This time it has an effect, she is now prepared to explore it together here and now.'

11 Deepening by bringing up the coaching relationship

(xliv)   'I am coaching a three-person team. I know the three people
          involved from projects, having worked for the organisation three
          or four times a year in previous years. The nature of the projects
          carried out by the organisation is such that the team members
          are used to operating alone under difficult conditions (Kyrgyzstan,
          Moldavia, Azerbaijan, etc.). Due to a new type of activity with
          different stakeholders, a different method (teamwork with inte-
          gral mutual interchangeability) and a different culture are
          required. During the first meeting, while identifying obstacles,
          one of them says about another: "Yes, T is great on content, but
          is completely unreliable and lacks any integrity". The third
          person, the director, responds with: "Fight it out between your-
          selves. I have known T the longest. I find him straightforward,
          rough but very honest". The dropping of this bombshell made
          me feel tense. I was at a loss for words. I ended the meeting early,
          rang up and suggested a team therapist and suspended the coach-
          ing until after the team therapy.'

(xlv)   'The client dragging her feet about getting herself out of the
          dysfunctional work situation she was in (which had already lead
          to one breakdown) who finally made the choice to move on
          when I told her, with firm compassion, that I'd have to move on
          as her coach if she didn't.'

(xlvi)   'On a number of occasions I've felt that I hadn't really made
          much progress with a client after several intensive sessions. In
          my view, the problem was deeper-seated and I couldn't help him
          enough. However, the client himself said he was satisfied with
          the progress made. Nevertheless, I wanted to recommend finding
          a therapist. In such situations I find it difficult to find a balance
          between (or to reconcile) following his perception and needs and
          expressing my opinion. It was a choice between: he has had
          enough for now and has gained a new perspective (and let's not
          undermine that) and if he steps up a notch he can really take a
          step forward (so let's be honest in my observations). I brought
          up both options, but suspect that it has a demotivating effect
          when you notice that a therapist is a bridge too far.'

(xlvii) 'It is a session with a coachee who, in six meetings, has already
          taken a number of steps in forming a picture of her future, her
          strengths and the steps she can take in order to make her dreams
          a reality. With every meeting, I see her self-confidence grow a
          little. During the last two meetings she admits that she is tired,
          shudders to think of everything that she discovered she can do/be

in the last meetings. She says she hasn't done her homework for the past few weeks, she's tired, nothing is working and she wonders if we shouldn't schedule at least another six meetings. I feel I'm not the person to supervise her now. She needs someone else's help. At the same time, I notice that she is acting dependent on me. I now have to choose. Do I keep her on or refer her to someone else?'

(xlviii) 'Dissatisfaction in myself about the level of personal contact in terms of the dissatisfaction and anxieties that the client was clearly showing. He kept talking at length about himself, from many angles, and wouldn't be drawn on the underlying, more difficult level. Plus, he walked out at my comment that it was perhaps necessary to start working on the more painful material. Then, by mutual agreement, in our third meeting he was finally referred for intensive personal supervision, which he has now completed with a positive outcome.'

12 Handling surprises as a result of exploring

(xlix) 'I was coaching someone around her career and we had used the Myers-Briggs Type Indicator as a way of thinking about preferences etc. We'd chosen this as she wasn't sure which way to go. We were just into looking at the Extraversion/Introversion preference (she had shown a slight Extraversion preference in her profile), when she got quite emotional and upset. The conversation ensued that she felt she more of an introvert but all her life she's been encouraged to be more extraverted and scolded for being more reflective and introverted as a child. It was quite a release for her to realise it was fine to be an introvert, and as we worked on this we were able to go on and explore career options with greater confidence. So I guess for me it's often the unexpected turns in the conversation which create the "critical moment". They aren't always comfortable and I don't know if I handle them as well as I should, but I think my strategy is to listen intently, allow silence, be with the individual and let them take the direction in the conversation and take it where they want to go. I also have a belief that things will work through to a positive conclusion which helps me if I'm feeling a bit stuck or unsure.'

(l) 'Around contracting and getting started. Client senior manager in a college, he had had three accusations for harassment against him which I understood were being handled in an internal process.

The Human Resources director had arranged with him and me for coaching, as these incidents seemed unusual and they thought this would help him. We arranged the first meeting by e-mail. I thought very carefully about the implications of these accusations and that our discussions were not part of this. The accusations were from women and I am a female coach, so how would this be for him and me? What boundaries might come into our conversation? The first meeting was exciting! We started by discussing what the intentions of coaching were as we understood them and how we had both got to this meeting. He said he thought I was part of the system out to get him as these accusations had been levelled at him in a special meeting to which he was summoned by his boss. A variety of kangaroo court. Coaching came from a similar direction. The nature of the accusations was surprising to me as they seemed to be about stress reactions, which could be bullying or heavy-handed. I realised I had been imagining sexual or racial harassment with a significant history. We both had to hear our individual surprise about the real and imagined context we found ourselves in and brought to the discussion. Then we were able to decide what would be helpful to him as the focus for coaching in a way that we could both trust each other.'

(li)   'The client was involved in a coaching programme designed to deliver promotion. A number of areas of behaviour were holding her back relating to influencing skills and her profile in meetings, but she had identified and worked on these progressively but no real breakthrough point had been achieved. She had always attended coaching meetings, but on one particular day had been asked to attend an all-day critical business meeting, and so needed to cancel the coaching sessions This was not known to me as a coach. However she decided to attend the coaching session and negotiated that she could attend the meeting but miss part of it to attend the coaching sessions. This was a high risk behaviour requiring use of influencing skills in a very visible way. She brought this issue to the coaching session having already negotiated her opt out. She was able to reflect on what she had achieved and the skills she used. This represented a critical moment in the coaching when several elements we had been working on came together. She has dared to try, was able to apply and reflect upon her skills. She had identified her own needs and those of the business and found a way to align them.'

13 Handling surprising transference phenomena

(lii) 'My coachee is a bank director. He suspects he head of his investment advisory group, a long term personal friend, of theft! His
question: How do I confront a close friend with such suspicion
without clear evidence? We are pondering effective options on how
to approach this delicate issue. We hear the ring tones of his mobile
phone. His secretary can hardly speak. Her information: The suspect
has committed suicide some minutes ago with a gun in his office.
My coachee breaks down and starts crying. I am stunned. I stay
silent, leaving him to his emotions of guilt, shame, despair now
breaking forth. Haven't we lost the cause? I can feel the void, a
nagging vacuum. For a long moment I feel stuck with my habitual
role identity as an executive coach: to know better than my coachees
how to effectively cope with difficult situations. We have a new
situation. And a different question: how to effectively cope with
this tragedy? To cope with the unexpected can be challenging.'

(liii) 'I was working with a senior civil servant. We had a contract for four
two-hour sessions. The fourth session came to an early conclusion.
I was concerned that as we were not using the full time allocated, I
was not meeting the needs of this individual. To my utter surprise,
at the end of the session he commented on how valuable the sessions
had been and asked if we could continue to work together. We have
now been working together for two further years. All of our sessions
are very focused and relatively short as this meets his needs.'

(liv) 'It was a first coaching conversation with a male client, who spent
half of the allotted time (2 hours!) crying. Every difficult point in
his life reduced him to tears, and I suspected that this would keep
happening. It put me in a strange sort of dilemma: on the one hand,
I could sense him crying out to be held and cherished. On the other
hand, everything in his story made it clear that physical intimacy
was absolutely forbidden, especially with men. I kept wondering if
I was experiencing transference and how responsible it is to give a
client a hug during a session. As I thought about this it became
clear in any case that I myself had no need to hug this man, rather
he was causing resistance. My suspicion grew that I was experiencing his own internal cry, which he himself did not want to acknowledge, but was indeed there. In view of the necessary professional
distance on the one hand and the idea that it nevertheless had to
be brought up on the other hand, I decided to share my thoughts
and feelings towards the end of the session. I knew I was taking an
enormous risk, but I also knew it had to be said. I was very anxious
about doing this, and it did of course cause enormous resistance in
him, which I was able to see for what it was. Then I started to list

with him how he could physically "set to work" more: doing sport, emotional exercises, etc. That touched a chord in him, because he was so keen to break out of his loneliness. At the same time, I knew I had messed things up with him by speaking openly about his still-concealed inner desires. A week after the session he rang to say that he would prefer a different coach. When I inquired further, it became clear that he was looking more for a father figure and that I did not fit the bill. I accepted that and matched him up with a father-figure coach, who continued the sessions successfully. He also went off to do more physical activities.'

(lv) 'Only recently I had a young coaching client whom I was seeing for a second time. During our first meeting we had gone very deep. It was at the end of a training course. She was relatively open and vulnerable at the time and I was able to reach her at that deeper level, even though she also came across as very anxious. Our second meeting was a month later. She seemed not to have an issue and to have come only because the appointment had been made. I asked her how she looked back on the first session. She was immediately on the defensive, said that it was a sort of "misunderstanding" in the first session and that I should think nothing of it. I expressed my surprise. She became more and more angry and started to accuse me of interfering and psychologising. I stated that it had not been my intention to push but to bring to her attention a curious change in her. What made it difficult for me was the fact that she had come a long way for this appointment. All very paradoxical. Should I continue and confront her defensiveness in a friendly manner, or should I call it a day? Of course, I put this to her. I knew the first session had done her good, but it had evidently made her anxious as well. The resulting insecurity, primarily due to her aggressive defence, was no basis for further exploration. We ended the meeting after 45 minutes.'

(lvi) 'It was our second meeting and he was reflecting to me what he had learnt about himself during the leadership programme he was participating in, and what implications this had for the direction he wanted his career/life to take in the future. Suddenly, with little warning, he started to cry. Initially he was very embarrassed and I felt a little uncomfortable about this, not sure how to respond. I like to think that I was able to offer him unconditional support and a sense that expressing emotion can be very beneficial. The tears proved cathartic and a productive coaching session ensued. When I met him for our next session, I was delighted in the difference in him. He was brimming with confidence and demonstrating a really high internal locus of control concerning his life and career, which he has continued to sustain.'

14 Handling counter-transference phenomena: 'can I actually help the coachee?'

(lvii)	'I sometimes get anxious when I'm with someone who is unusually intelligent, when I wonder at first if I can keep up with this person intellectually. Fortunately, so far I have always been able to enter into the conversation with the other person from a perspective of inner peace and not one of competition.'
(lviii)	'I was working with a client who was extremely successful in his career at a relative young age. He had it all, basically. Asking him the "miracle question" he realised that he was already living his miracle. I was stumped. Where do we go from here, what is the next step in this coaching relationship? Did he need coaching at all? The coaching session was then taken up with him talking about how limited his view of his potential was. "Potential" for him he noticed was not about career success (he already had that in spades and had very good prospects too), but it was about realising his true values about life and how to live accordingly. I have been seeing this client once a year following monthly then quarterly sessions in 2001 and 2002. He continues to be increasingly influential and highly regarded at a global level in his organisation. Recently he turned down a top job in his organisation because it did not fit in with his view of his future. He reports that that early miracle question is one he often reflects on and helps him make decisions about the direction of his career and lifestyle now.'

15 Handling counter-transference phenomena: 'I feel responsible for the coaching'

(lix)	'Very intelligent client, but I wasn't finding it exciting enough, asked about process here and now, results of each conversation and application. All were positive, and the contact very open. This man invariably had a very rational learning style and, time after time, appeared to have gained a lot from the sessions and put it to effective use and was good at comparing work situations with private experiences. The main problem was in fact my own anxiety ("We should be discussing feelings, it should be more exciting!").'
(lx)	'I sometimes get anxious when I notice that I'm approaching the other person with a lot of optimism and concern, while noticing internally that I am busy playing the role of rescuer.'

(lxi)   'It is tough when both parties are absolutely willing to make
          something of it, but I myself see little reaction or learning effect.
          In that case I think: I just don't know how it should be with this
          person. I assume I'm not making the correct diagnosis, probably
          because I do not have that specific diagnostic framework. But it
          may also be that, on closer inspection, I'm doing it "right", but it
          takes longer for the person to internalise his or her new insights
          and put them into words. I know one such person who doesn't
          display "rewarding" behaviour very easily. She never says: "Oh yes,
          that's helpful", or: "Now I understand it better", or: "That feels
          better already", or anything like that, and isn't really able to
          express what she is getting out of it, even if she wants to and I
          cautiously offer her some words to use. But a year later, other
          people were saying that she had changed and grown.'

(lxii)   'After some reflection I believe it is most exciting when someone
          takes important decisions after a coaching conversation, e.g. to
          quit his or her job; and then to wait and see what happens next.
          Of course, someone may already have been on the verge of quit-
          ting before the conversation and that was the final push they
          needed, but nevertheless.'

(lxiii)   'The coachee has been feeling for a while that she has to choose
          between: a) keeping her completely unassailable position as a
          consultant – with a lot of personal freedom, always choosing the
          monitor/evaluator role – or b) assuming joint responsibility for the
          future of the consultancy by working towards "becoming a partner",
          as some colleagues are suggesting. In conversations about career
          anchors, work/life balance, personal standards and values and the
          communicative strategies she has at her disposal, it has become
          clear to her that she has the ambition to become a partner, that
          she had already considered the step once before being pushed by
          her environment. She had considered all sorts of scenarios; from
          becoming extremely successful to going down, fighting bravely, in
          the battle against the prevailing culture. In her daydreams all of
          her scenarios seemed exciting and inspiring enough to warrant
          taking that step. Then she received the invitation from the board
          to discuss a partnership. At that point it is difficult (but in my
          view necessary) to keep the personal relationship built up between
          coach and coachee very businesslike. You would like to decide
          with her. I found the talking process whereby the coachee arrives
          at her decision particularly anxiety-provoking.'

16 Handling counter-transference phenomena: 'I want to drop out myself'

(lxiv) 'Because of all those different people and conversations, I can't remember what exactly I discussed with a coachee the previous time. It's difficult for him to understand, I think, to my distress!'

(lxv) '"Am I going on too long?", asked my client. I sincerely didn't think so, but my attention was diverted by something odd outside. I was able – after making my excuses – to turn things around in a positive sense: "You are more sensitive/perceptive than you described yourself before this first session!"'

(lxvi) 'A client – after the first exploratory meeting – rang up a day later, after waiting for me in vain for over half an hour in his freezing cold car. I was unable to pacify him, despite having the excuse that my car had broken down.'

17 Handling counter-transference phenomena: the coach's own emotions

(lxvii) 'Moments that can be better described as flow: when you are working with the coachee on solutions to his or her problems and the cooperation between you is excellent.'

(lxviii) 'I work with homework assignments, and ask the coachee to e-mail me a report every day on the application of new approaches. The coachee doesn't reply regularly. I send compliments back when I do receive an e-mail, and ignore it when I don't. Am I just after an easy life?'

(lxix) 'My most exciting client was a Nietzschean philosopher who surpassed my own frame of thinking and ability to put things into perspective by regarding objectives as moving panels.'

(lxx) 'Male coaching client aged around 34, adept at social skills, company director. The topic love/sex/unfaithfulness. An older woman he met at a dinner is courting him. He tells me about this and interrupts himself by asking me: "Have you ever been in love with a younger man?" I reply: "Pass." Him: "Why?" Me: "Before you know it you'll start speculating about it." (I meant about the ins and outs of my love life and the inappropriateness of that topic in this setting.) Him: "Speculating about what it's like to do it with you?" Me: "I didn't mean that." Him: "I've been doing that for a long time." Me – unsettled – "Back to the subject of your interaction with this woman, please." My discomfort was undoubtedly rooted in the fact that I thought I was safe hiding behind his mother transference and was suddenly being seen in a completely different capacity. A possible complication is the fact that he was a very attractive man. Just to be clear, I am 54.'

(lxxi) 'For years there has been a recurring motif in my coaching, working with long-term unemployed academics. The personal coaching took place on the heels of a management training course. Registering for that training was formally their own decision, but the social pressure to sign up was immense. The coaching process often dealt with personal standards and values that had become ingrained in the coachees and that they had stopped investigating and testing many years ago. It was impeding their personal development, so I often felt the need as the coach to confront them with alternatives to their current patterns of thinking. Discussions often led, especially when the coachee's established opinion started to waver, to an argument along the lines of: "Well, it's easy for you to talk, you have your steady job, your family and your career, I don't . . .". First, that wasn't entirely true: it wasn't a steady job, but a contract that could be terminated with a month's notice, but I didn't want to contribute that to the discussion. Second, it was a viewpoint I couldn't really agree with. I usually responded with a question such as: "Yes, and what does that mean for you?" The silence that would then descend, and that I myself was unwilling to break, was always something that I found exciting.'

(lxxii) 'I was on my second meeting with a coachee who was telling me that the child of someone he knew had died. This person was potentially interesting to him in connection with a career move. He was considering how to approach this woman in order to bring himself to her attention. Then he remembered that he had met her recently and they had spoken at the time about the death of the child. And he then observed that he was probably still in her memory, for that reason. Whereupon I thought: "It's as if you want to use the child's death to your own advantage. How calculating and unethical!" But I didn't say it, although it did feel that way. I think he felt it as well. He never mentioned it again . . . ! In short: I was not transparent, I was stranded with my own ethical standards and had an opinion that I did not express or check. Children and death is a sensitive subject. Next time, I would try to refer to it in a proper manner.'

(lxxiii) 'It relates to a recent coaching conversation where a manager had experienced the death of a colleague the previous week, had done a lot for the funeral and was still very emotional about it.

I myself had commemorated the death of my younger brother (a year ago) with my family in the past week, which was also an intense experience for me, especially because he meant a lot to me. The coachee revealed a lot of her distress during the session and it moved me greatly due to my own situation. In the coaching I found it difficult to give space to both of our emotions and direct the conversation in a professional manner at the same time.'

(lxxiv) 'A difficult piece of news and at the same time a "critical moment" in coaching. I receive bad news about my health; what I thought was an infection turns out to be pancreatic cancer. My whole world is changed . . . And I still have a few people in coaching, short-term and also medium-term, as a "leadership consultant". At the moment it is about my struggle: keeping contact, how do I set aside the coaching relationship? What will suit the other person, and what will suit me in this role? What will best serve the coachee? Refer as quickly as possible, because cancer is cancer. Or stay in contact, exchange information and make the transition to the next coach less abrupt? It takes an unconscious to meet an unconscious, and what will be transmitted from my unconscious at the moment may be more of a burden, from which I need to shield the coachee? Does honesty help?'

18 Handling questions and suggestions from the coachee

(lxxv) 'Someone else, a fast-rising manager with a lot of vision, once said after several sessions: "Oh, so I can ask something too!", although I always start openly and invite the other person just to start somewhere. But he evidently saw that as the umpteenth task in his pretty hard life, instead of feeling free to ask something. I learned from this: with melancholic people I now start by saying, would you like to say something or ask something? Anything is possible, it's your time. It can even be something very small, a tiny question, anything will do. When I said that to the manager in question he "warmed up" and proceedings suddenly moved along much faster and more smoothly.'

(lxxvi) 'If you limit coaching to one on one, I haven't experienced any critical moments, which probably says a lot about my style. I *have* experienced critical moments in team coaching sessions, which has to do with groups who don't want to take the path that I think is the right one or let fly at each other in an unsavoury fashion.'

(lxxvii)   'At the start of my career as a coach I found myself coaching a
           manager of a new service, whom I will call Peter. The role was
           a promotion for Peter, and although he had been managing the
           project developing the service, I, together with many others
           in our organisation (I was an internal consultant), had some
           doubts about his ability to actually run the service. We'd had
           about three coaching meetings in which we had concentrated
           on exploring the role, issues arising, learning needs etc. In our
           fourth meeting Peter announced he had been troubled by some-
           thing he wanted to share with me, because he had come to the
           conclusion he could trust me. He then explained that he was
           privy to some seriously compromising information about the
           senior manager who had appointed him in his new role. In fact,
           he had been asked by that manager to collude with a practice
           that was clearly in breach with the code of conduct of the
           organisation and was aimed as securing an even more senior
           role for the manager in question. Peter had done what had been
           asked of him. Although the game didn't pay off, he felt his
           promotion had been partly at least a result of collusion. Although
           he felt he was the right person for the job, his conscience didn't
           feel clear and he had been desperate to talk to someone. I found
           myself with the monkey on my shoulders and was at a loss as
           to what to do. In the end I kept his confidence but terminated
           our coaching relationship. The episode left a bad feeling. It
           undermined my confidence greatly and brought home to me
           quite how important supervision is – or at least access to a
           supervisor, which I didn't have at the time. As a result I con-
           tracted with my organisation to have access to an external
           supervisor.'

(lxxviii) 'As a career consultant for the staff of a large organisation I
           have also recently been sent employees who are threatened
           with dismissal for, say, outplacement. With one of these clients
           I had an extensive course of sessions in which I worked hard,
           of course, on mutual trust. On many occasions he had already
           expressed his appreciation for the supervision, he was even able
           to get criticism off his chest and we talked until it became clear
           to him what he wanted and how he could achieve it. Suddenly
           he asked if I would give him a copy of the reports that I prepare
           for the management of his department. He had known for a
           long time that I was sending them and was also made aware of
           their content in general terms each time. I hadn't expected this
           question from him and had become slightly more to-the-point

in my reports. What should I do? I found that I should have been able to predict this, but I hadn't been expecting it. It was a matter of trust and we both knew that in a split second. I then told him I couldn't do it: my relationship with the principal was also at issue here. "In what way?" That turned out not be an appropriate solution. To demonstrate that I was writing respectfully about him and the supervision, I read out passages from my last report to him. As I did so, I noticed that there was nothing in the report that I would not say to his face. In the end, I did give him a copy of my last report and the result was continuing openness and trust.'

Appendix C
Case Study: Tamara

In my experience of coaching, every assignment is different and unique, but for me this assignment is as typical as they come. It was selected entirely at random one day in the spring of 2006, when I determined I would make a case study of my *next* assignment, whatever it might be. All names and identifying details have been changed.

19 June 2006

Suddenly there appears in my inbox an e-mail from Tbilisi headed 'Advice', from someone who participated in an action learning group that I facilitated four years previously – let us call her Tamara. Her e-mail says that her maternity leave is almost over, after which she will be moving to the UK because head office has asked her to take on a more senior management position. She gives a brief outline of her new position, a new role created following a reorganisation by the powers that be. She describes how she put her team together herself, and how two people in her team had also applied for the post themselves. Then she writes, 'Anyway, it's all a bit daunting, and I feel I really need some coaching – would we be able to chat by phone at least once or twice?'

I write back the same day, congratulating her and saying how good it is to hear from her again, that I would be pleased to help her grow in her new role, and that I am generally an advocate of telephone coaching, although not always for a first session. I suggest that, after our first conversation, I draw up a written summary of our objectives and approach; finally, I cite a number of dates for a possible first discussion over the telephone.

19 to 23 June 2006

It takes another couple of e-mails and a voice-mail on her part before we have found a suitable date and she has obtained her boss's permission for the coaching. We are going to talk on 7 July and have set aside two hours for the conversation.

As is almost invariably the case with new assignments, I wonder why Tamara has chosen me (there is a world of uncertainties and fears of abandonment behind this: 'How can anyone ever choose *me* as a coach? I don't know anything, can't do much, and don't have much to say to someone born and brought up in Tbilisi. Not only that, but someone who has more experience in the UK than I do, and of course knows her own company immeasurably better than I do . . .'). It doesn't occur to me at first that I might have done something right when I facilitated her action learning group back in 2002/2003. Rather, I believe it has to do with the e-mail I sent her on 24 November 2003, some time after the end of the action learning episode, in the heydays of the Rose Revolution ('I often think of you when following the news about Georgia, and I am very happy that there will be a re-election for which I'll keep my fingers crossed!'). Two thoughts come to mind. 'You shouldn't send such revealing e-mails to clients, not even ex-clients,' and 'She must have chosen me on account of little marks of attention like these, not because I am capable of doing something in the area of coaching'.

7 July 2006

Less than three minutes in, I lose the telephone connection to Tbilisi and feel the tension mount: 'how can one coach when the conversation is regularly going to be cut off halfway through a sentence?!'. Even outside a coaching setting, it feels very unpleasant and unnatural to me when a personal conversation suddenly falls silent due to technical goings-on. Tamara, who's probably been through this a number of times (a preconceived idea about the Georgian telephone company), remains calm and collected; she had already said that she would try her mobile if we encountered any problems. When she rings again, on her mobile, the connection is fine from then on, for just under two hours.

Tamara talks in detail about her new role as Head of Operations. A couple of days later I summarise her account as follows for the purposes of our coaching contract.

'From our first meeting, I have taken two main outcomes for coaching, namely to:
• Transition well to your new role in the company, establish yourself in the new role and acquire confidence in it, confidence both with the requirements of the role and the two teams that the role links in with: the Direction Team and your own Operational Team.
• Achieve success in the new role, both in terms of its change agenda and in terms of your work-life balance.'

In the contract I suggest that these are subjects that lend themselves to being discussed coherently, e.g. by starting each coaching conversation with recent events and then moving on to the longer term in the second hour. I often suggest such a structure in my contracts (indeed, I have copied this text from an earlier contract), but as I write I realise that we haven't talked about an intended conversational structure, and I should in fact check this with Tamara.

Our first conversation turns out to evolve in reverse order: first the general picture, the new role, the context – and only later short-term events. We spend most time on a work conference that Tamara wants to organise with her new team in August. She is wondering whether to invite the team to Tbilisi. Together, we look at the signals that her invitation is sending out to the team, and I comment that it is understandable that her main 'rival' (an ambitious and enthusiastic team member who had also applied for her job) should prefer the UK to Tbilisi. She appears surprised by these more political, implicit aspects that I am bringing to the fore. I am curious to hear at the next session where the conference will take place. I am also aware that I am running the risk of becoming something of an 'expert', because Tamara and I both know that I have experience of facilitating work conferences.

Towards the end of the conversation I ask her why she chose me and what precisely she expects from me. I manage to make it sound entirely 'professional', but am aware that the question actually stems from my own uncertainty. Tamara cites three expectations:

1 suggesting different options;
2 challenging and 'seeing through' what she says;
3 contributing management theory.

I am aware that she is appealing to my subject expertise in the first and last of these points. It will sometimes be difficult to combine that expert role and the role of coach (asking naive questions, challenging, bringing out other perspectives, etc.).

Our common review of the first conversation remains a little vague to my mind: she says she found it positive, especially in terms of preparing for her team event in August.

8 August 2006

I experience a degree of tension again in the run-up to our second telephone coaching conversation: this time I am at Ashridge's London office, so I e-mail Tamara to ask her to ring a different number. She doesn't respond to my e-mail so I am not entirely sure what is going to happen. I ring Ashridge and ask someone there to answer my phone for me. Oh, the thrills of the telephone medium . . .

Five minutes after our agreed starting time, the tension is relieved. Tamara has received my e-mail in time, she rings the right number and we are able to get started.

The second coaching conversation mirrors the first very nicely in terms of content: this time, most of Tamara's concerns appear to be about the other team she belongs to: the Direction, so we discuss that this time. One metaphor that crops up, which we examine from several perspectives, is the 'tugging on the covers' going on between the various members of management, including Tamara. The conversation is also evenly balanced between work aspects and more personal aspects such as her imminent move to the UK with her family. At the end she comes back to the work conference, which is now to be held in the UK after all. When she expresses some doubts about who should wield the pen that day, whether she should request a secretary especially, I come out with a flood of arguments against that – very similar to my monologue the previous time about Tbilisi as the venue for the conference.

While I sit there saying all this, I notice that silence has descended at the other end of the line. Dare I mention that she has been sounding a bit 'flat' for the last ten minutes? It will be my first 'here and now' intervention in this coaching relationship. When I do say it, referring almost apologetically to the limitations of the telephone as a medium, she immediately confirms my impression. It is now five in the afternoon in Tbilisi and she has been hard at work since early in the morning.

I then offer her the option of winding up the conversation early. In the evaluation I help her again by – very unusually for me – being the first to give a review of the conversation. This 'helpful tendency' seems to be deeply ingrained in my personality: as soon as my coachee indicates tiredness, I take over the conversation and try to avoid her having to talk (or think!) any more. She seems to view the conversation very positively, though, describing it as 'talking about whatever comes into my head'. When I ask if she has been able to talk freely enough, because I interrupt her quite a bit (my own uncertainty raising its head again!), she confirms this with 'yes, and the interruptions are actually useful, otherwise I start to babble on endlessly'.

I am left with a slight feeling of guilt, as if I have been neglectful by not filling the last ten minutes of our appointment (compare with critical moment liii in Appendix B). I do feel satisfied about picking up and expanding upon the 'tugging on the covers' metaphor and the fact that I communicated my impression that she was coming across a bit 'flat'. I also write down a couple of topics that I want to explore the next time, such as the way in which she paints men as 'dumpers', 'knowing what they want and working on getting it' and 'obsessed by their own agenda', and more generally the association of gender and personality traits in her thinking about colleagues.

7 September 2006

Our first 'live' coaching conversation is also a renewal of our acquaintance after a gap of several years. It is strange, in the rather formal setting of the coaching room, to offer the spontaneous warm handshake that is my first impulse. But at the same time the austerity of the decor helps us get down to work quickly. Dispensing with any chitchat or reminiscences, we quickly get to the heart of Tamara's organisation.

In the course of this conversation I highlight for the first time something that I would really describe as a 'problem': Tamara's relationship with Neil, one of her fellow managers. When we come to examine Tamara's suspicions and examples, Neil is already, with Tamara not yet a month in the job, actively working against her and her department. Tamara strongly contrasts their styles, personalities and behaviours within the organisation. Her main reproach is that Neil thinks only for his department, and not for the greater whole. She describes herself as an 'organisationalist', someone who puts the interests of the organisation above those of her own department. She also describes Neil as belligerent, intimidating and edgy.

I feel obliged to query her somewhat black-and-white characterisations, especially of her own and Neil's motives. I suggest that she is perhaps just as ambitious, equally keen to present herself well, and is perhaps now opting for an 'organisationalistic' strategy because she presides over the smallest and weakest department. I note that I am balancing on the edge of acceptability with this observation, because Tamara takes a while to process it and comes back to it several more times.

At the end of the conversation I decide to bring up again the man/woman dynamic that she keeps coming back to. I ask her what it's like to be discussing that dynamic here and now with a man, and whether that is safe enough given her descriptions of how men present themselves in her workplace. She assures me that it's not a problem, but I notice later that I am not entirely at ease with this. Does she really have confidence that I am trying to imagine her situation 'from the inside'? Perhaps I should ask the question again next time, and explain how it is a bit difficult for me as a man to feel completely free to raise queries here – because there is always the risk that it may be misinterpreted; for example, as standing up for someone with whom I have more in common. She describes me in the review at the end, just before I draw attention to the fact that I am a man as well, as a 'neutral person', which is how I feel, so for the time being it seems we are alright with this.

After the conversation I wonder whether I did in fact make myself clear enough. Whether Tamara can see that when I query her assumptions (e.g. the assumption that she operates less politically than the people around her, or that she is not taken seriously as a woman in a male culture), I do not necessarily subscribe to the opposite assumption, but my main concern is to help her stand more firmly on her own feet. This prompts me to predict that 'I don't really understand what you're trying to say' may turn out to be one of her ways of defending herself against me.

5 October 2006

In this conversation it occurs to both of us that, so far, a new problem area has cropped up in each of our coaching sessions, that subsequently appears to be 'resolved' at our next session. Each time I think we're talking about something that we will have to discuss for many sessions to come, then the next session suddenly turns out to be about something completely different. In the first conversation Tamara's own team was the focus, in the second it was the Direction Team, in the third her Direction Team colleague Neil, and now it seems to be more about her other fellow manager, Paul. And there are other aspects of her role that occupy one conversation but then, at the next session, appear to have found a breakthrough. We both think this a good sign: Tamara's practice is evolving and she is tackling problems energetically.

It also strikes me that I am able to take this, fourth, conversation further; for example, by formulating hypotheses in relation to Paul, about the way he is 'put together': he isn't really into management and doesn't want to be, he focuses on other, more representative areas of his position and, as a result, avoids Tamara who reminds him of his own shortcomings in more managerial aspects of his role. I am aware that this is pushing it a bit: how can I formulate such bold hypotheses about someone I have never met? At the same time, however, I notice that Tamara becomes reflective after my comments and takes them into consideration.

Although each conversation introduces a new area for attention, a number of issues still arise with a degree of continuity, such as the tensions in establishing the new role that Tamara's department represents within the company. I have gradually become aware that hers is in fact the 'internal client' role, and that Tamara's small department therefore has to become a sort of front office, or 'linking pin', for everyone inside and outside the company. The competition for this role, which Tamara likened in our second conversation to tugging on the matrimonial bedcovers, goes on at many levels: in the Direction Team, with the existing external clients, and within the organisation at middle management level.

The way in which we discuss this topic in this conversation is in terms of the authority associated with her role: the client is ultimately 'king' in a properly functioning business, which makes the internal representative of the client a very authoritative person. It is as if others in the organisation are aware of this: on the one hand they are keen to make good use of Tamara's talents, so they have promoted her. On the other hand, there are clear indications that the 'established managers' don't want Tamara's star to ascend to quite the same degree within the organisation. For me an indicator for this is that Tamara's remuneration has remained the same and is well below that of her colleagues on the Direction Board, while Tamara's team is certainly not treated yet as a client within the organisation.

What I like about our collaboration is Tamara's independence: she opens the discussion eagerly, introduces a theme or a number of related themes, prattles away cheerfully about them, listens attentively when I join in and start to ponder them out loud, and is often quick to interrupt and elaborate. After our sessions she sets to work and overcomes obstacles in a way that appears to come entirely from herself and sometimes bears little relationship to the ideas we discussed between us. This does mean that it's not always clear to me what my own contribution is, or whether I am actually making a contribution, so my own uncertainty remains considerable. But at least not to the extent that I feel inhibited in what I say.

For example, at the end of this conversation, as we review the session, I draw a link with the action learning group where we worked together a number of years ago: 'How does this experience compare for you?' and she says: 'It is similar, though there are also differences. In that group I heard a greater variety of perspectives on my contribution and I changed role myself. Here I am much more like a "patient" visiting the "doctor". I think action learning is an undervalued tool, we should use it more in our organisation.' I note that I ask the question not for my own benefit but for hers (and that is the essential criterion for me, here), and that I do not get stirred up by the implicit criticism of this coaching journey in her reply. What she mentions are indeed differences between coaching and action learning, although it does occur to me a few hours later that coaching should have added value as a result of the 'professionalism' of the coach/doctor – and perhaps her comment reveals that she has not yet discovered that added value . . .

14 November 2006

As I prepare for this conversation, I note that I am very conscious of the fact that this one will be our last. I plan to suggest a procedure for a satisfactory conclusion incorporating evaluation; for example, by sending Tamara a 'review questionnaire' in two or three months' time and then having a final telephone conversation about the coaching. At the same time, I try to ensure that this coaching conversation is just as relevant as our previous sessions, to avoid drifting apart and becoming more reticent with each other right from the start of the conversation – as happens sometimes in 'ordinary' relationships when acquaintances realise that it is their final meeting. That is why I am keen to highlight this unique aspect of this conversation right at the outset.

At the start of the conversation a number of things happen at the same time. Tamara arrives rather flustered, and starts to talk in a rush about the department run by her colleague Paul and about his management style. For my part, I forget to offer her a coffee and instead busy myself taking notes as she talks. I do make sure to mention the fact that it is our last agreed session within the very first minute. Then I realise that I am sitting there drinking coffee while she goes without, whereupon I await the end of her sentence and go downstairs to make coffee. When I return she is still a bit flustered in her speech and gestures, but the 'coffee break' has helped to slow the conversation down a little. We settle relatively quickly into our normal, more reflective rhythm. In retrospect I do think it a shame that I was unable to let her initial flustered state continue and then go on to explore it. I was too busy with my own desire to mention the end of our journey in those opening minutes.

Later, the conversation follows the same pattern as in previous sessions: the main themes from the last meeting have been addressed and changed in a positive sense. Tamara therefore suggests another new area for attention. This time the 'spotlight' is on the director of her organisation, i.e. her own manager, someone who has remained in the background to date in our conversations. In fact, Tamara does not introduce her director as a topic of conversation, but talks more broadly about the organisational culture and the function (or dysfunction) of her Direction Team. I am the one who steers the conversation more towards her director, as the person with ultimate responsibility in these areas, and I ask her some questions about his role and his style.

The fact that it is not the director, but the lingering 'old-fashioned' culture and dysfunctional nature of the team that are raised as a subject of conversation, appears to be partly explainable by Tamara's relationship with the director. It was he who gave her this opportunity and promoted her, and who is always appreciative of her suggestions and ideas. He is regularly available for two-way discussions and, more generally, he is her line manager, so she accepts his leadership much more as a given, rather than subjecting his style to critical reflection as she does with the others. It takes some insistence on my part, therefore, before we are able to consider the part played by the director in the ineffective teamwork.

At one point she says, for example, that the director has been in post for *only* three years, that he came in from outside the organisation three years ago, so he's not had very much impact yet. And she lists a long series of changes that have 'happened to' the organisation, which have probably prevented him from finding his management feet yet. I remind her that three years is a long time, not a short time, for a CEO to make an impact: most CEOs remain in post for less than four years. Then she slowly opens up about the absence of a sense of direction or vision, and about the fact that meetings are hardly ever about things that are relevant, and that Neil recently called the team a 'confederation of warring tribes'.

After subjecting team and leader alike to examination, we explore how Tamara herself might have an impact and raise the subject of how the team functions, and what has held her back from doing so thus far. She sees the following factors as preventing her from having that impact:

1 the need to conform with the new team;
2 the team's fear of emotions and open conflicts; and
3 her own anxiety about coming across as one of the combatants rather than as a constructive source of reflection.

What I myself find interesting is how some typical aspects of the organisational culture of this organisation are a reflection of its primary process, and the tensions generated by that primary process (Menzies, 1960).

At the end of the conversation we spend some more time discussing Tamara's move to the UK, the effects of that transition on her family life, and her long-term career perspectives. It does me good to discuss this type of more personal topic as well. I feel that she is standing firmly on her own two feet and we agree that, if she manages to have a genuine, demonstrable impact in her new management role within a year, a career as a general manager, inside this organisation or elsewhere, will be open to her.

We part on very positive terms. Tamara mentions the very same three expectations identified in our first conversation (see above) as elements that have stood out for her. I cite the pattern of the alternating 'spotlight' on a different aspect of Tamara's role and practice as a positive element, mainly because we found on each occasion that the field spotlighted last time had undergone a significant improvement. When I mention that I didn't always see the connection between her achievements and the coaching conversations, Tamara interrupts me. She emphasises that ideas considered during the coaching were hugely important. I believe she is saying this for my benefit, to leave me with a feeling of satisfaction at the end of our last session.

One of the recurring patterns at the end of a coaching relationship is playing itself out before my eyes: how we work together in such a way as to give ourselves a pleasant 'leaving-do atmosphere', and we both participate in a 'flight into health' (Malan, 1979) for the coachee: we are both convinced that Tamara is doing very well and will continue to do very well. As if neither of us will soon be feeling the twinges of doubt again . . .

The idea of sending a short questionnaire in two or three months' time and then having another telephone conversation about how things are going appeals to Tamara, so there is to be a further coda to our relationship. My initial doubt after the conversation is whether I suggested this idea out of a need of my own to remain somehow part of her future, or out of an authentic need for a natural conclusion after sharing so many personal and relevant issues with Tamara. I will stick with the latter as there is nothing much that can be changed about it now, anyway.

Response from coachee after reading the case study

'I enjoyed reading this! I think our critical moments were quite similar. I found this an accurate description of the issues and the coaching journey itself. Thanks again for a very enjoyable coaching experience. I did indeed find it helped my achievements, I think you are being too modest. I was very impressed that for an outsider you had such a quick grasp of our organisational issues. But then as you say, they are probably quite typical.'

Appendix D
Verbatim Transcript: Ken

These are the first 10 minutes of the 22nd executive coaching session with Ken, who is the manager of forty senior sales managers, who in turn manage tens of staff each. This coaching journey began in early 2004, and was initiated when Ken took on this role, his first senior management role. He was promoted from being one of the most successful sales managers to being their boss. We initially agreed five coaching sessions, and have extended our coaching relationship several times. Sessions 23 to 27 are pencilled in our diaries for the first half of 2007.

I still remember vividly how I came out of our first conversation thinking to myself: 'This man does not need coaching. He is doing exceptionally well.' From that very first conversation on I have often felt appreciation for the ways in which Ken fulfils his role. I have therefore always been careful to keep my objectivity and critical faculties, and have brought my work with this client to supervision twice, the second time about half a year ago with the explicit question whether we should continue this coaching relationship, and to what degree I might be 'colluding' with him and his agenda, to the detriment of his learning.

At the same time, the coaching has always seemed very relevant, as much challenging for Ken as it was supportive, and has delivered important fruits, particularly over the last year. In this last year, Ken has found himself increasingly in conflict with his boss, in danger of being excluded from the senior team by him and fearful for his position in the organisation. These events have thrown up a lot of issues for Ken, and he has been tempted to leave the organisation or return to the role of sales manager.

Gradually, Ken has grown in recent months into a position where he is more accepted and involved by his boss, while at the same time speaking out more openly against parts of his boss's policy, and is more self-assured if he doesn't agree with something. This has helped him to retain the full support of his own staff through taxing times. I believe the regular coaching sessions that are now taking place once every six weeks have helped him to become more assertive and confident in building this stronger position.

The fragment below, which is a literal transcript including repetitions and 'ums and ers', spans 10 minutes chosen by the two of us at random. My exact suggestion was 'let's record the first 10 minutes of our next session'. These 10 minutes seem fairly typical of the way we work together. After this fragment we spent just under 5 minutes drawing up a sort of agenda for the rest of the session, as we always do at the start of our sessions. My commentary is in the right-hand column. As always with Ken, my question on reading this fragment is 'am I too understanding, do I take Ken's words and his arguments against his boss too much at face value, without challenging them?'

Verbatim transcript	Running commentary
Literal transcript of precisely 10 minutes at the start of the coaching conversation	My thoughts during the coaching conversation and afterwards on reading the transcript and listening to the tape.
Normal print: Ken	Normal print: my thoughts during the conversation
Italic: Erik	Italic: my afterthoughts on reading the transcript and listening to the tape
Yes Ehm eh. We discussed I think in the past – ehm ehm – whether it was, ehm you know, whether we should continue with eh eh the coaching exercise and eh and we kind of took stock and I *Yes* . . . remember saying that I was finding it incredibly useful and helpful, and interestingly it has come up, and, 'cause Nick, my boss, has said that eh	He's bringing up our coaching relationship itself. That is going to be interesting, and multi-layered. That means he's as good as talking about us when he talks about his work relationships. I think he's trying to help me here with my re-accreditation, by saying such positive things about the coaching.

Verbatim transcript	Running commentary
he wanted me to look at ehm alternative ways of getting the management support, if you like, or career development support that I needed. *Aha* Ehm. He – his concerns were about the ehm, the cost, saying that our organisation had available to it ehm eh internal coaching ehm, which eh our business could get free of charge ehm, so I kind of explained to him that from my perspective it would be a huge step backwards to change the eh coaching that I was having on the basis that it takes a long time to build up a *Mm (affirming)* . . . relationship and knowledge and the style of coaching that's appropriate etcetera etcetera. Ehm. The cynical side of me wonders whether it's because of some of the conflict that I'm having with him; *Yes?* . . . and whereas I, I don't ever go back and say, I've reached this decision because, or, *Yes* . . . you know, or decisions have been made, etcetera, I have on a, a number of occasions when we've kind of been talking about ehm my relationship with him and how that, sort of, you know, if you like, the breakdown of our position happened in our relationship and my position in his (breathing in) mind, ehm, and in trying to resolve that, I've kind of mentioned a couple of times about you know, about things that I've learnt about how I work etcetera etcetera through coaching, so *So is your sus-sus-suspicion then that you might be showing a similar, eh sorry: a different type of behaviour towards him,*	(Ken knows that this transcript will be used for my re-accreditation). It's about his relationship with Nick again. Interesting how our subject-matter has narrowed this year, since the conflicts with Nick began. I am very careful here about giving my opinion on what sort of 'management support' Ken needs. I am aware that I am an interested party: I'd like to continue the coaching but don't want to talk about it here. It's entirely up to him whether or not to continue the coaching. I notice I give an affirming 'Mm' here, I hope that's not inspired by my own interest. I notice he uses the word 'conflict' and recall that it was me who first used that word between us, around four sessions ago I said he seemed to be avoiding the word 'conflict' but that was what it appeared to be. I notice that he now uses the word very freely. I wonder how freely he uses it with his boss. *Here he sounds a bit cautious and searching; he seems to be shy to talk about the coaching relationship.* *I also notice I start to stutter a bit here.*

Verbatim transcript	Running commentary
I think I prob . . . I think I am . . . *and that he might be responding to that and not to the cost?* That that is my suspicion, my suspicion is that it isn't about money, because he's come back and suggested a number of courses, or in fact, interestingly enough, he said 'these are courses that Liz has suggested you might want to go on'. Now Liz is our training officer. Mm-mm And I, I was interested by two points there really. One was the fact that this is a lady who I've probably sat in maybe two or three meetings with and I've certainly never had any one-to-one discussion with her about anything, Mm-mm . . . so I was interested on what basis she was judging her opinion on what courses I should go on (ha-ha) *O – So this was her recommendation actually?* Well this is what Nick, *He said, okay* he said. *Okay – yes* I was a bit baffled by the fact that somebody who I can't, Mm with whom I've had no first-hand dealings – *So it must have been on the basis of what Nick has told her would be helpful to you? Something like that?* *Yeah, yeah.* Yeah. Ehm. So, some interesting thoughts there . . . and whereas – *You said two, two points?* Yes, well, the first one was to say I was interested that ehm. I suppose it was the same point really. One was that it, he should be deferring to her opinion on what	Interesting slip of the tongue: I use 'similar' instead of 'different'. I think it betrays the fact that I am being critical and part of me doesn't think he has made all the changes that he professes to have made and could make. In particular, that part of me seems to be saying that he is still behaving very similarly towards Nick as before. However, I agree with the essence of my summary: he has changed, and Nick does not like it. *There is a similarity here between Ken and Nick, however much Ken may not like it or want to see it. Nick talks to Liz about Ken, and now Ken is talking similarly to Erik about Nick. Liz and Erik are both 'interfaces'. Avoidance on both sides. Later, I try to make this more explicit.* *Also, Ken disqualifies Liz here; and his main complaint is that Nick disqualifies Erik. With so many similarities between Ken and Nick, it is not surprising I used the word 'similar' in my slip above.* I am conscious that Ken is implicitly inviting me to laugh here. I do not want to be drawn into laughing, as I feel that would imply agreement with the things he is saying. And I do think his is sometimes a one-sided perspective on the situation and his conflicts, which is of course to be expected from someone who is involved in that conflict every day. Instead, I opt to clarify further and to keep listening.

Verbatim transcript	Running commentary

Mmm

. . . course it it was in the first place.
Ehm. And apart from that, why, why
isn't it him as my immediate
manager,

Mm *(affirming)*

| | Again, I find myself affirming what Ken |

talking through with me the issues that
he thinks that he may experience and
therefore he thinks these are the
issues that I need to look at and
therefore, why don't I, you know, so
I, I kind of just felt again that there
was a little bit of a eh reluctance on
his part to talk to me at all

Mm

about me (ha-ha).

*And did . . . yeah . . . Did you discuss that
with him?*

I didn't, no. Ehm. (pause)

*So the reluctance was, came a little bit
from both sides then?*

Well, I think it was a very brief, ehm, a
very brief meeting,

Aha

and my tactics at the moment are to to
try and eh ehm eh. There is enough
conflict going on between us at the
moment,

Mm

My tactic is to try and focus any conflict
on something which is, yeah, on the,
on the most important areas if you
like,

Yes

so if there are business-critical decisions
going on and we are in disagreement,
I'd rather argue about that,

Yes

rather than get into kind of the
rather more in-depth analysis,
which is, you know, perhaps about
ehm our relationship and my eh my
development, if you like, but I think
that's more of a longer-term
discussion . . .

Yes

Running commentary (right column):

Again, I find myself affirming what Ken
says, in my tone of speech. It is so
easy to collude with the coachee,
especially if there is so much
appreciation.

On reading this fragment later, I am
able to challenge his reasoning: he
ascribes 'a little bit of a eh reluctance'
to Nick but in my view the same
could be said of him about having an
open conversation with Nick. So,
another similarity between Nick and
Ken: avoidance on both sides.

*Here, I make this explicit and bring out the
fact that I see similarities in the way Ken
and Nick handle their conflict. This is
probably the most challenging thing I say
in the fragment, so Ken's immediate
defensive response is not surprising.
Interestingly, he says in his defence that
he'd rather challenge Nick on more
important matters, but then, at the end
of the session, he admits that this is one
of the more important matters. It is
humbling to realise that there are so
many points of view on a single fragment
of coaching, so many things that I only
realise retrospectively . . .*

Verbatim transcript	Running commentary
and . . .	
So if I may, for a moment, just, ehm, just, just suppose, if this is not about cost-saving, which he says it is, eh then as you said the only other thing it can be about is that through the coaching he perceives you becoming stronger, eh or ehm more conflictuous, or something like that, eh and he would like to to stop that by – not by talking to you as you say – but by stopping the coaching. Is that your, is that your hypothesis let's say?	I want to clarify what Ken is saying, exactly.
My hypothesis is that it's entirely that it is an avoidance	*When I listen back to this, I am struck by the fact that I insert Nick's wish to 'stop' Ken going forward. Also, I now see this slightly differently, I don't agree with myself any more that this is the 'only other thing it can be about': it could still be simply and constructively about Nick genuinely trying to find other development opportunities for Ken. In the fragment I go along with Ken's more cynical interpretation of Nick's suggestions. Am I still clarifying?*
Yes	
by him,	
Yes	
to tackle the real issue.	
Mm. Which is that you become a stronger adversary in his – let's say, that's the real issue for him,	
I I think so.	
then?	
I I think so.	
Mm.	My use of stronger language: 'conflictuous', 'stopping the coaching', 'adversary', is on purpose. I sense that Ken is experiencing this rather in those terms than in the more polite, circumspect descriptions that he offers, and I want to make that more explicit.
Eh I think, you know, for – sorry, sorry to	
No, go ahead –	
Well, actually, the second point we get to is (A) he is coming to ehm the conclusion as to the course I should be doing, but (B) it doesn't stand up as an excuse that it is about money, because the two courses he recommends I do are very expensive courses, and they are more expensive than I've spent on coaching so far this year and so, it isn't about money.	I interrupt my coachee here. Not a good thing for a coach to do, according to most handbooks. I press ahead, although I want to stick with my summary of the two 'adversaries' and to explore the essence of their relationship. Instead, Ken still prefers to offer more details and arguments.
Hm	
There's no way that it can be about money if he's suggesting I spend more than I currently have. Ehm. But yes, it does, ehm, it does follow in my view a pattern that he exhibits with all conflict, which is to just avoid it and assume that it, you know – when there's something that he feels difficult to deal with	

Verbatim transcript	Running commentary
Yes Ehm I don't think he tackles it head on. *Yes and I think you did speak with him about that particular pattern* Hm *before,* Yeah *so it's not entirely avoided by you at least, or by the two of you, 'cause you have spoken with him* Indeed *about the fact that he avoids lots of* Yeah yeah *real issues.* And I have a, you know, a number of, you know, yet again, of e-mails, to which I'm awaiting a response. *Hm* When he'll respond to two of the what three e-mails that I've sent in the last hour, but not the one, it's not as if he hasn't read it, or – but it's too difficult for him to respond to, eh, but it needs urgent attention. I've got a couple of those. Ehm. So there is, I think there is this pattern that it's, you know, that, in his mind, it's gonna be another conflict he doesn't want into, doesn't want to think about it, just eh, ignore it, and . . . So ehm, I agreed that I would look at, ehm, ways of, ehm, of reducing the amount I was spending on my personal development, *Aha* which may mean not going on an expensive course, potentially, because that will reduce. Haha Haha (both laugh) Ehm, I don't know what, where we'll go with this. Ehm. I don't – I I think it will be something that he'll have said and now've forgotten about. And again, it will also be something that I would, you know, I would be prepared to have a battle with him about, . . .	*I think I am manipulating a bit here. I am 'balancing' my earlier challenge about the similarity between Nick and Ken in terms of conflict avoidance, helping Ken off the hook with that, almost complimenting him and Nick on what they have explicitly discussed between them. I am still struggling with the degree of similarity and difference between Ken and Nick.* Ignoring my somewhat empty compliment, Ken sticks with the 'avoidance' that he perceives, or likes to perceive, in Nick. And he resorts to some sarcasm here, which I collude with, by laughing heartily with him. Where am I going with this? He seems to have the same thought: 'where are we going with this?'

Response from coachee after reading the case study

'My first reaction on reading this was horror at the number of times I said *ehm*..., followed by an awareness of the complexity of the internal dialogue going on for Erik. There are comments and insights made in the transcript that would not normally come out during coaching and I can't decide whether it would be useful if they did. I also felt the urge to respond to Erik's commentary and frustration that I couldn't.'

Appendix E
Code of Conduct for
Executive Coaches

The purpose of this Code of Conduct[1] is to establish and maintain professional standards for executive coaches and to inform and protect their individual clients, organisations seeking their services and members of the public.

Ethical standards comprise such values as integrity, competence, confidentiality and responsibility. Coaches who subscribe to this Code accept their responsibility to clients and colleagues. The client's interest is paramount, but where coaches have a conflict of responsibilities or an ethical dilemma they must rely on their own personal and professional judgement. The Code of Conduct is therefore a framework within which to work rather than a set of instructions.

1 General principles

This code assumes that
1 Coach and coachee enter into an equal relationship which is used intentionally for the benefit of the coachee.
2 Coachees ultimately know best what is best for them and can decide for themselves what they do or do not want, both in their private and in their professional lives; coachees are therefore also responsible for the choices that they make and accountable for their actions.
3 The responsibility of the coach is to give the coachee an opportunity to explore, discover and clarify ways of living and working more satisfyingly and resourcefully.

---

[1] This is the Ashridge Code of Conduct for Coaches, drawn up by Charlotte Sills, Ina Smith and myself, and building on the ethical guidelines introduced in Chapter 15 of *Coaching with colleagues* (De Haan & Burger, 2005).

4 During coaching the goals, resources and choices of the coachee
   have priority over those of the coach.

2 Code of ethics

The purpose of the Code of Ethics is to clarify the ethical principles
that executive coaches respect in their work with coachees.

Responsibilities
- Coaches are responsible for observing the principles embodied in
  this Code of Conduct.
- Coaches accept responsibility for encouraging and facilitating the
  self-development of the coachee within the coachee's own network
  of relationships.
- The coach takes account of the developmental level, abilities and
  needs of the coachee.
- The coach is aware of his/her own cultural identity and that of the
  coachee and of the possible implications of any similarities and
  differences for the coaching.
- Coaches are responsible for ensuring that they are not dependent
  upon relationships with their coachees for satisfying their own
  emotional and other needs.
- During coaching the coach will not engage in non-coaching relationships, such as friendship, business or sexual relationships with
  their coachees. Coaches are responsible for setting and monitoring
  the boundaries between working and other relationships, and for
  making the boundaries as explicit as possible to the coachee.
- The coach will cooperate in the handling of a complaints procedure
  if one is brought against him/her, and make sure that reasonable
  arrangements have been made for professional liability.

Competences
- Coaches recognise the power inherent in their position: they realise that they can exert considerable influence, both consciously
  and unconsciously, on their coachees and possibly also on third
  parties.
- Coaches are aware of the limitations both of their coaching and
  their personal skills and take care not to exceed either. They refer
  a coachee to a colleague, if necessary, and maintain a professional
  network to that end.

- Coaches commit themselves to training in coaching and undertake further training at regular intervals during their careers.
- Coaches seek ways of increasing their professional development and self-awareness. Coaches monitor their coaching work through regular supervision by professionally competent supervisors, and are able to account to individual clients, colleagues and client organisations for what they do and why.
- Coaches monitor the limits of their own competence.
- Coaches, along with their employers and client organisations, have a responsibility to themselves and their clients to maintain their own effectiveness, resilience and ability to help clients. They must be able to identify any situation in which their personal resources have become depleted to the extent that they must seek help and/or withdraw from coaching, whether temporarily or permanently.

3 Code of practice

This Code of Practice is intended to provide more specific information and guidance in the implementation of the principles embodied in the Code of Ethics.

Management of the work
- Coaches should inform clients as appropriate about their training and qualifications, and the methods they use.
- Coaches should clarify with coachees the number and duration of sessions and fees. They should also explore a client's own expectations of what is involved in coaching with him/her.
- Coaches should gain the coachee's permission before conferring with other people about the coachee.
- Coaches should abstain from using any of the information that they have obtained during coaching for their own personal gain or benefit, except in the context of their own development as a coach.
- If there is another internal client (e.g. a manager or HR officer), coaches must ensure before the coaching starts that all parties have the same information concerning the goal and structure of the coaching and the intended working method. The coaching can proceed only if there is agreement between them with respect to its goals and structure. If there is any change in the situation or the assignment, the coach formally revises the arrangements with all parties.

- Coaches who become aware of a conflict between their obligations to a client and their obligation to an organisation employing them will make explicit the nature of the loyalties and responsibilities involved.
- In situations where coaches have a difference of opinion with the client or other involved parties, they will maintain a reasonable attitude and keep dialogue open.
- Coaches work with clients to terminate coaching when the clients have received the help they sought, or when it is apparent that coaching is no longer helping them.

Confidentiality
- Coaches regard all information concerning the client – received directly, indirectly or from any other source – as confidential. They protect their clients against the use of personal information and against its publication unless this is authorised by the client or required by law.
- Treating information 'in confidence' means not revealing it to any other person or through any public medium, except to those on whom coaches rely for support and supervision.
- If coaches believe that a client could cause danger to others, they will advise the client that they may break confidentiality and take appropriate action to warn individuals or the authorities.

Advertising/Public statements
- The coach obtains the agreement of the client before using the name of the client's organisation or other information that may identify the client as a reference.
- Coaches do not advertise or display an affiliation with an organisation in a manner that falsely implies sponsorship, validation or approval by that organisation.
- Coaches do not make false, exaggerated or unfounded claims about what coaching will achieve.

Appendix F
Intake Instruments and Checklists

One of the common factors that plays a role throughout the coaching process – i.e. not only at the start when it is more formally under discussion – is *contracting*. There are many aspects of contracts that are worthwhile exploring (Sills, 1997). For example, it is worthwhile distinguishing between the contract:
- for the coaching (long-term);
- for the coaching session (medium-term);
- for this moment (short-term, i.e., contracting as a conversational technique).

This Appendix contains three *checklists* that may help in contracting, for the three main parties:
- the coachee;
- the coach;
- the organisation (often in practice the coachee's manager or HR director).

The checklists are primarily concerned with the psychological contract, an aspect that can be only partly formalised in a document for signing. The checklists may help to establish whether the various parties have an understanding of each other's aims and expectations, and are able to agree on them.

1 For the recipient of coaching

In the end, the choice of the right coach is mainly determined by the belief that the coachee can work with this coach, because they 'click', and the expectation that the coachee can learn something from and with this person.

This checklist contains a number of other considerations that may help in choosing the right coach. To this end, work through the questions in the flowchart in Figure F.1. Note: if the answer to a question is *yes* try following the light arrow; if the answer is *no* try to move on according to the dark arrow.

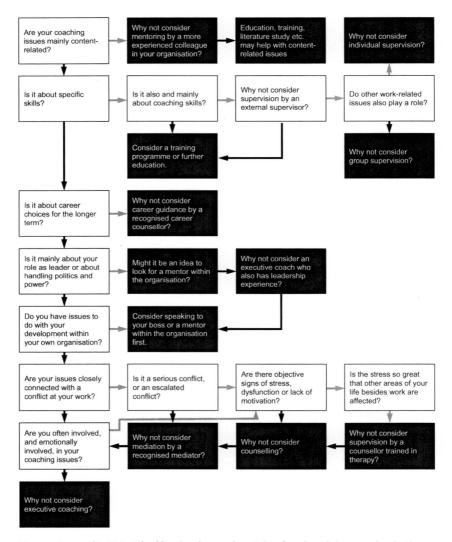

Figure Appendix F.1 *Checklist for the coachee. This flowchart helps you decide if your issues are suitable for executive coaching, and which coach to choose. Follow the pale arrows if the answer to the question is 'yes' and the darker arrows if the answer is 'no'. Dark-coloured rectangles contain advice.*

2 For the coach

When the coachee has completed the first checklist, he or she can work through the next checklist with the coach. This is a relational checklist, which works through the most important conditions relating to the coachee, the coach and the relationship between coach and coachee – largely following the 'common factors' discussed earlier (see Chapter 3).

The checklist also follows the thought-experiment in Chapter 1. I have kept the checklist as short and realistic as possible. There are many

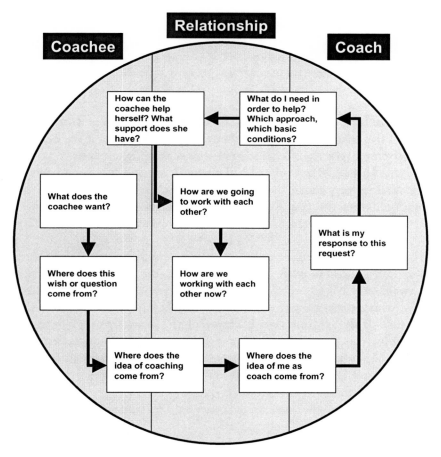

Figure Appendix F.2 *Intake checklist for the coach. This flowchart will enable you to make a quick assessment and take decisions about the contracting when faced with certain questions.*

other questions that the coach can ask at the start of a coaching journey, and many other dimensions that could be added to a full case history. This checklist approximates most closely to what happens in practice, and also puts the relationship between coach and coachee at the centre from the outset.

On the basis of this list, a whole range of practical questions can be asked which shape the contract further, such as with whom to contract, how many sessions, how frequently, how to measure or evaluate the impact, and so on.

3 For triangular contracts

Triangular contracts are the order of the day in coaching conversations, although sometimes not all of the parties realise that they are entering into a triangular contract, or how difficult a triangular contract can be.

The coaching situation always involves at least three parties: the coach, the coachee and the coachee's organisation – or, if the coachee is self-employed: the coachee's customers, suppliers, clients and colleagues. In fact, the work-related network around a coachee can be regarded in very much the same way as the organisation around the coachee: from the coach's viewpoint, all organisations are primarily networks of relationships, or 'ongoing conversations' (Shaw, 2002).

The three parties present enter – formally and informally – into three different contracts with each other: between coach and coachee, between coach and organisation, and between coachee and organisation, with a contract with an 'organisation' being a very complex thing in itself. If the organisation is represented mainly by one person; for example, the coachee's manager, the triangular situation involves three people, which makes the situation slightly more straightforward. If two people are closely involved in the coaching, such as the manager and the HR director, the situation quickly becomes very complicated: between four people there are as many as 6 relationships, so in fact 6 – formal and informal – contracts!

The following checklist is intended as an aid for the coach in managing triangular situations. It goes without saying that it is equally important

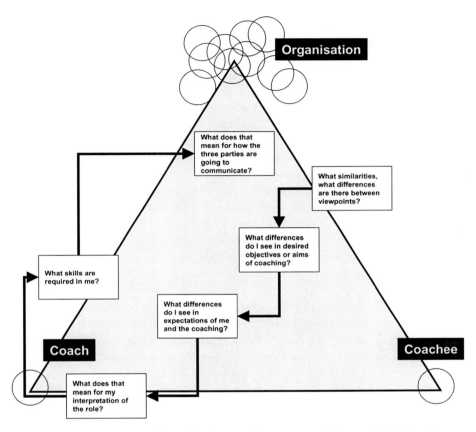

Figure Appendix F.3 *Intake checklist for triangular contracts, for the coach. This flowchart can help to gain a quick idea of tensions between the three parties and also gives ideas for the contracting.*

for the coachee and the representatives of the organisation to manage their sides of triangular contracts as well as possible, and similar questions may help for them.

1   Start with the relationship between coachee and (representatives of) the coachee's organisation. This is the side of the triangle that is in fact furthest away from the coach. What agreements have been made between these parties about the coaching, and what differences of opinion do you observe?

2   What do those observed differences mean for the aims or outcomes of coaching? What outcomes does the coachee primarily want? What outcomes does the organisation primarily want? And how do

    I meet that challenge as a coach: to what extent can I help both of
them to get what they want?

3 What expectations do the different parties appear to have of the
coaching? What is motivating them to enter into a contract with
me as their coach?

4 What does that mean for my interpretation of my role? What role
am I going to play for the coachee? What role am I going to play
for the organisation, or for different parties in the organisation?

5 Which susceptibilities or valencies of mine (see De Haan, 2005)
might the different parties appeal to?

6 What does all of this mean for the way in which all of the parties
in the triangle should communicate with each other? How often
should they liaise with each other, and on what?

Figure F.3 shows the same checklist for triangular contracts again, in
the form of a diagram.

You can run through the checklist at the start of a coaching contract,
but you can also return to it later, when tensions arise in triangular
contracts. This also applies to the other two checklists, for the coachee
and the coach: it can help to revisit them if questions arise concerning
the mutual relationship and the contract. See Chapter 7 and Appendix
B for examples of tensions in triangular contracts. Triangular relationships and contracts are a frequent subject for discussion in supervision
as well.

Literature

Ahn, H. & Wampold, B.E. (2001). Where oh where are the specific ingredients: A meta-analysis of component studies in counseling and psychotherapy. In: *Journal of Counseling Psychology* 48.3, pp. 251–257.

Armstrong, D. (2004). *Organization in the mind: psychoanalysis, group relations and organizational consultancy*. London: Karnac Books.

Baritz, L. (1960). *The servants of power: a history of the use of social science in American industry*. New York: Wiley.

Berglas, S. (2002). The very real dangers of executive coaching. In: *Harvard Business Review* June 2002, pp. 86–92.

Berman, J.S., Miller, C. & Massman, P.J. (1985). Cognitive therapy versus systematic desensitization: is one treatment superior? In: *Psychological Bulletin* 97, pp. 451–461.

Berne, E. (1972) *What do you say after you say Hello?* New York: Grove Press.

Beutler, L.E., Crago, M. & Arizmendi, T.G. (1986). Therapist variables in psychotherapy process and outcome. In: S.L. Garfield & A.E. Bergin (Eds.), *Handbook of psychotherapy and behaviour change 3rd Edition*. New York: Wiley.

Beutler, L.E., Machado, P.P. & Allstetter Neufeldt, S. (1994). Therapist variables. In: *Handbook of Psychotherapy and Behavior Change*, 4th Edition (eds S.L. Garfield & A.E. Bergin), pp. 229–69. New York: Wiley.

Billow, R.M. (2000) Bion's 'passion'; the analyst's pain. In: *Contemporary Psychoanalysis 36*, pp. 411–426.

Bion, W.R. (1963). *Elements of psychoanalysis*. London, William Heinemann.

Bion, W.R. (1965). *Transformations*. London: William Heinemann.

Bion, W.R. (1970). *Attention and interpretation*. London: Tavistock Publications.

Bion, W.R. (1973–1974). *Brazilian lectures*. Published in 1990 by Karnac Books, London.

Blackman, A. (2006). Factors that contribute to the effectiveness of business coaching: the coachee's perspective. In: *The Business Review* 5.1, pp. 98–104.

Briggs Myers, I., McCaulley, M.H., Quenk, N.L., Hammer, A.L. (1998). *MBTI Manual*. Palo Alto (CA): CPP.

Brunning, H. (2006). *Executive coaching: a systems-psychodynamic perspective*. London: Karnac.

Carlberg, G. (1997). Laughter opens the door: turning points in child psychotherapy. In: *Journal of child psychotherapy* 23.3, pp. 331–349.

Casement, P. (1985). *On learning from the patient*. London: Tavistock Publications.

Cattell, H.B. (1989). *The 16PF: personality in depth*. Champaign (Ill.): Institute for personality and ability testing.

Cohen, J. (1988). *Statistical power analysis for the behavioural sciences*. Hillsdale (NJ): Lawrence Erlbaum Associates.

Corsini, R. M. & Wedding, D. (1989). *Current Psychotherapies*. Itasca (Ill.): Peacock.

Crits-Christoph, P. & Mintz, J. (1991). Implications of therapist effects for the design and analysis of comparative studies of psychotherapies. In: *Journal of Consulting and Clinical Psychology* 59, pp. 20–26.

Curd, J. (2006). *Coaching behaviours questionnaire: internal consistency and norm group profiles.* Ashridge Centre for Coaching Internal Report.

Day, A. Haan, E. de, Blass, E., Sills, C. & Bertie, C. (2007). Critical moments in the coaching relationship: does supervision help? In: *Human Relations* (submitted).

De Haan, E., Bertie, C., Day, A. & Sills, C. (2008). Critical moments of clients of coaching: towards the 'client model' of executive coaching. In: *Consulting psychology journal: practice and research.* Submitted.

De Haan, E. & Burger, Y. (2005). *Coaching with colleagues: an action guide for one-to-one learning.* Chichester: Wiley.

De Haan, E., Culpin, V. & Curd, J. (2008). Executive coaching in practice: what determines helpfulness for coachees? In: *Consulting Psychology Journal: Practice and Research,* submitted.

De Haan, E. & De Ridder, I. (2006). Action learning in practice: how do participants learn? In: *Consulting Psychology Journal: Practice and Research* 58.4, pp. 216–231.

De Haan, E. (1997). *The consulting process as drama: learning from King Lear.* London: Karnac Books.

De Haan, E. (2005). *Learning with colleagues: an action guide for peer consultation.* Basingstoke: Palgrave Macmillan.

De Haan, E. (2006). *Fearless consulting: temptations, risks and limits of the profession.* Chichester: Wiley.

De Haan, E. (2008a). 'I doubt therefore I coach' – critical moments from coaching practice. In: *Consulting Psychology Journal: Practice and Research,* Spring 2008, in press.

De Haan, E. (2008b). 'I struggle and emerge' – critical moments of experienced coaches. In: *Consulting Psychology Journal: Practice and Research,* Spring 2008, in press.

De Haan, E. (2008c). Becoming simultaneously thicker and thinner skinned: the inherent conflicts arising in the professional development of coaches. In: *Personnel Review* 37.5, in press.

DeYoung, P. A. (2003). *Relational psychotherapy: a primer.* New York: Brunner-Routledge.

Downey, M. (1999). *Effective coaching.* New York: Thomson Texere.

Dumont, F. (1991). Expertise in psychotherapy: inherent liabilities of becoming experienced. *Psychotherapy* 28, pp. 422–428.

Duncan, B.L., Miller, S.D. & Sparks, J.A. (2004). *The heroic client.* San Francisco: Wiley.

Evers, W.J.G., Brouwers, A. & Tomic, W. (2006). A quasi-experimental study on management coaching effectiveness. In: *Consulting Psychology Journal: Practice and Research* 58.3, pp. 174–182.

Eysenck, H.J. (1952). The effects of psychotherapy: an evaluation. In: *Journal of Consulting Psychology* 16, pp. 319–324.

Fairbairn, W.R.D. (1952). *An object-relations theory of the personality.* New York: Basic Books.

Farrelly, F., and Brandsma, J. (1974). *Provocative Therapy.* Cupertino, Calif.: Meta Publishing.

Feldman, D.C. & Lankau, M.J. (2005). Executive coaching: a review and agenda for future research. In: *Journal of Management* 31.6, pp. 829–848.

Fineman, S. (1985) *Social work stress and intervention.* Aldershot (V.K.): Gower.

Flanagan, J.C. (1954). The critical incident technique. In: *Psychogical Bulletin* 51, pp. 327–358.

Foucault, M. (1983). Parrhesia: free speech and truth. Six lectures delivered at the University of California at Berkeley. Edited by Joseph Pearson: *Fearless speech* (2001). Los Angeles: Semiotext(e).

Freud, S. (1894). Die Abwehr-Neuropsychosen. In: *Neurologisches Zentralblatt* 10 & 11.

Freud, S. (1904/1924). *Zur psychopathologie des Alltagslebens* – 10. *weiter vermehrte Auflage* (1924). Vienna: Internationale Psychoanalytische Verlag.

Freud, S. (1912). Ratschläge für den Arzt bei der psychoanalytischen Behandlung. In: *Zentralblatt für Psychoanalyse* Band II.

Freud, S. (1913). Zur Einleitung der Behandlung. In: *Internationale Zeitschrift für ärztliche Psychoanalyse* Band I.

Frisch, M.H. (2001). The emerging role of the internal coach. In *Consulting Psychology Journal: Practice and Research* 53.4, pp. 240–250.

Garvey, B. (2006). The meaning of mentoring and coaching. In: *Conference Proceedings of EMCC International Conference November 2006*.

Goodman, G.S., Magnussen, S., Andersson, J., Endestad, T., Løkke, C, & Mostue, C. (2006). Memory illusions and false memories in real life. In: S. Magnussen & T. Helstrup (Eds.), *Everyday Memory*. London: Psychology Press.

Gould, R.A. & Clum, G.A. (1993). A meta-analysis of self-help treatment approaches. In: *Clinical Psychology Review* 13, pp. 169–186.

Grant, A.M. (2006). Workplace and executive coaching: a bibliography from the scholarly business literature. In: D.R. Stober & A.M. Grant (Eds.), *Evidence based coaching handbook*. Hoboken (NJ): Wiley.

Gray, L.A., Ladany, N., Walker, J.A. & Ancis, J.R. (2001). Psychotherapy trainees' experience of counterproductive events in supervision. In: *Journal of Counselling Psychology* 48, pp. 371–383.

Greene, J. & Grant, A.M. (2003). *Solution-focused coaching*. London: Momentum Press.

Greenson, R.R. (1965). The working alliance and the transference neuroses. In: *Psychoanalysis Quarterly* 34, pp. 155–181.

Grencavage, L.M. & Norcross, J.C. (1990). Where are the commonalities among the therapeutic common factors? In: *Professional Psychology: Research and Practice* 21, pp. 372–378.

Grissom, R.J. (1996). The magical number .7 ± .2: meta-meta-analysis of the probability of superior outcome in comparisons involving therapy, placebo and control. In: *Journal of Consulting and Clinical Psychotherapy* 64, pp. 973–982.

Harrison, R. (1963). Defenses and the need to know. In: *Human relations training news* 6.4, pp. 1–3.

Hawkins, P. & Shohet, R. (1989). *Supervision in the helping professions: an individual, group and organizational approach*. Buckingham: Open University Press.

Heimann, P. (1950). On counter-transference. *International Journal of Psychoanalysis* 31, pp. 81–84.

Heron, J. (1975). *Helping the client*. London: Sage Publications.

Homer (8th century BC). *Odyssey*.

Horvath, A.O. & Marx, R.W. (1990). The development and decay of the working alliance during time-limited counselling. In: *Canadian journal of Counselling* 24, pp. 240–259.

Horvath, A.O. & Symonds, B.D. (1991). Relation between working alliance and outcome in psychotherapy: a meta-analysis. In: *Journal of Counseling Psychology* 38.2, pp. 139–149.

Jung, C.G. (1921). *Psychologische Typen*. Olten (Switzerland): Walter Verlag.

Kampa-Kokesch, S. & Anderson, M.Z. (2001). Executive coaching: a comprehensive review of the literature. In: *Consulting Psychology Journal: Practice and Research* 53.4, pp. 205–228.

Kets de Vries, M. F. R. (2005). Leadership group coaching in acton: The Zen of creating high performance teams. In: *Academy of Management Executive* 19.1, pp. 61–76.

Kline, N. (1999). *Time to think: listening to ignite the human mind*. London: Cassell.

Kolb, A., & Kolb, D.A. (2006). Facilitator's guide to learning. *Hay Group Internal Report*.

Kolb, D.A. (1984). *Experiential learning: experience as the source of learning and development*. Englewood Cliffs (NJ): Prentice-Hall.

Lambert (1992). Psychotherapy outcome research. In: J.C. Norcross & M.R. Goldfried (Eds.), *Handbook of psychotherapy integration*. New York: Basic Books.

Lambert, M.J. & Bergin, A.E. (1994). The effectiveness of psychotherapy. In: S.L. Garfield & A.E. Bergin (Eds), *Handbook of psychotherapy and behaviour change 4th Edition*, pp. 143–89. New York: Wiley.

Lambert, M.J. and Arnold, R.C. (1987). Research and the supervisory process. In: *Professional psychology: Research and Practice* 18.3, pp. 217–214.

Lapworth, P., Sills, C. & Fish, S. (2001). *Integration in counselling and psychotherapy: developing a personal approach*. London: Sage.

Lawson, D. (1994). Identifying pre-treatment change. In: *Journal of Counseling and Development* 72, pp. 244–248.

Lawton, B. (2000). 'A very exposing affair': explorations in counsellors' supervisory relationships. In: B. Lawton & C. Feltham (Eds.), *Taking supervision forward: enquiries and trends in counselling and psychotherapy*. London: Sage.

Lipsey, M.W. & Wilson, D.B. (1993). The efficacy of psychological, educational, and behavioural treatment: confirmation from meta-analysis. In: *American Psychologist* 48, pp. 1181–1209.

Luborsky, L. (1976). Helping alliances in psychotherapy. In: J.L. Cleghorn (Ed.), *Successful psychotherapy*, pp. 92–116. New York: Brunner/Mazel.

Malan, D.H. (1979). *Individual psychotherapy and the science of psychodynamics*. London: Butterworth.

Mann, C.C. (1994). Can meta-analysis make policy? In: *Science* 266, pp. 960–962.

Maroda, K. J. (1998). *Seduction, surrender and transformation: emotional engagement in the analytic process*. Hillsdale (NJ): The Analytic Press.

Martin, D.J., Garske, J.P. & Davis, M.K. (2000). Relation of the therapeutic alliance with outcome and other variables: a meta-analytic review. In: *Journal of Consulting and Clinical Psychology* 68, pp. 438–450.

McGovern, J., Lindemann, M., Vergara, M., Murphy, S., Barker, L. & Warrenfeltz, R. (2001). Maximizing the impact of executive coaching: behavioural change, organizational outcomes, and return on investment. In: *The Manchester Review* 6.1, pp. 1–9.

McLennan, J. (1999) Becoming an effective psychotherapist or counsellor: are training and supervision necessary? In: Feltham, C. (Ed.), *Controversies in Psychotherapy and Counselling*. London: Sage Publications.

McNeal, B.W., May, R.J. & Lee, V.E. (1987). Perceptions of counsellor source characteristics by premature and successful terminators. In: *Journal of Counseling Psychology* 34, pp. 86–89.

Menzies, I.E.P. (1960). A case-study in the functioning of social systems as a defence against anxiety: a report on a study of the nursing service of a general hospital. In: *Human Relations* 13, pp. 95–121.

Merton, R.K. & Barber, E.G. (2003). *The travels and adventures of serendipity: a study in sociological semantics and the sociology of science*. Princeton (NJ): Princeton University Press.

Miller, A. (1979). *Das Drama des begabten Kindes und die Suche nach dem wahren Selbst*. Frankfurt am Main: Suhrkamp.

Miller, S.D., Duncan, B.L., Sorrell, R., Brown, G.S., & Chalk, M.B. (2005). Using outcome to inform therapy practice. In: *Journal of Brief Therapy* 5.1.

Mitchell, S.A. & Aron, L. (Eds.; 1999). *Relational psychoanalysis: the emergence of a tradition*. Hillsdale (NJ): The Analytic Press.

Nanamoli, B. (1991). *The path of purification*. Translation of the *Visuddhimagga, the classic manual of Buddhist doctrine and meditation*. Kandy (Sri Lanka): Buddhist Publication Society.

Nietzsche, F.W. (1888). *Ecce Homo*. In: G. Colli & M. Montinari (Eds.), *Sämtliche Werke – Kritische Studienausgabe in 15 Bänden, Band 6*. Munich: Deutscher Taschenbuch Verlag, 1980.

Norcross, J. (1993). Tailoring relationship stances to client needs: an introduction. In: *Psychotherapy: Theory, Research and Practice* 30, pp. 402–403.

Norcross, J.C. & Goldfried, M.R. (Eds.; 1992). *Handbook of psychotherapy integration*. New York: Basic Books.

O'Neill, M.-B. (2000). *Executive coaching with backbone and heart: a systems approach to engaging leaders with their challenges*. San Francisco: Jossey-Bass.

Olivero, G., Bane, K.D. & Kopelman, R.E. (1997). Executive coaching as a transfer of training tool: effects on productivity in a public agency. In: *Public Personnel Management* 26.4, pp. 461–9.

Peltier, B. (2001). *The psychology of executive coaching: theory and application*. New York: Brunner and Routledge.

Pemberton, C. (2006). Coaching to Solutions. Oxford: Butterworth-Heinemann.

Plato (4th century BC). *Meno*.

Porter, M.E. (1979). How competitive forces shape strategy. In: *Harvard Business Review*, March/April 1979.

Proctor, B. (1988). Supervision: a co-operative exercise in accountability. In: M. Marken & M. Payne (Eds.), *Enabling and ensuring supervision in practice*. Leicester: Leicester National Youth Bureau and Council for Education and Training in Youth and Community Work.

Project MATCH Research Group (1998). Therapist effects in three treatments for alcohol problems. In: *Psychotherapy Research* 8, pp. 455–474.

Ragins, B.R., Cotton, J.L. & Miller, J.S. (2000). Marginal mentoring: the effects of type of mentor, quality of relationship, and program design on work and career attitudes. In: *Academy of Management Journal* 43.6, pp. 1177–94.

Reason, P. (1994). *Participation in Human Inquiry*. London: Sage.

Rice, L.N. & Greenberg, L.S. Eds.; (1984). *Patterns of change: intensive analysis of psychotherapeutic process*. New York: Guilford.

Rogers, C.R. (1957). The necessary and sufficient conditions of therapeutic personality change. In: *Journal of Consulting Psychology* 21, pp. 95–103.

Rogers, C.R. (1961). *On becoming a person: a therapist's view of psychotherapy*. London: Constable.

Rogers, C.R. (1980). *A way of being*. New York: Houghton Mifflin.

Rosenzweig, S. (1936). Some implicit common factors in diverse methods of psychotherapy: 'At last the Dodo said, "Everybody has won and all must have prizes."' In: *American Journal of Orthopsychiatry* 6, pp. 412–415.

Roth, A. & Fonagy, P. (1996). *What works for whom? A critical review of psychotherapy research*. London: The Guildford Press.

Safran, J.D., Crocker, P., McMain, S. & Murray, P. (1990). Therapeutic alliance rupture as a therapy event for empirical investigation. In: *Psychotherapy* 27, pp. 154–165.

Safran, J.D., Muran, C.J. & Wallner Samstag, L. (1993). Resolving therapeutic ruptures: a task analytic investigation. In: A.O. Horvath & L.S. Greenberg (Eds.), *The working alliance: theory, research, and practice*. New York: Wiley.

Schein, E. H., Schneier, I. & Barker, C.H. (1961). *Coercive persuasion*. New York: W.W. Norton & Company.

Schlaefli, A., Rest, J.R. & Thoma, S.J. (1985). Does moral education improve moral judgment? A meta-analysis of intervention studies using the defining issues test. In: *Review of Educational Research* 55.3, pp. 319–352.

Schutz, W.C. (1958). *FIRO: A three-dimensional theory of interpersonal behaviour*. New York: Rinehart & Company.

Scogin, G. Bynum, J. Stephens, G. & Calhoun, S. (1990). Efficacy of self-administered treatment programs: a meta-analytic review. In: *Professional Psychology: Research and Practice* 21, pp. 42–47.

Scoular, A. & Linley, P.A. (2006). Coaching, goal-setting and personality type: what matters? In: *The Coaching Psychologist* 2.1, pp. 9–11.

Searles, H.F. (1955). *The informational value of the supervisor's emotional experience*. In: *Psychiatry* 18, pp. 135–146.

Shapiro, D.A. & Shapiro, D. (1982). Meta-analysis of comparative therapy outcome studies: a replication and refinement. In: *Psychological Bulletin* 92, pp. 581–604.

Shaw, B.F., Elkin, I., Yamaguchi, J., Olmsted, M., Vallis, T.M., Dobson, K.S., Lowery, A., Sotsky, S.M., Watkins, J.T. & Imber, S.D. (1999). Therapist competence ratings in relation to clinical outcome in cognitive therapy of depression. In: *Journal of Consulting and Clinical Psychology* 67, pp. 837–846.

Shaw, P. (2002). *Changing conversations in organisations: a complexity approach to change*. London & New York: Routledge.

Sills, C. (Ed.; 1997). *Contracts in counselling*. London: Sage.

Skiffington, S. & Zeus, P. (2003). *Behavioral coaching*. New York: McGraw-Hill Professional.

Smith, J.A. (2003). *Qualitative psychology: a practical guide to research methods*. London: Sage.

Smith, M. (2003). The fears of the counsellors: a qualitative study. In: *British Journal of Guidance & Counselling* 31, 229–240.

Smith, M.L. & Glass, G.V. (1977). Meta-analysis of psychotherapy outcome studies. In: *American Psychologist* 32, pp. 752–760.

Smith, M.L., Glass, G.V. & Miller, T.I. (1980). *The benefits of psychotherapy*. Baltimore: Johns Hopkins University Press.

Smither, J.W., London, M., Flautt, R., Vargas, Y. & Kucine, I. (2003). Can working with an executive coach improve multisource feedback ratings over time? A quasi-experimental field study. In: *Personnel Psychology* 56, pp. 23–44.

Snyder, C.R., Michael, S.T. & Cheavens. J.S. (1999). Hope as a psychotherapeutic foundation of common factors, placebos, and expectancies. In: M.A. Hubble, B.L. Duncan & S.D. Miller (Eds.), *The heart and soul of change: what works in therapy*. Washington (DC): APA Press.

Stern, D.N. (2004). *The present moment in psychotherapy and everyday life*. Norton, New York.

Stern, D.N., Sander, L.W., Nahum, J.P., Harrison, A.M., Lyons-Ruth, K., Morgan, A.C., Bruschweiler-Stern, N. & Tronick, E.Z. (1998). Non-interpretive mechanisms in psychoanalytic therapy: the 'something more' than interpretation. In: *International Journal of Psycho-Analysis* 79, pp. 903–921.

Stevens, P. (2004). Coaching supervision. In: *Training Journal* 1, pp. 18–19.

Stroeken, H.P.J. *Kleine psychologie van het gesprek* [*Brief psychology of the conversation*]. Amsterdam: Boom.

Sullivan, H. S. (1953). *The interpersonal theory of psychiatry*. New York: Norton.

Tallman, K. & Bohart, A.C. (1999). The client as a common factor: clients as self-healers. In: M.A. Hubble, B.L. Duncan & S.D. Miller (Eds.), *The heart and soul of change: what works in therapy*. Washington (DC): APA Press.

Thach, E. C. (2002). The impact of executive coaching and 360 feedback on leadership effectiveness. In: *Leadership & Organization Development Journal* 23.3/4, pp. 205–214.

Wampold, B.E. (2001). *The great psychotherapy debate: models, methods and findings.* Mahwah (NJ): Lawrence Erlbaum.

Wampold, B.E., Mondin, G.W., Moody, M., Stich, F., Benson, K. & Ahn, H. (1997). A meta-analysis of outcome studies comparing bona fide psychotherapies: empirically, 'all must have prizes'. In: *Psychological Bulletin* 122, pp. 203–215.

Wasylyshyn, K.M. (2003). Executive coaching: an outcome study. In: *Consulting Psychology Journal: Practice and Research* 55.2, pp. 94–106.

Watzlawick, P., Beavin, J., & Jackson, D.D. (1967). *Pragmatics Of Human Communication.* New York: W.W. Norton.

Weil, A. (1995). *Health and healing.* New York: Houghton Mifflin.

Whitmore, J. (1992). *Coaching for performance: GROWing people, performance and purpose.* London: Nicholas Brealey.

Yalom, I.D. (1992). *When Nietzsche wept.* New York: HarperCollins.

Index